We truly value our partnership
with you. Thank you for your
continued support over the years.

Best Wishes,

*Peter A. Brooke*

# A
## VISION
## FOR VENTURE
## CAPITAL

. . .

# A
# VISION
# FOR VENTURE
# CAPITAL

. . .

REALIZING THE PROMISE OF
GLOBAL VENTURE CAPITAL AND
PRIVATE EQUITY

**PETER A. BROOKE**

WITH DANIEL PENRICE

NEW VENTURES PRESS
Boston
*In association with*
University Press of New England
Hanover and London

NEW VENTURES PRESS
In association with
University Press of New England,
One Court Street, Lebanon, NH 03766
www.upne.com

Printed in U.S.A.

5 4 3 2 1

Library of Congress Cataloging-in-Publication Data
Brooke, Peter A.
A vision for venture capital: realizing the promise of global venture capital
and private equity / Peter A. Brooke with Daniel Penrice.
p. cm.
"In association with University Press of New England."
Includes bibliographical references and index.
ISBN 978-1-58465-799-6 (cloth : alk. paper)
1. Venture capital. 2. Private equity. I. Penrice, Daniel. II. Title.
HG4751.B76    2009
332'.04154—dc22    2009026505

University Press of New England is a member of the
Green Press Initiative. The paper used in this book meets their
minimum requirement for recycled paper.

TO ANNE

# CONTENTS

. . .

# FOREWORD

. . .

Peter Brooke has written an important book about the birth of an important economic phenomenon — the profession of investing money in private companies and actively helping them succeed. When applied to early-stage companies, we call the practice venture capital. When applied to more mature firms, we call the practice growth equity or leveraged buyouts. Peter was there at the beginning. He helped create the industry, not just in the United States but also around the world. I think of Peter as the Johnny Appleseed of private equity, the all-encompassing term we apply today to the phenomenon. He started two of the important players in the industry, TA Associates and Advent International. Peter was and is a missionary — he viewed private equity as a force for economic development and positive social change. He was and is tireless in taking his message anywhere and everywhere.

We take so many things for granted today. I am writing this foreword on a personal computer using word-processing software. If I make a typing mistake, I fix it quickly and easily. When I am done writing this piece, I will send it off using an integrated e-mail program. If I need to look something up, I go to the Internet and search billions of sources instantaneously. Alas, it was not always so. Before Peter and his colleagues invested in companies like Wang Laboratories, the same process involved clunky typewriters, messy corrections, fewer drafts, and using the postal service. Wang developed an integrated word-processing capability that changed all our lives. Peter and his fellow venture capitalists helped launch or build companies like Lotus Development, Microsoft, Cisco, Federal Express, and Google. It's hard to imagine a world without those companies and the products and services they created.

This book operates at a number of levels. It tells the story of an extraordinary man, one who is creative, persistent (even dogged), visionary, competent, courageous, and a talented leader. He has changed the world for the better. The book also describes how an industry came into being.

Peter is one of a handful of men who created a profession out of an ad hoc process that had always existed but never had the impact it could have. By that I mean that essentially every company ever formed required some outside capital. There were angel investors in companies like Ford Motor and Eastman Kodak. What Peter and a handful of fellow pioneers did was to turn something individuals did into something professional organizations did and did well.

Peter played a significant part in the earliest years of the venture capital industry, in the 1950s, in eastern Massachusetts, as he and others grew the business of growing businesses. Putting up money was only part of the challenge. He understood that nascent entrepreneurs need more than financial support; they also need advice and assistance from management professionals, as well as connections to wider networks of investors, customers, and suppliers to help their companies thrive. Peter provided these and much more, initially as a lender, then as an equity investor on behalf of wealthy individuals, and finally, in 1968, as the founder and leader of TA Associates, a firm that grew rapidly and, in turn, spawned other successful firms and trained many investment professionals.

During Peter's long and distinguished career, the venture capital industry grew from one populated by a handful of small firms and a total annual investment of a few million dollars to one today characterized by sophisticated firms with investments surpassing $240 billion. As a result, hundreds, if not thousands, of important publicly traded and private companies founded in the United States since 1970 have relied on venture capital investments to accelerate their launch and increase their odds of success.

Peter understood from the outset that helping new ventures get under way was only one use of investment capital. In the 1950s and 1960s, a "venture" did not necessarily connote a start-up or what today is called an early-stage investment. TA Associates invested in many established companies that needed capital to expand, and the firm provided the same advisory and networking services for these companies as for new ventures. Over time, TA Associates and other firms it spawned helped hundreds of companies grow while becoming more efficient and profitable. Meanwhile, participation in mature, later-stage companies far surpassed amounts invested in start-ups, especially after buyouts and leveraged buyouts proliferated, beginning in the 1970s and 1980s. Today, more than $500 billion is invested through private equity firms.

The extent and impact of private equity investments are staggering and, of course, controversial in light of today's credit crunch and financial crisis. To Peter's credit, however, the firms with which he has been associated avoided both heavy reliance on debt financing and ostentatious displays of personal wealth. In fact, while Peter's firms and investors in their funds have done extremely well, this reflects the great good — the enormous positive economic and social impact — achieved in the United States and around the world. As *A Vision for Venture Capital* makes clear, Peter believes that venture financing is a vital key to economic development, growth, and renewal. When firms carry out this fundamental mission, a host of benefits follow to companies that grow and create jobs, and to societies that benefit from increased prosperity and its offshoots.

Initially, Peter's field of vision took in New England. Later it expanded to the eastern United States, and then overseas. In the 1970s, Peter was one of the very first American financiers to bring professional venture financing to Western Europe, helping to establish the first network of venture capitalists in France, Germany, Belgium, and the United Kingdom. He worked closely with national and multilateral economic development agencies including the World Bank and the European Bank for Reconstruction and Development.

In 1984, Peter founded Advent International, one of the very first global firms to spread venture financing and private equity beyond North America and Western Europe to Eastern and central Europe, Asia, and Latin America. None of this was easy, as Peter had to deal with skeptical investors, intimidating legal and institutional barriers, and significant cultural differences. He persisted and eventually prevailed, however, and the world is more productive, prosperous, and hopeful because of it.

Today, Peter's legacy is manifested literally all over the world — directly in Advent's global offices and investments and indirectly as other firms have followed his lead to set up international and global funds. Meanwhile, Peter is continuing to do what he has always done. With his son John he founded Brooke Private Equity Advisors to fund commercialization of health-care technology originating in the impressive medical community in St. Louis. Peter's vision and methods also inspire and inform not-for-profit organizations such as Endeavor, founded by Linda Rottenberg to identify and support high-impact entrepreneurs in emerging markets in Latin America, Africa, and the Middle East. As a result, today, it is not far-fetched for promising entrepreneurs in nearly every country, on and off the beaten paths, to believe they can attract capital and expertise to help build their businesses.

In short, Peter is a remarkable man, one of a handful in the last half century who truly changed the world. Like a select few of his peers, the great pioneers of a great industry, he operated behind the scenes, content to let others take credit for the growth of great companies and the prosperity they generate. Now that he has told the story of his pathbreaking career, we have much to learn from Peter. His vision is as vital and compelling today as it was in the 1950s, when he first set out to lend money to engineers in garages and Quonset huts in Cambridge, Massachusetts. The story of why and how he embarked on this path, and of how his career and firms he led made a difference in the world, makes for dramatic and compelling reading.

WILLIAM A. SAHLMAN
*Dimitri V. D'Arbeloff–MBA Class of 1955 Professor of
Business Administration and Senior Associate Dean for External Relations,
Harvard Business School*

# INTRODUCTION

• • •

In June 1947, when I was seventeen years old and just finishing my junior year at Phillips Exeter Academy, I had no idea that my life's work would involve international venture capital and private equity. In retrospect, it looks to me as if my course may have been set back then. On June 5 that year, a Thursday, my father took me out of school and hauled me to Cambridge for Harvard's commencement exercises. My main interests in life at the time were sports and girls, and I sat fidgeting through the long hours of ceremonies, including the twelve minutes for which the day is now chiefly remembered. That afternoon, General George C. Marshall, the former army chief of staff who had led the Allies to victory in World War II and then become President Truman's secretary of state, delivered the famous address in which he announced what would become the Marshall Plan for the economic reconstruction of postwar Europe.

In his speech, Marshall talked about the economic devastation visited upon Europe by the fight against "the arbitrary and destructive Nazi rule." I knew a little about the recent war and about the Nazis. My father had left his home in England at the age of sixteen, shortly before the outbreak of World War I, and come to the United States, but he still had two brothers in England when the Germans unleashed the Blitz in 1940. During the war, my parents and I followed the daily reports, hoping that my uncles and their families would survive (which they did, fortunately). After the war, my father was concerned about rebuilding Britain and worried that not enough capital was being employed to do so. So he must have been intensely interested to hear General Marshall say that "Europe's requirements for the next three or four years . . . are so much greater than her present ability to pay that she must have substantial additional help or face economic, social, and political deterioration of a very grave character."

It wasn't until my junior year at Harvard College four years later — by which time I was taking mostly history and government courses, and had developed an especially keen interest in European history — that the magnitude of what had happened that day began to occur to me. The Marshall Plan had been launched, and by the time I graduated from Harvard in 1952, its effects were already becoming apparent. The United States had shown foresight and courage through its willingness to risk helping its former enemies as well as its allies, and the risk would pay off as the postwar era continued to unfold. The Soviet Union rejected the offer of U.S. aid and forced countries such as Poland and Czechoslovakia to do so as well. Yet billions of dollars in assistance flowing to West Germany, Italy, and the rest of Western Europe proved critical in reviving former trading partners and, as Marshall had hoped, "restor[ing] the confidence of the European people in the economic future of their own countries and of Europe as a whole."

Although I became a venture capitalist in the late 1950s, I did not at first understand the connection between this career choice and the Marshall Plan. My focus in the beginning was local rather than global: I wanted to provide capital for small, innovative companies with the potential for lifting New England out of the economic doldrums. Venture capital, in the sense in which the term was used then, involved identifying small companies with good growth prospects and good management, providing them with financial support and management advice, and watching some companies succeed and others fail. It was and is exciting, but not for the reason commonly believed. Many people think that venture capital and its offspring, private equity, are only about making money. To me, they are about using foresight and taking risks in order to build the successful enterprises that are the lifeblood of an economy, and being rewarded for contributing to their success. In so doing, venture capital and private equity managers play a vital role in promoting economic growth and general prosperity. I have long believed that they can do this not only in the United States, where modern venture capital was invented, but virtually anywhere in the world. My vision for venture capital has been to take these powerful tools for economic development and to use them to create greater prosperity in countries everywhere.

I was part of the first wave of venture capitalists in the United States, initially as a banker and later as head of my own venture organization, TA Associates, which I founded in the late 1960s. In the early 1970s, I finally began to see a connection between Secretary Marshall's speech and my own career, as I became interested in taking venture capital financing overseas. I believed that venture capital could be a tool for unlocking innovation and entrepreneurship, improving existing companies, and stimulating economic growth and development around the world. I do not claim to have foreseen all the changes that would take place in the world over the next twenty-five years and more, such as the revolution in communications technology and the deregulation of global financial markets that have done so much to create today's international market-place. Surveying the landscape at the time, however, I saw no reason why venture capital could not succeed in other countries as it had in the United States. I didn't know if I would make any money — none of us who started venture capital firms in the 1960s knew, at the time, if we would make any money here at home. I just wanted to combine my vocation (finance) with my avocation (history), and to watch economic history unfold.

The idea of helping others not by handouts but by aiding them in build-ing their economies was central to the Marshall Plan, which, in a sense, was a giant venture capital fund.[1] The United States didn't tell recipients of Marshall Plan aid what to do with it any more than a venture capital-ist investing in a new company dictates how an entrepreneur should use the capital. Rather, it let these countries use the aid as they saw fit, de-pending on their own particular needs. The plan also created mechanisms for stimulating trade. There was an element of self-interest involved — we wanted Europe to recover economically so that Europeans would be able to buy our goods. But as the historian Tony Judt has observed, "this self-interest was distinctly enlightened." The United States was trying to boost its own economy and create future economic competitors at the same time; as Judt puts it, "the Marshall Plan would benefit the USA by restor-ing her major trading partner, rather than by reducing Europe to an impe-rial dependency."[2] Our motives were honorable as well as pragmatic, and the recognition of this created goodwill toward the United States in coun-tries whose weakened condition might have caused them to resent us. In the annals of postwar history, the Marshall Plan stands out as a proud ex-ample of Americans acting in ways that gained us, at least for a time, admi-ration around the world.

Today, over sixty years after the inauguration of the Marshall Plan, global competition and new opportunities in global markets mean that countries everywhere want to foster the growth of innovative, technol-ogy-based businesses as well as to improve the efficiency, profitability, and growth prospects of their existing companies. The failure of socialism to lift people out of poverty and significantly improve their standards of living, and the benefits that economic globalization has brought to people in emerging and less developed countries, have demonstrated that a vibrant private sector capable of deploying capital and good ideas from wherever they are available is the key to sustainable economic growth and development.[3] In the meantime, venture capital and private equity have indeed spread — or, in some cases, just begun to spread — all over the world, thereby helping people on every continent to compete in today's global economy by becoming more innovative and efficient. And it is not just American venture capitalists who have been responsible for this, as many countries have developed, or begun to develop, their own home-grown venture capital and private equity industries.

I am proud to have played a role in pioneering this development, which seems to me to offer one of the best ways of making economic globalization work for both developed and developing countries. Today my vision for venture capital remains what it has been for the last thirty-five years, ever since I first began to realize that the Marshall Plan gave me a model for what I wanted to accomplish on a global basis. I believe that this vision can — and hope that it will — inspire venture capital and private equity managers today who want to do good in the world while doing well for themselves.

## SUMMARY OF THE BOOK

I have written this book for two purposes: to tell the story of how I developed my belief in venture capital as a tool for global economic progress and worked to spread it internationally; and to share my ideas about how venture capital and private equity managers — better known today for the fortunes the most successful of them have made than for the good they have done — can best carry the work of global economic development forward by using their problem-solving skills with adventurousness and creativity.

In keeping with this twofold purpose, I have divided this book into two parts. Part I, "Pursuing the Vision," tells the story of my career in venture capital and private equity, first in the United States and then internationally. It covers the founding and development of the two venture capital/private equity firms I have established in my career, TA Associates and Advent International; the stories of TAA and Advent, in turn, trace the establishment and growth of the international network of venture capital firms that I began building at TAA and the development of Advent into a global private equity firm with investment operations in North America, Europe, Latin America, and Asia. Part II, "Sustaining the Vision," draws upon my fifty years of experience in venture capital and private equity to address three issues that are key to these industries' ability to fulfill their potential as I see it: adding value, leadership in venture capital/private equity organizations, and the exploration of new frontiers in venture capital and private equity today.

## "VENTURE CAPITAL" AND "PRIVATE EQUITY": A NOTE ON TERMINOLOGY

Before proceeding any further, I need to clarify my use of the terms *venture capital* and *private equity*, which can mean different things in different contexts. From the time of the invention of organized venture capital in the 1940s until approximately the late 1980s, "venture capital" meant simply investment in small companies with growth potential, whether at the start-up stage or later in their development. Early Boston-based venture capital firms such as American Research & Development, Greylock Partners, and TA Associates all made both early-stage and later-stage investments in their early years. This approach was also pioneered at Warburg Pincus, cofounded by Lionel Pincus and Eric Warburg in 1966 to make private investments in companies at all stages of development. At whatever stage of a company's life they invested, these firms focused on adding value and building well-managed, sustainable businesses. Thus in discussing the industry during this time period I will employ the then-current terminology and use the term *venture capital* to encompass both early-stage and later-stage investment in such companies.

After the rise of the leveraged buyout in the United States in the mid-1980s (which I discuss in chapter 8), it seemed necessary to begin distinguishing between this type of investment, which increasingly involved the restructuring of large public companies, and investment in small, usually technology-based start-ups. Thus "venture capital" came to refer to the latter type of investment, while "private equity" gradually came to denote the investment of risk capital at the other end of the spectrum, that is, buyouts. Either term could be, and was, used to describe investments that fell somewhere in the middle: for example, providing mezzanine (pre-IPO) financing for companies about to go public, or expansion capital to mature companies.

In the United States, "venture capital" now almost always means investment in start-ups, while "private equity" refers to investment in mature companies and, especially, buyouts. (In Europe today, "private equity" is still sometimes used in the broad sense of equity investment through private channels as opposed to the public markets, so that "venture capital" becomes a subset of private equity. As private equity in the American sense has become more of a force in Europe, however, the term has increasingly become synonymous with *buyouts*.) In this book I generally observe this distinction in talking about events of the last two decades. To avoid cumbersomeness, however, I sometimes use the term *venture capital* to mean both "venture capital" and "private equity" when there is no need to distinguish between the two. Thus, for example, in the title of this book, *A Vision for Venture Capital*, I am really talking about a vision for both venture capital *and* private equity.

I do wonder if, as some have suggested, it would be best if both venture capital and private equity in the contemporary sense were just called "venture capital" again. The term *private equity* lends itself too easily to the image of shadowy, backroom machination with which the industry has been characterized of late. And as I hope to show in this book, private equity investing, when undertaken with the goal of making mature companies more efficient and competitive, can be just as venturesome as venture capital investing. Or perhaps we need to revive the term *risk capital* to describe what both venture capitalists and private equity managers provide. While investing in start-ups is a chancier business than investing in mature companies, no legitimate form of investment is without risk. And when investment venture capitalists and private equity managers do their jobs properly, both take risks in order to create the kinds of sustainable companies that create jobs and prosperity.

PART I

# PURSUING THE VISION

. . .

# CHAPTER 1

# BECOMING A VENTURE CAPITALIST

· · ·

When I was young I never planned on becoming a venture capitalist, or even on going into business. I would become known in my later years as a "missionary" for venture capital, but it took me several years to discover my mission. In the summer of 1951, just prior to my senior year at Harvard, I had a conversation with my father about what I intended to do after graduation. My father, a doctor, always wanted me to go to medical school, but I was completely baffled by organic chemistry when I took it in my sophomore year of college. I had finally convinced my father of my lack of fitness for medical studies when I accidentally started a fire in the chemistry lab and he was billed five hundred dollars for the damage. In any case, when he asked me that summer before my senior year what I planned to do with myself, I talked about going to Harvard's graduate school of arts and sciences to pursue a master's in history. My father insisted that this was no way to get anywhere in life, so I said, "Why don't I go to Harvard Business School?" I threw this out as a pure gambit, something the two of us could agree on without either of us being able to declare victory. We did agree, so I applied to HBS and was accepted.

I disliked the business school and did nothing to distinguish myself there except to walk out on a class taught by General Georges Doriot, the founder of the American Research & Development Corporation and the father of modern venture capital. It was his legendary course "Manufacturing," in which Doriot announced on the first day of class, "Gentlemen, if you don't read *Scientific American* cover to cover, every word of *Business-Week* and all the rest of the business press, if you can't work nights and weekends, you shouldn't be here." He said a lot of things that were not of particular interest to me, so even though I was sitting in the first row I got up and walked out. A few days later we passed each other in the hall, and

Doriot said to me, "You know, people don't usually do that to me." So I explained that I was coaching the Eliot House football team at Harvard that fall, that I would be coaching lacrosse in the spring, and that I had just met an extraordinarily attractive woman — my future wife, Anne, as it turned out. I don't know what the General thought of this explanation, but when I came into contact with him in later years I always sensed a certain coolness toward me on his part.

After business school Anne and I were married, and I spent two years in a cushy desk job in the army while living at home. When I got out of the army in 1956, still without any particular ambitions, I landed a job at the First National Bank of Boston — then the thirteenth-largest bank in the United States and the largest in New England — through a friend of Anne's father. The Credit Department, where I began, was on the second floor, and here we trainees — a faceless gang of well-washed boys, ambitiously dressed in white button-down shirts, skinny ties, and dark suits our wives had pressed the night before — sat in rows, pushing numbers and waiting for promotions. My first job was "spreading statements." This meant taking figures from an auditor's report and arranging them in a bank form. This, in turn, allowed a quick analysis of the pertinent numbers: cash flow, accounts receivable, and inventory levels — the areas where one can detect negative trends that can lead to trouble. Most of the companies we analyzed were moribund local outfits that weren't going anywhere — dead-end textile firms and shoe manufacturers, once prosperous but now dying as the shoe business moved to St. Louis and the textile trade to the Carolinas.

I got a real business education there in the Credit Department from a clerk named John Walsh, whom all the officers treated condescendingly but who knew a great deal more than he was given credit for. When he spread an income statement and balance sheet, John could explain what was behind the figures better than anyone I had ever met; I can still hear his descriptions of what happens when raw materials come into a plant, how value is added in the manufacturing process, and how the raw materials come out as finished goods that go into inventory and are shipped. He identified all the trigger points to worry about — knowledge that would serve me well when I later became a loan officer and then, eventually, a venture capitalist. Despite the efforts of John and others who tried to help me, however, I simply couldn't find my way at the bank. The prescribed way of getting ahead was to do the same thing everyone else was doing, but just a little better — an approach that had no appeal to me.

I was on my way to being fired late in 1957 when, in a last-ditch effort to find some use for me, I was assigned to the bank's Special Industries Group, which was run by a controversial, charismatic White Russian named Serge Semenenko. Someone must have said to someone, "We might as well give Brooke one last chance. Let him work on a deal with Semenenko and see what the kid can do." Semenenko's department was not on the main track to the executive office suite. He was a vice chairman of the bank and a genius lender, but he had a flamboyant lifestyle that was frowned upon by some of the bank's more straitlaced senior officers. For example, he occasionally rented *Shemara*, the 860-ton yacht belonging to the gaudily extravagant Sir Bernard Docker (chairman of the Daimler Company from 1938 until his sacking in 1956) and his wife Lady Docker (the former Parisian café dancer Norah Collins); it was rumored that Semenenko stocked the boat with starlets obtained as fringe benefits from the loans he was then making to the movie industry.[1]

In any case, Semenenko gave me the project of analyzing the acquisition of Pratt & Whitney Machine Tool Company by Penn-Texas Corporation. There was nothing particularly exciting about this assignment. However, I had just learned from a friend in the Personnel Department that the officers considered me distinctly mediocre. This suddenly tripped a switch in my head, and I decided to show everybody I was smarter and more determined than the other new recruits. I began leaving home in West Concord at five in the morning and getting to my desk before anyone else. I talked to Pratt & Whitney's officers, employees, customers, and suppliers. I developed a highly informed sense of the company. I completed the analysis in six weeks and concluded that, all else being equal, Penn-Texas should go ahead with the acquisition. Semenenko approved a term loan on the basis of my work, but not before saying to me, "You know, that's one of the best pieces of analysis that's ever been done here." This was in the spring of 1958.

The pat on the back was welcome, but I was chafing at the bit. I wanted my own business, my own list of clients. And I had already figured out that that wouldn't happen as long as I was in Semenenko's department. When you worked for Serge, you worked on Serge's deals. I have always looked for ways of making end runs — learning the rules of the game, understanding how they can be circumvented by writing my own rules, and then doing so. And so now I plotted an end run. How could I get around the knot of young trainees all lined up and waiting for their promotions?

How could I get to the top of this heap without clawing my way? I began to think about the bank's fundamental mission. How does a bank decide where to lend money? What gave New England a competitive advantage? What was the real asset of our region? And was the bank serving that asset by lending to it?

Like every other bank in the region, First National Bank of Boston recognized that the few local manufacturers in the textile, garment, leather, and shoe industries that were still holding on were ticketed for oblivion. As a result, FNBB was doing most of its lending outside New England. Before the rise of Route 128, Silicon Valley, and other high-tech meccas, the fastest-growing region in the United States was the Southwest, and it was here — where the oil was plentiful and the labor cheap — that FNBB was doing business. In addition, Serge Semenenko was making large loan commitments to the movie industry, which of course is based in Southern California, three thousand miles away. Exporting capital outside the New England region, however, did nothing to foster the kind of economic activity within New England that would lead to the bank's long-term prosperity. It seemed obvious to me that the business of the bank should be to finance the only valuable raw material we had in the region — namely brains.

Massachusetts was in the economic doldrums in the late 1950s, but the seeds of what would someday be known as the Massachusetts Miracle had been sown during World War II at the Massachusetts Institute of Technology. Founded in 1861, MIT had actually been a proving ground for commercial ideas long before the war thrust it into the forefront of military-related research. By then, companies such as Arthur D. Little and Raytheon had already been spawned by MIT-trained engineers and spun off. Then came the war, and with it $117 million in federal moneys channeled to MIT for development of such decisive, state-of-the-art technologies as radar and self-aiming antiaircraft systems. After the war the defense work continued. Federally funded research organizations such as Lincoln Laboratories, MITRE Corporation, and Draper Laboratory were spun off, and smaller companies with expertise in defense technology (many of them also spin-offs from MIT) sprouted throughout the region.[2] This activity intensified after the Soviet Union launched Sputnik I and Sputnik II in the fall of 1957, setting off what would be known as the "space race." Suddenly the federal government was funding anything and everything that smacked of high tech, and MIT, Harvard, and any number of the small tech companies in the Boston were awash in government contracts. I had been exposed to some of this activity and acquired some sense of the trends during my two years in the army, when my job was to audit defense contracts.

Midway through 1958, a year when unemployment in Massachusetts reached 13 percent, I wrote a paper criticizing FNBB for not lending more to the growing number of research-based companies in the Boston area. My paper made two key points. First, it demonstrated what should have been obvious — that increased regional lending would mean increased deposits for the bank. As an example, I cited a loan to a textile company in North Carolina, where the proceeds were deposited in a North Carolina bank. From there they circulated throughout the local economy in North Carolina, not in our own local economy. It was a self-defeating strategy. Instead, I argued, FNBB should lend the money to Boston companies, which would then deposit their funds with us so that we could make other loans. What I was demonstrating in the case of the First National Bank of Boston was what every first-year economics student learns — that getting money into circulation has a multiplier effect on an economy.

The second point I made in my paper was that the bank should be proactive and aggressive in lending to Boston's high-tech sector. Being proactive meant lending more money at lower rates than the competition. Because high tech represented the future of the region and its financial community, the First National Bank of Boston would have to take the lead in high-tech lending. The bank needed a marketing strategy if it was to become the dominant player in this field.

My paper was not a work of genius. It simply took a fresh look at what was going on all around us. Yet when I gave a speech in the Credit Department based on my paper, I was greeted with stony stares and a few suppressed snickers. That didn't bother me, however. I was convinced that high-tech lending was the only way the bank could build its future business while fostering a healthy regional economy. This was the beauty of it: the bank could benefit itself while benefiting the region.

Fortunately, there was one man at the bank who believed as I did. He was Bill Brown, an assistant vice president who thirteen years later became president of the Bank of Boston, FNBB's successor. Brown reported to Bill Raye, one of the four top lending officers at the bank. Raye was still somewhat fixated on lending outside the region, although Brown had begun to win him over to what he referred to as technology-based lending. I took my paper to Brown and Raye, and they agreed that it was a pretty good piece of work. In October 1958, I was invited to join them "on the main banking floor" to form what became known as the High Technology Lending Group.[3]

Raye and Brown were concerned that the more traditional lending officers at the bank would not understand some of these high-tech companies, and they wanted to make sure the bank didn't let promising companies fall through the cracks. So they made it a policy that no one in the bank could refuse a loan to technology-based borrowers without Raye's or Brown's approval. The three of us became known inside the bank as the "space men," an allusion to the importance of the aerospace industry in the Boston area's nascent high-tech sector.

A second new policy that the bank instituted after the formation of our High Technology Lending Group was the acceptance of government research contracts as collateral for loans. The federal government was contracting at this time with small, undercapitalized companies. It was front-end loading the contracts, then providing progress payments. For instance, a professor could leave his university job with his prized doctoral student and begin an instrumentation company with a modest amount of his own capital — say $10,000 — and manage a $250,000 contract that the federal government would virtually prepay; the first installment would come before the work was even started. So with very little capital, these companies were able to get into business. And there was essentially no risk for the bank, because a government contracting officer would accept almost any proposal as long as it pushed the technology forward. The FNBB loans were of short duration, usually only 90 or 180 days, and a high-tech manager would practically have to commit a felony not to have the funds available from the government to pay the bank back. But this was still a great leap forward in what was an ultraconservative financial environment at the time.

The third policy the High Technology Lending Group instituted to get business from the new high-tech companies in the region was to lend them more money than any of our competitors would, and at lower rates. Quite simply, it amounted to a policy of grabbing 100 percent market share, or close to it, by giving the customer more product at a lower price. What's more, there were a number of lower-caliber underwriters in New York at that time who would flog anything with a transistor in it. Thanks to these so-called investment bankers, the bank could get its loans paid off in just about every case. These underwriters knew a hot commodity when they saw one. The benefit to the bank of an underwriting was twofold: our loan was paid off, and the proceeds of the underwriting meant a flood of cash to the debtor client, which became demand deposits in the bank. In fact the bank balances that resulted from the public offerings of securities by loan customers of the bank outstripped the loans to these customers by several orders of magnitude. The bank was not paying for this money. These were demand deposits, free of interest, which could then be loaned again at market rates.

In the small but influential High Technology Lending Group, I was the youngest gun and the most entrepreneurial. In venture capital circles today, "proactive deal-sourcing" has become a cliché, but in the late 1950s I virtually invented it. I became known as the guy who would charter a heli-copter and scatter my business cards along the length of Route 128. I never actually did this, but I might as well have. I was in the office Monday and Friday, but the other three days of the week I was on the road, chasing down every nickel-and-dime high-tech operator in every abandoned mill building in eastern New England. I found my prospects by poring over Dunn & Bradstreet reports and searching any Standard Industrial Classi-fication (SIC) code that had something to do with electronics or defense. I rank-ordered these lists by company size, ordered D&Bs on my target companies, studied them every free minute I had, and went after them. I found out virtually everything I could about a company before calling. The D&B included the director list, and if I knew any of them, or knew anyone who knew any of them, I'd call and ask about the company. I read the product literature; I talked with customers and suppliers, so that when I finally made my cold call, it was anything but cold. I already knew why the prospective client company should bank with us. And it usually did. I discovered I was a good salesman — though nothing makes you a good salesman like offering more product at a lower price.

Virtually the whole field was open to me, and I took much of it. One young technology company in the region whose business I didn't get was Digital Equipment Corporation, founded as a Lincoln Labs spin-off in 1957 by Ken Olsen in an old textile mill in Maynard, Massachusetts. Digi-tal was a portfolio company of American Research & Development, the first modern venture capital firm, and General Doriot, its founder, was also on the board of the Shawmut Bank, which meant that Digital became

Shawmut's captive lending client. I did, however, get business from one
of the other leading high-tech companies in Massachusetts in that era, although not without a lot of persistence.

Much of the high-tech business in those days, as today, was in East Cambridge in the area around MIT. In a second-floor loft on Hurley Street was
a still-young company called Wang Laboratories that I had researched and
that seemed to be first-rate. I made three cold calls at the company trying to get in to see its founder, Dr. An Wang. He had a secretary who was
like a stone wall, however, and who offered me no assistance toward my
objective. The first time I went to see Dr. Wang, I sat outside his office for
nearly an hour, all for naught. The second and third times I stopped by, I
waited just as long, if not longer, but still without success. It wasn't until
my fourth visit to the company, one day in 1958, that my persistence paid
off. An alarm went off somewhere on the premises, and everyone in the office, including me, went running around to the back of the building to see
what was the matter. There we saw that a big piece of equipment that the
shipping bay crew was trying to load onto a truck had slipped off its dolly.
I joined the group that was trying to push the piece of equipment back
onto the dolly and into its harness and suddenly realized that I was stand-
ing shoulder-to-shoulder with Dr. Wang. When we finally succeeded in
getting the equipment onto the truck, my efforts had earned me five minutes with him.

Dr. Wang thanked me for my help and asked me what I wanted—his
secretary had never said anything about me to him. He then told me that if
I wanted to talk about banking I should call his lawyer, Chuck Goodhue of
Goodwin Procter and Hoar. That was the end of the meeting. I promptly
made an appointment to see Goodhue and, when I did see him, offered
to double Wang's line of credit, from $25,000 to $50,000, to take Dr. Wang
off the back of the note, and to do it all for a quarter of a point under what
Wang was paying Merchant's Bank at the time. This was an offer Dr. Wang
couldn't refuse, and I became his banker.

Soon after our relationship commenced, I became puzzled by the fact
that Wang Laboratories manufactured only one-of-a-kind products designed to do specific tasks for one particular customer, the U.S. government. At the time, the closest Wang had to a mass-produced product was
a tape reader used in the numerical control of machine tools. Its major
customer for the product was the Cleveland-based machine tools manufacturer Warner & Swasey, whose director of research, Myron Curtis, told

me that An Wang was extraordinarily prolific when it came to product ideas but lacked any strategy for marketing. Meanwhile, Wang Laboratories was beginning to grow, and Dr. Wang was asking me for more money than the bank could lend without exceeding his credit line. I decided that I needed to raise equity for Wang, which would then allow me to loan the company more money. I also thought that Myron Curtis and Jim Hodge, Warner & Swasey's chairman, could be valuable advisers to Dr. Wang. And so, in 1959, I arranged for Warner & Swasey to acquire 25 percent of Wang Laboratories for $50,000 cash and the establishment of a $100,000 subordinated loan.

I thought this investment was a good deal for everyone. It certainly was for Warner & Swasey, whose $50,000 investment in Wang Laboratories was eventually worth $100 million. Dr. Wang also benefited significantly, not only from receiving the expansion capital he needed but also from Jim Hodge's wise counsel for the more than twenty years that Hodge sat on the Wang Laboratories board. This was not the way Dr. Wang saw it, however. In his autobiography *Lessons*, published in 1986, Wang complained that he had sold 25 percent of the company "for too little" and "given myself the handicap of minority controls." He said that he hadn't needed the money and that he regretted the "alliance" with Warner & Swasey "almost at once"; the relationship, he claimed, made no strategic sense, and he had learned nothing useful from it. Dr. Wang had a very selective view of history by this point, which was not long before the company to which he had devoted almost his entire working life became unglued.[4]

Building the high-tech program at the First National Bank of Boston was great fun, and a good example of deciding on a strategy and simply executing it. Our competition was aware that we were cleaning their clocks, and when they became aggressive with their loan proposals, we let them have the ones we didn't want. In 1959, about eighteen months after nearly being fired, I was made a loan officer — a significant promotion. I suspect I was made an officer out of sheer expediency. I started bringing in so much business — all of which had to be initialed by Raye or Brown or another senior officer — that pretty soon none of my superiors could keep up with it all, and they simply had to make me an officer so that I could initial my own notes! The First National Bank of Boston was the first of many foreign cultures I had to figure out, and I had done so. The experience confirmed me in a dawning belief that you've got to be a bit of an iconoclast to accomplish anything significant. You've got to think that you can do something better than somebody else, that you can change something, and that there is no barrier that you cannot scale.

During my time at FNBB, I lent $10 million and lost only $15,000 of that, and the new deposits these loans generated exceeded $30 million. The timing had turned out to be perfect for the High Technology Lending Group, whose success was recognized nationally. The group would continue to prosper for years afterward by providing financing for small, innovative companies in New England. It expanded dramatically in the 1970s and '80s and really distinguished FNBB: the companies it financed included not only Wang Laboratories but also Unitrode, Teradyne, and Analog Devices. One could easily say that the commercial banks in New England fueled the growth of the region and were as much a part of its renaissance as was venture capital.[5]

Nevertheless, after three years with the High Technology Lending Group I was getting restless. The continued rush to regain America's technological edge over the Soviets, the Kennedy administration's strong support of the U.S. space program, the heightened interest in and the funding of science curricula across the country in secondary schools and in colleges and universities — all this, along with the tremendous success the High Technology Lending Group had enjoyed, indicated to me that the high-tech world was just beginning to bud. The big opportunities, I began to think, were not going to be for those who made loans but rather for those who supplied equity capital and could benefit from the growth of the companies in which they invested when the value of those companies' shares rose.

At FNBB I was also beginning to get to know some of the handful of people who were actually in the venture capital business in those days. All the companies I loaned money to were technology based. Because they have intangible assets that are difficult for traditional lenders to value, and generally lack the track record and positive cash flow that traditional lenders want to see, young technology companies typically find it difficult to obtain debt financing and thus need to obtain equity capital from investors such as venture capitalists. (For reasons explained above, FNBB's high-tech lending in the late 1950s and early 1960s was virtually risk-free, although as prudent lenders we were careful not to allow the companies to which we made loans to take on too much debt.) In working with such companies, I became close to those who were providing equity capital at that time: Georges Doriot's American Research & Development (ARD) and wealthy families in New York such as the Rockefellers, the Phippses, and the Whitneys.

This was my real introduction to venture capital. I would lend money to a company, and if I thought it was particularly attractive and making good progress, and the loans were exceeding reasonable limits, I would take that company to one of the family venture capital providers in New York to see if the family would like to invest. One of the particularly successful companies I helped in this way was Thermo Electron, founded by George Hatsopoulos in 1956 on the basis of an idea he had, while a graduate student in mechanical engineering at MIT, for a device that would directly convert heat to electricity. The account executive for Thermo at FNBB in the late 1950s approached me for suggestions about an equity source for the company. So I introduced Hatsopoulos to Brady Security and Realty in New York, which was the investment company of Nicholas Brady's father. (Nick, who went on to become secretary of the treasury under Presidents Ronald Reagan and George H. W. Bush, was apprenticing at Dillon Reed at the time.) The Bradys, in turn, introduced him to Laurance Rockefeller, who invested $1 million in the company.

There was a good deal of altruism in what some early venture capitalists, including the Rockefellers, did at this time. They wanted to prove that advancing technology and making money were not mutually exclusive. So they started to make investments in the 1950s without knowing whether they would work or not, or what the exit would be. (It wasn't until the over-the-counter market became somewhat more active in the late 1950s and the early 1960s that such investments could be taken public.) They didn't expect to make a lot of money in this field. Their first stabs proved successful, so they tried more of that kind of investing. In so doing, they helped pave the way for the success of the venture capital industry,[6] which had its first major success when Digital Equipment Company went public in 1966, making ARD's share in the company worth over five hundred times its initial investment. Indeed, as syndicate investors with ARD and later with firms such as Greylock and TA Associates, the Rockefellers and their fellow venture capitalists from New York, the Whitneys and the Phippses, became a pivotal factor in the creation of a successful venture capital industry in Massachusetts.

Those investors were also a good example of what I was already doing. For in lending money to small high-tech companies, helping them attract equity capital, and advising them on management decisions, I was, in effect, already a venture capitalist at FNBB. The crucial thing I learned at the bank was the importance of providing entrepreneurs with management advice and assistance. As I have explained, the use of government research contracts as collateral essentially eliminated the financial risk in lending to many of the Boston area's high-tech start-ups. My role as a banker resembled a venture capitalist's not so much in its financial aspects as in its operational ones. For I found that being a brilliant technologist, on the one hand, and knowing how to commercialize an invention and successfully manage a business, on the other, were two entirely different matters. I had never run a business myself, but I had been to business school, learned how to analyze a company's strengths and weaknesses, and discovered that I could help many entrepreneurs simply by bringing business sense to the table. Even as shrewd and successful an entrepreneur as An Wang sometimes needed management advice. Indeed the company he founded and loved so much eventually ran aground when, against the advice of myself and my fellow directors, he appointed his son Fred as his successor rather than someone who was qualified for the job.[7]

Another example of an entrepreneurial venture that badly needed management assistance was a company called U.S. Sonics, a customer of mine at FNBB that I eventually introduced to Bessemer Securities, the Phipps family's investment arm. U.S. Sonics was founded by an MIT Ph.D. in one of the little garages on E Street in Cambridge — a typical MIT start-up. The company manufactured ceramic transducers, components of electronic devices. After Bessemer had made an equity investment in the company that paid off my loan, I continued to follow U.S. Sonics. When Bessemer came back to me and asked me to renew U.S. Sonics' line of credit, I told Bessemer that it would have to guarantee any new loans that I made because of my lack of confidence in U.S. Sonics' management. It was becoming obvious to me that the product did not meet the quality standards demanded of it; inventory and overhead were increasing, the company was burning cash, and the configuration of the balance sheet was becoming more and more precarious. In addition, the management rejected any advice I gave it out of hand. In short, the company was doing just about everything that an emerging enterprise should not do.

In the end, getting Bessemer out of that investment became my first task when, in the spring of 1961, I left FNBB after accepting an offer from Jack Kingsley, Bessemer's president, to come to New York and run the firm's venture capital operation. Charlie Lea, who would later be the key venture investor in Federal Express, had just left Bessemer for F. S. Smithers & Co., creating the opening at Bessemer. Although I was grateful to the First National Bank of Boston for the opportunities it had given me, I relished the chance to become a bona fide venture capitalist — so much so that I was willing, at first, to leave my family behind in Concord Monday through Friday. I soon realized, however, that in addition to extracting Bessemer from its investment in U.S. Sonics, my job was to rationalize the firm's venture capital portfolio and get it out of the venture capital business entirely if that seemed to be the appropriate course of action. Since I had not left the bank and sacrificed time with my family to get out of an industry I was so excited to join, I made sure that my analysis of Bessemer's participation in venture capital would not lead Kingsley to conclude that he should exit the business.

I loved the work at Bessemer, where I learned the venture capital business and invested in some companies that were very successful — for example, the electronics companies Unitrode and Crystalonics. By the end of 1962, however, I was tired of commuting back and forth between Concord, Massachusetts, and New York. My family was happy in Concord, where my wife Anne and I had recently built a new house, and I decided it was time to come home. Ogden Phipps and Jack Kingsley gave me an eighteen-month contract to follow all the New England–area investments Bessemer had made, which were considerable. When I came back to Boston, I didn't have a job, but I had their contract in my pocket, which was a real seal of approval from one of the major venture capital players in the country. So I had no problem getting offers from Hayden Stone, the investment bank,[8] and Paine Webber when I approached them and asked them if they would be interested in starting a venture capital management company.

Hayden Stone's Boston office, which was somewhat peripheral to this Wall Street bank's overall operations, was interested in starting a local venture capital activity. The manager of this office, David Stone, had his own ideas as to how to go about this, but I did not think that he understood the venture capital business well, and I was concerned that he would interfere with the way I wanted to do things. Paine Webber, founded in Boston, was a much more substantial organization. After I interviewed with Paine Webber and received an offer, I called Bill Brown at FNBB and told him I was going to go to work there. Brown warned me that this would be a serious mistake: "They'll be giving you close supervision and the last thing you could handle is close supervision," he correctly observed. He went on to say, "I've got a friend, Claire Pontius, at Tucker Anthony and R. L. Day who is always looking for new fertile fields to get into. Go see him." After I interviewed with Tucker Anthony, a prosperous Boston brokerage firm, Brown invited Claire Pontius and the firm's managing partner, Bill Claflin, to lunch at the bank and said to them, "You would be silly not to hire this guy." The reason I took Tucker Anthony's offer was that, unlike both Hayden Stone and Paine Webber, its managers didn't know anything about the venture capital business and realized that they didn't know anything.

Going to Tucker Anthony was a big step backward, and not only in pay. I was coming from New York, the world center of finance, where I had been working for one of the major national players in the venture capital business, to a Boston brokerage operation — a backwater, really. The firm had formed a company called Tucker Anthony & Co. whose purpose was to develop a corporate finance activity, but the fellow they had put in charge had been let go a year or two before I arrived, and the company was basically just a shell. I was charged with developing a business in mergers and acquisitions and in the private placement of venture capital securities. I was starting with virtually nothing. However, I did have the advantage of a clean piece of paper. I could build TA's corporate finance and venture capital business without anyone interfering.

I assigned my Bessemer contract to Tucker Anthony (TA), and we started building a corporate clientele, of which TA & Co. had none at that point. I was just a one-man shop, and developing a corporate finance business was not easy. TA & Co. did not have the heft to be the primary underwriter of a security, so when I found a new corporate client, I would have to take the business down to an investment bank like White Weld and negotiate a deal with the bank. It would run the books and bring the deal to the marketplace, and we would split the fees. Moreover, TA did not have the type of clientele interested in buying the securities of technology-based companies. I therefore had to go out and merchandise them myself, or interest the TA salesmen in marketing the securities to their clients. I had not only to find each tech-based company and convince it to do business with TA but then go out and sell the issue. It was on-the-job training and hard work, but it prepared for me for what I wanted to do next, which was to launch my own venture capital firm.

Venture capital in the modern sense, with investment managers raising funds from third parties as opposed to wealthy individuals and families investing their own money, was invented in Boston but was still a relatively new phenomenon in the mid-1960s, when I began looking for an opportunity to start my own firm. It is no accident that venture capital as an organized enterprise was born in eastern Massachusetts or that, as it was being invented there, it was viewed as a tool for economic development. As Boston venture capitalist Tom Claflin (who started his career with me at TA Associates forty years ago) has observed, the Massachusetts Bay Colony, established in 1628, essentially was a venture capital deal. The region's long history of innovation and risk taking includes the traders of colonial Boston, the seafaring merchants of the China trade in the early Republic, and the founders of the New England textile industry in the early nineteenth century.[9] Alexander Graham Bell received funding for his early research, and for the founding of Bell Telephone Company, from what we would now call "angel" investors in late-nineteenth-century Boston.

By the early twentieth century, however, New England had begun to experience economic decline. Its aging textile mills had become increasingly uncompetitive, and manufacturers in the textile and garment industries were being lured to the South by lower labor costs, lower taxes, and similar advantages. The region's once-prosperous leather and machine tool industries were also faltering. Business and civic leaders began looking for ways to attract or create new businesses to fill the growing economic void. In the years just prior to the start of World War I, the Boston Chamber of Commerce formed a short-lived industrial development corporation, a first, unsuccessful attempt to figure out how to foster the development of new firms and industries to replace the ones that were beginning to leave eastern Massachusetts. Then in 1925, as the exodus of textile, garment, and other manufacturers accelerated, the New England Council was founded under the leadership of the Boston merchant Lincoln Filene. Four years later, a council report stated that "the growth of industry in New England can best be promoted by local enterprises financed by local capital."

However, as the report also observed, attracting such capital for the financing of young enterprises posed serious challenges:

> The small company which has made good on a small scale and which wants to grow probably always has been and always will be in a difficult position. It often has no security except its own future possibilities to offer. . . . It needs additional capital for expansion of plant or operations and feels that it is entitled to capital. Nevertheless, the furnishing of such help is considered in many quarters as outside the bank's function, making it necessary for the company to go without the needed capital or to sell stock or to find additional private capital. If it chooses to sell stock, it often pays a prohibitive price for its capital; if it succeeds in interesting private capital, this ordinarily necessitates surrendering control of the business — in many cases into hands less expert in its actual management.[10]

The need the report identified was for what we would now call expansion capital rather than start-up financing. But the New England Council's study identified the precise reason why — if young, entrepreneurial companies were to have a chance to grow and prosper — venture capital (and what we now call private equity) had to be invented. The first modern venture capital firm appeared in Boston in 1946 when Georges Doriot, MIT president Karl T. Compton, Federal Reserve Bank of Boston president Ralph Flanders, and Massachusetts Investors Trust chairman Merrill Griswold (all of whom had served on the New Products Committee established by the New England Council in 1939) founded the American Research & Development Corporation (ARD). With anxiety about the strength of America's economic institutions and the prospects for postwar prosperity running high in the wake of the Depression and World War II, ARD's founders wanted to help commercialize some of the advanced research undertaken as part of the war effort in government laboratories and universities such as MIT and Harvard. In the model that Doriot created, the venture capitalist, although a minority investor in most cases, was not simply to be a passive investor but was to be actively engaged in the strategic planning and direction of the companies in which he invested, serving as the partner of the entrepreneurs with whom he worked. The techniques ARD developed, including staged investment in new or growing firms and taking seats on their boards of directors, are still the standard ones used by venture capitalists today.

Venture capital is something we now take for granted in the United States, but the way Georges Doriot approached it created some confusion. As two historians of Doriot's pioneering venture capital organization have observed, "At its core ARD carried an apparent contradiction: it was meant to create the social good of new economic activity, yet it had to be profitable."[11] The role of the venture capitalist, for Doriot, was to promote technological advancement, innovation, and new industries while also creating wealth for investors and for venture capitalists themselves, to prove that technological advancement and making money were not mutually exclusive. General Doriot's message was a clear and attractive one to a generation of young men (venture capitalists were all men in those days) who were motivated to help build a vibrant American economy. In the years after World War II, this was as much of an imperative for the United States as it was for Europe. For with memories of the Great Depression still vivid and the Cold War in full swing, Americans were determined to show that capitalism was the best system for creating shared prosperity.

The idea of benefiting society while also making a profit was something that Boston's financial establishment, which had become quite conservative, did not latch on to right away. The notion of doing good while doing well is one that the descendants of the New England Puritans should have easily grasped, but the estate trustees with their gold watch chains were more bent on conserving the fortunes made in the China trade in the nineteenth century than on helping to create new ones. It was not easy to convince a financial establishment paralyzed by the "prudent man" rule to invest in new technologies and new enterprises, and ARD just barely raised the $3 million it needed to get started. Even MIT, which backed ARD at first, cut back its support by the mid-1950s.[12]

ARD was the only venture capital firm in Boston for nearly twenty years after its founding, and the only one in the United States for most of that time. In 1964, the oldest existing venture capital firm on the West Coast, Sutter Hill Ventures, was cofounded by Paul Wythes and William H. Draper III. (Draper's father, William H. Draper, Jr., had been a founder of Draper, Gaither & Anderson, the first West Coast venture firm, started in 1958.) A year later, one of Georges Doriot's protégés at ARD, Bill Elfers, teamed up with Dan Gregory (they would soon be joined by Elfers's ARD colleague Charlie Waite) to found Greylock Partners in Boston. With investors that included Sherman Fairchild, founder of Fairchild Semiconductor, the Watsons of IBM, and members of the Corning family,

Greylock's first limited partnership, Greylock & Co., raised just under $10 million and invested in companies including Damon Engineering, Millipore, Teradyne, and Continental Cablevision.

I first met Elfers while I was still at Bessemer Securities and he was Doriot's right-hand man at ARD. While building the book of business at TA & Co., I got to know him well. He took me to lunch a couple of times and asked me questions such as "Do you mind traveling?" and "Do you mind working weekends?" I did not know what he was driving at and flatter myself by wondering if it had anything to do with joining him when he left ARD to found Greylock. Probably not, since Bill soon found an outstanding partner in Dan Gregory, who later became a much-admired industry leader. Elfers also knew that I had a burning desire to found my own firm when I had the opportunity. A few years later, when I founded TA Associates, Bill, one of the truly great men in the early days of venture capital, would show me his limited partner agreement and help me in many other ways to get the firm up and running.

Meanwhile, one of the investments I made while at Bessemer Securities was in Damon Engineering, a small company that had done very well producing frequency-control systems for the military but whose founders, David Kosowsky and Carl Hurtig, were interested in diversifying into the medical field. In 1967 I arranged a private placement in the securities of International Equipment Company (IEC), a manufacturer of blood centrifuges. Its investors included Greylock, Bessemer, the Rockefellers, and Charlie Cunningham (my successor as head of the High Technology Lending Group at FNBB). Bill Elfers was aware of Damon's interest in the medical equipment field and suggested that Damon and IEC would be a good fit. Kosowsky and Hurtig readily accepted this advice. Bill was highly regarded in financial circles as a strategist and for his wisdom. He also possessed that patina of elegance, confidence, and rectitude that distinguished the East Coast venture capitalist. He was hard to resist. In any case, Damon and IEC were merged, and a subsequent public offering was very rewarding for the shareholders of the combined companies.

Also in 1967, I introduced Bill Elfers and Greylock to An Wang, and Bill and I worked together on a plan for a private issue of common stock in Wang Laboratories. The IPO market temporarily took off as we were formulating this plan, and An Wang decided that a public offering would be a better route to obtaining capital than a private financing. However, I did arrange for Greylock to buy a substantial block of shares in the underwriting, a windfall for Greylock since the value of the stock increased threefold in the immediate aftermarket.[13]

Meanwhile, the fact that Tucker Anthony & Co. acquired a clientele including names such as Damon, Wang, and some other excellent companies only a few years after starting virtually from scratch reflects the success of its corporate finance and venture capital activity. Indeed, Tucker Anthony & Co. was doing so well that, by 1967, the IRS let us know it was time for us to distribute the money we were making to our shareholders. When it was determined that paying a single liquidating dividend would have tax advantages over paying out a string of dividends year after year, I approached the shareholders (the partners of Tucker Anthony & Co., Inc.) with a proposition. I suggested that they remain with us, keeping enough of their liquidating dividend to pay their taxes. Everyone agreed, and the $2 million that remained after taxes became the cornerstone investment in a new fund, the first fund formed by my first true venture capital organization, which I named TA Associates. I was finally in business for myself, in charge of my own destiny.

TA Associates was the name of the new firm, but what to name the new fund? One evening in December 1967, I pondered this over cocktails with Chuck Goodhue, with whom I had negotiated a line of credit for Wang Laboratories when I was at the First National Bank of Boston and who now represented Tucker Anthony and R. L. Day and TA Associates. One acronym we devised, for Tucker Anthony and R. L. Day Ventures, came out TADVEN when we scribbled it on a napkin. That looked a little too much like TADPOLE to us, so we swung the T around to the end and had ADVENT, a religious term invented without religious motivation during the season of that name. As we will see, however, it would require more than a little faith — from investors, entrepreneurs, and those of us at TA Associates ourselves — to make the dreams I had for the organization become a reality.

# CHAPTER 2

# BUILDING TA ASSOCIATES

. . .

We eventually raised a total of $6 million for TA Associates' first fund, which we named Advent Company. Besides the partners of Tucker Anthony and R. L. Day, the investors included those Tucker Anthony clients for whom I had made successful investments in the past, others who were acquainted with Tucker Anthony and R. L. Day, and a few international investors. Investors from abroad (mostly French families to whom I was introduced by a French partner of Tucker Anthony and who contributed $2 million) entered the fund through a special partnership called Advent Bermuda.[1] I negotiated a 25 percent interest for myself in both partnerships.[2]

TA Associates opened its doors in 1968. It seemed a promising time to be setting up a new venture capital firm, in many ways. The venture capital industry in the United States was still relatively young but already had some impressive achievements to its credit. Digital Equipment Corporation in Massachusetts, in which ARD had invested $70,000 in 1957, had gone public in 1966, at which point ARD's investment was worth $38.5 million.[3] This caught the attention of investors on the East Coast. On the West Coast, Fairchild Semiconductor — which back in 1959 had introduced the first commercially successful version of the integrated circuit — gave birth in 1968 to Intel, which would go public only three years later. Both Fairchild and Intel had received venture capital backing from Arthur Rock, a now-legendary investor who had been a student of Georges Doriot's at Harvard Business School. The year after TA Associates was established, two other now-prominent firms, Venrock Associates on the East Coast and the Mayfield Fund on the West, were both founded. Two of the most storied West Coast firms, Kleiner Perkins Caufield & Byers and Sequoia Capital, would begin operations in 1972.

Despite the exciting prospects some of us saw, however, this was not yet a time when people were lining up to get into the venture capital business. In fact you had to be kind of a nut to get into it, because it wasn't even an industry yet, let alone the household word it is today. When somebody asked my wife Anne what I did, she didn't know how to describe it. (She finally started telling people that I was an investment banker.) And so when I recruited my first team for TAA, I just tried to find people who were interested in joining me and who I thought could be trained.

TAA's first employee was Tom Claflin, whom I had actually hired at Tucker Anthony & Co. the preceding year. Tom was the son of a cousin of Bill Claflin, who was the head of Tucker Anthony. He seemed interested in learning about venture capital and looked like a bright young guy, so I said, "Well, come on board." I found my second employee, Kevin Landry, the same way: his father-in-law was a great friend of a partner at Tucker Anthony. Kevin, who has led TAA ever since I left to form Advent International in 1984 and is now one of the leading private equity managers in the United States, was getting his MBA at the Wharton School when I met him and told him that I was in the venture capital business. Kevin replied, "Boy, I love the venture capital business!" As he now says, he thought that was a better response than "What's the venture capital business?"

Looking back at the earliest days of TA Associates and the team of greenhorns I assembled there, one could legitimately wonder what we had to offer besides capital. When I started TAA, I had ten years' experience investing in new and growing companies and a long list of contacts that would prove helpful in recruiting managers and locating other kinds of assistance for our portfolio companies. But Kevin and Tom were kids just out of business school with no experience to speak of, particularly the kind of operating experience that gives venture capital and private equity managers direct insight into the problems faced by the managers of their portfolio companies. I suppose you could say that, in other respects, my young associates in the early days of TAA had few qualifications as venture capitalists compared with young people entering the business today. There were no courses in venture capital and entrepreneurship in business schools at the time, and no opportunities like there are now for starting businesses with nothing more than a bright idea and a little knowledge of Internet technology.

Eventually I would build a team that included such talented investment managers as Bill Egan, Craig Burr, Grant Wilson, David Croll, Andy

McLane, Jacqui Morby, Roe Stamps, Steve Woodsum, and others. For several years after TAA's founding, however, even as the team acquired more investment experience, I remained the only one who could raise capital and, crucially, provide revenues from sources other than fees on capital under management to cover the salaries of the team and build out the firm. What those sources of revenue would be I had to figure out on my own, as there were few existing models for starting a venture capital firm with limited resources.

Actually, the $6 million I had raised for Advent Company seemed to me like a hell of a lot of money in 1967. Greylock and Co., Bill Elfers's first venture fund, had started up in October 1965 with only $4.8 million (although it would eventually have nearly $10 million to invest). Still, the 2.5 percent management fee on our $6 million amounted to only $150,000 per year — hardly enough, even then, to keep a venture team together. (Today it wouldn't pay the cell phone bill.) Advent II, which closed in 1972 and was a tough sell to the prospective new investors I approached, would be a $10 million partnership. At the same 2.5 percent rate it would add $250,000 to our annual income base, but that still wasn't enough. I would raise Advent III in 1978, just before Advent II began producing the high returns I had hoped for, and was hard-pressed to secure $15 million in capital. I did get a crucial assist at that point from Boston University's can-do president John Silber, who saw to it that the university found a way to invest $1 million of its endowment at a time that institutions such as Harvard — which came in with an investment of $1 million at the very end of the fund-raising for Advent III — were still hesitant about investing in venture capital.

In retrospect, it is hardly surprising that investors were reluctant to put their money into venture capital in the 1970s. The industry was new and did not have much of a track record. It would take five to seven years from the time of investment in a venture capital fund before the results would begin to be known, and venture capital managers would ask investors in one fund to invest in a second before the performance of the first one could be assessed. Until 1979, when the Labor Department clarified the "prudent man" rule in the Employee Retirement Income Security Act (ERISA) of 1974, pension funds were actually barred from investing in such relatively risky vehicles. Prior to 1978, when Congress returned the capital gains tax rate to 28 percent, investors would also have paid the 49.5 percent rate that had been in effect since 1969. Moreover, a decade that saw the American withdrawal from Vietnam, the Watergate scandal, and long years of inflation and recession was hardly conducive to economic vibrancy and optimism. The stock market was underwater, and there was no evidence that a share of the gains from an IPO would be worth anything. Before it became evident that many of the conglomerates formed amid the mergers-and-acquisitions craze of the 1960s and '70s were underperforming, many economists and business leaders assumed that the future of the world economy was going to be dominated by a few dozen giant corporations. As the economy emerged from recession in the late 1970s, the stock market rebounded, and the country regained its optimism, the results of the patient labors of capable venture capitalists would eventually become visible. Until that point, however, an investment in venture capital required an extraordinary amount of trust.

In any case, the relatively small size of these first three funds meant that on top of all the work of building and training a team, prospecting for investments, and being actively involved in managing them, I had to develop alternative sources of income for the firm. For the first ten years after its founding, TAA continued to function as the corporate finance arm of Tucker Anthony, which gave us fee income from our relationships with clients such as Wang Laboratories, Damon Engineering, and Unitrode, as well as others in which TA Associates would invest including Guilford Mills, Worcester Controls, and Taylor Rental. In addition, TA Associates managed special venture capital accounts for F. S. Smithers & Co., Massachusetts Mutual Insurance Company, and a few others. I also developed my own clientele for consulting and mergers-and-acquisitions work. It was a busy time.

In prospecting for investments, I did have the benefit of relationships with entrepreneurs and companies that I had developed at FNBB, Bessemer, and Tucker Anthony. For example, I encouraged an entrepreneur whom I had backed at Bessemer, Crystalonics founder Bill Frusztajer, to start the BBF Group, a group of electronics companies in which TAA invested. Otherwise, to find prospective deals — *any* prospective deals — for TAA, I had to do what I had done when launching the High Technology Lending Group at FNBB: work the telephone, make cold calls, and sell myself to entrepreneurs. Except that now, instead of having the First National Bank of Boston behind me willing to lend them money at low rates of interest, I had to convince prospective clients that a new, untested venture capital firm named TA Associates could help them succeed by taking an equity share in their companies.

I also had to cast my net as widely as possible, looking not just for technology companies but for small companies in any industry that seemed capable of growth and needed capital and management assistance. It is important to remember that the term *venture capital* (as I have explained in the introduction) meant something different in the late 1960s and early 1970s than it has since come to mean. When I founded TA Associates I remained interested, as I had been since my days at the First National Bank of Boston, in providing new, technology-based companies with start-up financing and management assistance. I still believed that such companies were the key to reviving and renewing the New England economy. Yet neither the technology business nor the venture capital business had progressed to the point where hundreds of business plans from technology entrepreneurs came in over the transom of a venture capital firm every year. Those days were still a long way off. In the late 1960s, telling someone that you were a "venture capitalist" usually just provoked blank stares, even though by this time high-tech companies were accounting for almost 10 percent of total employment in Massachusetts.

Moreover, none of us at TAA in those early days knew much about technology. This was true of East Coast venture capitalists as a group: we were generalists, not technologists. We also took a portfolio approach to venture investing that emphasized diversification and protection of our investments. Most of TAA's investments, indeed, were in companies that had a revenue base and were profitable or moving toward profitability. We differed in these regards from our colleagues on the West Coast. While Arthur Rock and Tommy Davis were generalists with backgrounds in finance, they were joined early on by people like Tom Perkins and Don Valentine, managers with backgrounds in the technology industry. The West Coast venture capitalists concentrated on technology investments and were not averse to supplying seed and early-stage capital. They looked for the next great technology companies that would change the world. This reflected the pioneering spirit of those in the West and their deep knowledge of technology and how to introduce it into the marketplace, as well as of the special skills involved in managing a young high-tech firm. They were good at what they did, and gained an edge that they have never relinquished.

That said, however, and as the successful West Coast venture capitalists themselves have demonstrated, an understanding of technology will only take a venture capitalist so far. While it is important to know something about technology—increasingly so today, given the complexity of technology and the speed of technological change—it is essential to know how to identify market opportunities, size up entrepreneurs, and develop relationships with entrepreneurs in which information and ideas flow freely. These are not skills that can readily be taught—venture capital is an art, not a science. But a venture capitalist who has such skills can add substantial value to a business by supplementing the knowledge and talents of an entrepreneur, even without knowing everything there is to know about a particular product or technology.

While I hoped to help my young recruits at TA Associates develop all the abilities they would need to succeed, we were all able to offer entrepreneurs an understanding of finance and other aspects of business and a genuine interest in helping them succeed. A look at some of the companies in the portfolios of TAA's first two funds, in any case, shows the range of industries in which we invested. The portfolios of these funds, Advent Company and Advent II, included everything from high-tech companies such as the BBF Group and the Tandon Corporation to firms in communications (including Continental Cablevision), business services, furniture manufacturing, and retail, to name just a few. Approximately half of the portfolio companies in the first two TAA funds were technology based.

The kinds of challenges we faced at a time when venture capital itself was new and high-tech entrepreneurs, in particular, distrusted and even resented venture capitalists are exemplified by TAA's early investment in a company called ECRM. In the late 1960s, MIT professors Sam Mason, Bill Schreiber, and Don Troxel developed a new optical character recognition technology. Schreiber had gone to the First National Bank of Boston to talk about financing, and my former colleagues at FNBB had referred him to Tucker Anthony and R. L. Day. I thought the technology had potential, so we formed a development partnership, which was a vehicle that existed in those days enabling investors to write off their investment against ordinary income. Advent Company, the first limited partnership managed by TA Associates, was an investor along with the MIT entrepreneurs, who invested $10,000 each—not an insignificant amount for them at that time. When the development partnership proved that the technology actually worked, we formed ECRM (which stood for Electronic Character Recognition Machinery) in 1969 to exploit it in the newspaper industry.

Bill Schreiber and Don Troxel had been persuaded that their optical character recognition technology had applications in the newspaper business by Mel Fennell of the Associated Press. Fennell had contracted with the two MIT professors for technology support on an AP project and was convinced that their equipment could be used to improve the efficiency of newspaper production. When the capitalization of ECRM was completed, Fennell joined the company to be its president and to develop its marketing and sales strategy. Mason, Schreiber, and Troxel seemed to respect his industry knowledge and experience. When I took my seat on the company's board of directors, however, I began to find out how the three MIT professors viewed us, the venture capitalists. Sam Mason, otherwise a very reasonable man, charged that for TA Associates to have acquired the share of the company that it had was "close to rape." He let me know that he considered us not partners but suppliers, in this case suppliers of capital, and that he expected our advice to have little impact on the company's success. He would tolerate my presence on the board, but barely. Our relationships with Schreiber and Troxel were cordial but guarded, at least at the beginning.

ECRM introduced preproduction prototypes of its electronic character reading machinery at an American Newspaper Association meeting in 1970, and interest in the product began to build. At this time Mel Fennell, who had indicated from the beginning that he was not interested in being president of a manufacturing company but only in selling ECRM's equipment to the newspaper industry, resigned and returned to his home state of Oklahoma to enter the ranching business, his first love. This caused us to undertake the first of what would be a long, arduous series of searches for effective leadership for the company.

Along with Dr. Amran Rasiel, a director of ECRM, I embarked on this first search for a CEO and identified Ronald Noonan, the head of a business unit of Digital Equipment Corporation. Noonan joined the company in 1971 and oversaw its rapid growth and the successful introduction of its shares to the over-the-counter market in 1972 through C. E. Unterberg, Towbin. Unfortunately, shortly after the company went public, Noonan became ill and was unable to continue running ECRM, which was having trouble fulfilling the growth expectations of its shareholders. And so the search for a new leader began all over again. Next we brought on Bruce Cooperman, a manager of a business unit of Xerox, who joined ECRM in 1973 but lasted only a year.

As an interim step, we then hired a well-regarded Boston businessman, John Callahan, to take the post of CEO until a search for a permanent replacement for Cooperman could be launched. I found Callahan through a company in which TA Associates invested in 1973, S. W. Industries, where he was vice president for mergers and acquisitions. Before that he had been a partner with Arthur Andersen. In 1974 he had started his own consulting business, John B. Callahan & Associates, in which TA Associates took at 50 percent stake. When we asked him to take over ECRM temporarily, Callahan settled in and considered remaining as the permanent CEO until he was hired away to become head of the gaming company World Jai-Alai at the end of 1974. Perhaps we should have done more due diligence on him before investing in his consulting firm and hiring him to run ECRM. It later emerged that Callahan had been living a double life at least since the early 1970s, building a reputation in Boston as a crack accountant and consultant by day, consorting with local mobsters, including the infamous James "Whitey" Bulger, by night. While heading up World Jai-Alai, Callahan laundered $10,000 a week in skimmed profits from the company's fronton in Hartford, Connecticut, for Bulger and his partner Stephen "The Rifleman" Flemmi. Callahan's minions at the company kept up the skimming after he was fired in 1976, and when a new owner, the Tulsa businessman Roger Wheeler, began to suspect what was going on, Bulger had him murdered. It further emerged that Callahan had been involved in plotting Wheeler's murder, making him a man who knew too much as far as Bulger was concerned. Callahan's unusually varied business career came to an end in July 1982 when his body, with two bullets in the head, was found in the trunk of a silver Cadillac in a parking garage at Miami International Airport.[4]

At any rate, after Callahan moved on from ECRM to even riskier ventures, Dr. Rasiel and I undertook another search process, one that eventually led us to an executive named Dan Fisher. This management turmoil, needless to say, was not helpful to ECRM. The company, which was a market leader, lost its position and was not able to recover for years afterward. It was sold in 1978 to Addressograph Multigraph, and although both the venture capital investors and the MIT professors made money in the deal, it was hardly enough to compensate for the agony we had all endured.

During theses struggles, the MIT entrepreneurs could easily have become hostile to us. As time went on and the company went from crisis to crisis, however, the MIT crowd actually came to appreciate how difficult it was to manage an enterprise of this nature, and that we were breaking our backs to make it succeed. We might not have been smart, but we did not

quit. At the end of the day I think we gained their grudging respect. Don Troxel finally said to me, "Well you know, after this whole exercise, I really appreciate what you guys have done. You hung in there." This was quite an admission for him to make, considering how suspicious of us he and his two MIT partners had been at the beginning.[5]

TAA's investment strategy proved to be sound, and the execution was sharp. The performance of its funds was strong from the start and escalated rapidly. Advent Company, our first fund, outperformed most venture funds of its vintage with an IRR (internal rate of return) of 8.65 percent, while Advent II had an IRR of 21.48 percent. Advent III, which we launched in 1978 with $15 million, invested in companies including Biogen, Comcast, and McCormack & Dodge and would become an even bigger success with an IRR of 39.98 percent, which led to TA Associates rapidly accumulating a great deal of capital to manage. Advent IV would be capitalized at $70 million in 1979, and Advent V at $165 million in 1982. Funds raised from Orange Nassau in the Netherlands, the Bemberg Group in Paris, and the Industrial Bank of Kuwait, as well as a substantial fund raised by a financial adviser in Munich, the Matuschka Group, gave TAA in excess of $150 million to manage in the early 1980s. This placed TA Associates among the venture capital managers with the largest amount of capital under management by 1983.

TA Associates' investment in Biogen is notable for having come out of one of two programs in corporate venturing in which TAA became involved in the mid-1970s, a time when we still did not have enough capital from institutional investors under management to support the operations of the firm. As Paul A. Gompers and Josh Lerner have documented in their book *The Money of Invention*, corporate venturing activity has ebbed and flowed since the late 1960s with the vicissitudes of the IPO market. After what Gompers and Lerner call a "first wave" of corporate venturing activity that lasted from the late 1960s to the early 1970s, a second wave arose in the late 1970s.[6] Just after the first wave had subsided and before the second had quite begun, TAA entered the field of corporate venturing. In 1975, Advent Company and Advent II were coming out of the recessionary period of the early '70s with strong portfolios that promised excellent returns for its investors. The firm's client relationships were growing because of its prominence domestically and increasing awareness of what it was doing internationally. Attracted by TAA's investment successes and international relationships, both the Xerox Corporation and International Nickel Company (INCO) approached the firm about starting dedicated venture capital programs.

TAA's relationship with INCO would have significant impact not only on its own fortunes but also on those of Advent International, for which corporate venturing would become an important mainstay after its founding in 1984. Given the highly cyclical nature of the nickel business, INCO was seeking opportunities to diversify. Its strategy was to do so through internal R&D, acquisitions, and venture capital investments that would help the company identify new areas into which it might move. INCO's point man for executing this strategy was the far-sighted and energetic Raymond Schaeffer, who had taken on this job despite being close to retirement. With the capital that INCO placed with TAA we opened a separate account and, in partnership with Schaeffer, embarked on one of the truly successful forays into corporate venturing.

At the invitation of Kleiner Perkins, the lead venture capital investor in the immensely successful Genentech, the INCO/TAA account invested in that company.[7] One of the resources we used in evaluating the Genentech technology prior to investing was Harvard's Walter Gilbert, who would receive the Nobel Prize in chemistry in 1980. On the flight back to the East Coast after a visit to Genentech, with whose technology Gilbert had been impressed, Ray Schaeffer suggested to him that INCO and TA Associates establish an East Coast knockoff of Genentech. Gilbert agreed and, together with Schaeffer, drew up a list of experts in the field of bioscience on the East Coast and in Europe. The list included Phil Sharp of MIT and Charles Weissman of the Institute for Molecular Biology in Zurich. I actually went to Zurich with Schaeffer when he signed up Weissman to become an adviser and shareholder of the new company, Biogen. The Biogen board included, among others, Ray Schaeffer, Kevin Landry of TA Associates, and Moshe Alafi, a noted health-science investor. This group was instrumental in attracting corporate investors and participants in the technology developed by Biogen, including Schering Plough and Monsanto.

Gilbert, who became president of Biogen when the company was launched in 1979, had an attitude toward venture capitalists that was refreshingly different from the hostility we had sometimes encountered when dealing with an earlier generation of academic scientists. He understood that the advice and contacts provided by Schaeffer, Landry, and Alafi were essential to the commercialization of the research provided through Biogen's technology advisory board. He had no problem with INCO and TA Associates having a substantial share in Biogen in return for developing the marketing strategy for the technology and capitalizing the company. He knew that he and Phil Sharp couldn't negotiate with Monsanto or Schering Plough for commercial rights or for share ownership in the company. So he told us, "Okay boys, go at it." Gilbert's approach was increasingly typical of academic entrepreneurs in the late 1970s. The MIT and Harvard faculties did not necessarily embrace venture capitalists, but they now appreciated us for what we could bring to the table.

Given the capital requirements of a biotech company, INCO could never capitalize on its position in Biogen. It had substantial financial requirements in the nickel business and for the other ventures we were recommending. Schaeffer and Kevin Landry would duplicate the founding of Biogen in 1981, when the INCO/TAA account invested in ImmunoGen. Once again, however, the capital requirements proved to be too great. INCO was unable to become a factor in the biotech field and finally abandoned the effort. It never made another serious move to diversify after Schaeffer retired in the early 1980s.[8] Yet the TAA program was very successful for INCO from a financial standpoint — INCO made twenty-five or thirty investments through the TAA account, and probably ended up making as much money from these investments as from the nickel business during some of these years. The program also produced significant fee income and capital gains for TAA.

TA Associates grew and developed rapidly in the course of the 1970s and early 1980s, but the venture capital industry was growing and changing as well, and staying in the game meant meeting some significant new challenges. For example, although the firm's generalist approach, and investment across a variety of sectors, had served us well in our first two funds, by the mid-1970s it was becoming clear that some sector specialization was called for as well. It was at this point that Grant Wilson, a very bright and innovative investor, came to TAA from the John Hancock Insurance Company, where he had convinced his superiors that what was important in the cable television and broadcast industries was not the traditional balance sheet but rather the ability of an asset to create a positive cash flow.

I hired Grant for two purposes: to develop a private placement activity that would supplement TAA's revenues, and to start a cable television investment activity for TAA. Our investment in Continental Cablevision in 1970 (which Greylock had led) had been a home run, and the industry was attractive: its market was expanding rapidly, and its heavy depreciation created a shelter that generated strong positive cash flow.

In 1976, not long after he joined the firm, Grant convinced me to hire David Croll, who had previously been a loan officer at the First National Bank of Boston, concentrating on loans to the broadcasting and cable television industries. While at FNBB, Croll had collaborated on credits with Wilson and John Hancock, the bank taking the short-term obligations, the Hancock taking the long. When Wilson left TA Associates to go into business on his own in the late 1970s, David developed a distinct media and communications unit, with its own sector-centered strategy, within TAA, a team that became a leader in cable television financings with investments in companies including American Cablesystems, American Radio Systems, Columbia Cable, and Crowley Cellular. David brought in Rich Churchill, Bill Collatos, who later formed Spectrum Equity Investors, and Steve Gormley, who later founded Great Hill Partners. This was an early example of a team approach to an industrial sector. While each associate found and executed investments, they all worked together under the close supervision of Croll. The sector approach that David developed provided gains that were crucial to the good results produced by TA Associates' fourth and fifth funds — funds that, thanks to the media and communications group, managed to perform in the top quartile. (Results from the early-stage sector for TA Associates and the industry as a whole would not be particularly attractive in the early 1980s.)

As TA Associates stood on the verge of the breakthrough success it would enjoy in the early 1980s, however, the partnership was in the process of changing. Kevin Landry, who had become a partner in Tucker Anthony and R. L. Day and TA Associates in 1972, was gradually assuming increasing responsibility for the investment side of TAA's activities and would become a managing partner (along with David Croll) in 1982. Others were not sticking around quite so long, however. Barriers to entry in the venture capital business are low, and talented, ambitious, entrepreneurial venture capital managers are easily drawn to the idea of setting up their own shops. For example, although I had made Grant Wilson a partner at TAA only a year or two after he joined the firm, he left to start his own investment operation soon thereafter. Then, in 1979, Bill Egan and Craig Burr left TAA to form their own firm, to be joined shortly thereafter by Jean Deléage of Sofinnova, the French venture capital firm whose founding I describe in the next chapter. Bill and Craig had joined TAA in the early 1970s, and when Tucker Anthony's 75 percent interest in Advent Company and Advent II was acquired in 1978, they were admitted to the TA Associates partnership along with David Croll. Losing Bill Egan was an especially sad thing for TA Associates. Bill was a good investment man, the best we had, and a wise man. He brought a balance of seriousness and fun to the firm, both of which were sorely missed. Bill, Craig, and Jean were very successful. Their firm, Burr, Egan, Deleage & Co., became an important investor in information technology, communications, and in the health-care sector.[9]

Happily others within the firm were developing and were able to fill the gap until Roe Stamps joined us from the First Chicago Investment Corporation. Andy McLane developed a sector expertise in computers, computer peripherals, and telecommunications, and Jacqui Morby became one of the country's leading computer software investors. Andy and Jacqui became partners in the firm and were joined by Roe Stamps in 1979 and Steve Woodsum in 1981. The firm would change again in 1984, when Stamps and Woodsum left to found their own firm, Summit Partners, which like Burr, Egan, Deleage in its day has been immensely successful.

Having hired, groomed, and then said good-bye to talented venture capitalists such as Bill Egan, Craig Burr, Roe Stamps, and Steve Woodsum, I have often been asked how I felt when my protégés at TA Associates left. My feelings about this were complex. At first I felt rejected. Then I wanted to get back into the marketplace to raise more funds than my new competitors. Eventually I would come to accept, with some reluctance, that these individuals were entrepreneurs like me, doing what came naturally to them. Finally I would feel proud of these old colleagues who had gone out in the world and made it on their own. I am still proud of them today.

With all the hard work I put into building my own venture capital firm at a time when the future of venture capital itself was still uncertain, I should have been satisfied to focus all my attention on that task alone. However, given my belief that venture capital was all about economic development,

I did not think I had the luxury of simply cultivating my own garden at TA Associates. At the First National Bank of Boston I had concerned myself with how, in my role as a lender, I could contribute to the economic revival of New England. Similarly, while building TAA I was keeping my eye on the bigger picture — namely, the state of the Massachusetts economy and the role of venture capital in promoting the state's and the New England region's economic health.

By the end of the 1960s, as I have mentioned, Massachusetts's industrial base had undergone some significant diversification owing to the rise of a high-tech industry, which by then accounted for nearly 10 percent of total employment in the state. The IPO of Digital Equipment Company in 1966 provided evidence of the great potential of the computer industry in Massachusetts. Two years later, three engineers from Digital left the company to cofound Data General, which went public only a year later. Prime Computer, in which Greylock invested, and Computervision would both be founded in the early 1970s, and that decade generally, like the 1960s, was a fertile period for computer-related start-ups in Massachusetts. Venture capitalists in Boston and New York could definitely claim some of the credit for this welcome development. Indeed, the Boston venture capitalists who were around in those days are not shy about claiming credit for turning the New England region into a center of high-tech innovation.

Not long into the 1970s, however, the Massachusetts economy as a whole began to deteriorate. In early 1972, despite all the new high-tech companies that had been created in the previous decade, unemployment in Massachusetts reached 8 percent. The state had lost over 112,000 manufacturing jobs in its traditional industries over the preceding five years. For all its early promise, high tech was simply not ready to plug such a hole in the state's employment base. Moreover, as the winding down of both the space program and the Vietnam War slowed the flow of federal R&D contracts to the state, it became evident that its still relatively young high-tech industry was too dependent on government work. Local financial institutions, hit hard by the downturn, began to withdraw their support for emerging companies. Venture capital, only a few years after the brief euphoria of the Digital IPO, was becoming difficult to raise. If the progress made in the 1950s and '60s in fostering the creation of innovative new companies and industries in Massachusetts was to continue, something would have to be done to help jump-start a process that had stalled.

In 1974, when Michael Dukakis was elected to his first term as governor of Massachusetts, unemployment was over 9 percent and rising. It would hit 11.2 percent during his first year in office. One of the more serious problems facing the state at this point was that there was simply not enough capital for smaller emerging companies, or medium-size companies that needed expansion capital, or companies that needed senior debt from commercial banks. A lot of the businesses that TA Associates had helped to start in the late 1960s and early 1970s were suffering. Many could have gone out of business. Oddly enough in these circumstances, there were people in the mid-1970s — including many Boston venture capitalists — who were saying that there were too many venture capitalists around. I remember attending a meeting at the Federal Reserve Board of Boston where other venture capitalists were saying this kind of thing, and I got up and told them, "No, there aren't enough venture capitalists. There's not enough capital in the venture community. There are so many opportunities here that we need more capital, not less."

In 1976, the Dukakis administration issued an economic development plan for the state that identified access to capital for Massachusetts firms as a critical priority. That same year, at my own urging, the New England Regional Commission, which Governor Dukakis then chaired, asked TA Associates to investigate the capital gaps in the region. The study, which I wrote, confirmed that lack of capital was inhibiting the growth of many of the most promising companies in New England. The "capital gap," in fact, existed at all levels of financing, from early-stage and expansion capital to subordinated debt and senior debt. To illustrate this point and the effect that the lack of investment was having on regional business, I wrote case studies of particular companies that were being handicapped by their inability to access equity or loan capital.

The capital gap study succeeded in establishing that Massachusetts, along with the rest of New England, had a serious structural problem that required an institutional response. As part of its economic development strategy, the Dukakis administration created two task forces, one on capital formation and another on high technology. Ray Stata, the founder of Analog Devices, chaired the High Technology Task Force, and Governor Dukakis asked me to chair the Task Force on Capital Formation for Economic Development. Our task force reviewed my capital gap study and concluded that the state had to help create new sources of investment capital to foster the creation and growth of innovative companies.

At this same time, it happened that the domestic life insurance industry — an important factor in the Massachusetts economy — was seeking relief from a tax on gross investment income as well as other taxes that were putting companies domiciled within the state at a disadvantage in relation to out-of-state competitors. Both our capital formation task force and the Dukakis administration saw in this circumstance an opportunity to further the state's economic development goals. Citing my capital gap study, both the task force and the administration advocated repealing the gross investment tax in exchange for an agreement by the state's life insurance companies to place $100 million in a new entity that would invest in Massachusetts businesses and to promote job creation. When the Massachusetts Capital Resource Company was founded in 1977, the idea behind it was new: MCRC was to be a private company engaging in regional and community-based investment. It now provides expansion capital for Massachusetts-based companies in the manufacturing, technology, and services sectors that have annual revenues of between $1 million and $100 million. Since the mid-1980s, MCRC has invested over $530 million in more than 270 companies.[10] The deal that made this possible was a good trade-off for both sides.

Another recommendation of the capital formation task force led to the creation, in 1978, of the Massachusetts Industrial Finance Agency and the Massachusetts Technology Development Corporation. MTDC was founded to help fill the capital gap specifically for the start-up and expansion of early-stage companies in Massachusetts. Between 1980 and June 2006, MTDC, which supported itself on the returns from its investments, invested more than $72 million in 122 companies.[11]

Given my belief that the ultimate purpose of venture capital is to stimulate economic development, and the fact that helping to reinvigorate entrepreneurship in Massachusetts was in venture capitalists' self-interest, it seemed clear to me that the venture community in Boston ought to support these initiatives by the Dukakis administration. My effort to do so was a lone one, however. I could not even convince my partners at TA Associates that spending time on the project made sense. They reluctantly provided case material from their portfolio companies to bolster my contention that there was a capital gap, but that was all. They were not alone in their lack of enthusiasm. No one in the Boston venture community was particularly interested in these public-sector efforts to provide capital that the private sector was not then furnishing, capital that was vital to

stimulating innovation, employment, and economic development in our
state. I had been interested in economically targeted investing since the
1960s. When I founded TA Associates in 1968, I visualized the firm playing
an important role in developing the New England economy. I had hoped
to convince others in the venture community that stimulation of the local
economy through the establishment of MCRC and MTDC would not
only be civic-minded but would help revive the climate for entrepreneurship in the region.[12]

American venture capitalists, like others in the business community,
still sometimes exhibit an almost reflexive hostility toward the public sector, in the belief that government should never intervene in financial markets (except when it comes to bailing out big financial institutions that
have made colossal blunders, as recently in the case of Bear Stearns, AIG,
and Citigroup). While it is true that capital markets will eventually respond to improved economic conditions and promising investment opportunities, there is often a delay in this response. In such circumstances,
the public sector can provide vital support, as it did in the 1970s in Massachusetts and, before that, in the 1950s when the federal government
passed the Small Business Investment Act. It is interesting to note that
in these two responses the catalyst for the provision of capital was the
public sector. However, the management of the capital was provided by
the private sector. (In the case of MTDC, investments by management
required participation by bona fide venture capitalists.) A Keynesian intervention at times when there is dislocation in markets can be useful,
although, as we shall see, the public sector cannot jump-start a successful
venture capital industry in the absence of the right set of institutions and
cultural attitudes.

There is another point to be made here. While venture capitalists are
focused on maximizing returns for their investors, as they should be, there
should also be room in their thinking for such subjects as economic development, job creation, and the general welfare in the places where they
invest. Do not misinterpret what I say: maximizing returns is their first obligation. However, they have other obligations as well. Many people in the
industry will disagree with me about this. Free-market economists argue
that business in general serves society by making a profit and should not
concern itself with social responsibilities. This is not the way I see it. There
is a way to play a constructive role in society as a whole without sacrific-
ing investment returns. My failure to persuade the Boston venture capital

community to follow my lead in the 1970s would not be the last time I would try and fail to bring others along as I pursued my ideas about applying venture capital in a broader context.

In any case, the Massachusetts economy recovered from the slump of the mid-1970s and soon afterward gave birth to the "Massachusetts Miracle" of the 1980s. The economic rebirth of the state resulted from a variety of factors. Enlightened cooperation between the public and private sectors was one key element. Another was the presence of outstanding universities that have furnished both a research base for innovation and a plentiful supply of highly skilled workers. And a strong local venture capital industry played a significant role. This can be seen from a list of some of the Massachusetts companies in which the Boston venture community invested in the 1970s and '80s: Wang Laboratories, Unitrode, Prime Computer, Teradyne, Millipore, Cullinet, Apollo Computer, Stratus Computer, PRI Automation, McCormack and Dodge, Biogen, Genzyme, and Continental Cablevision.

As the Massachusetts economy revived and the venture capital industry in Boston began to take off in the early 1980s, however, I began to get restless again. Looking back on what TA Associates had accomplished since its founding, I thought the record was pretty remarkable given that we had raised three increasingly large funds and invested them quite successfully. As we began raising even larger sums of money in the early 1980s, however — $70 million in 1980 for Advent IV, and $165 million in 1982 for Advent V — to me the business wasn't as much fun as it had been before. It wasn't as thrilling as being on the knife-edge all the time wondering whether you were going to make a living or not, having to scramble just to keep the team together. Fortunately, however, I had already caught sight of a whole new horizon for TA Associates and myself across the Atlantic, where the Marshall Plan had revived the economies of Western Europe and where I now continued pursuing my vision for venture capital.

CHAPTER 3

# GOING INTERNATIONAL

## FRANCE AND BRITAIN

. . .

Even as venture capital was beginning to establish itself, first on the East Coast and then on the West, in the 1960s and early 1970s, it remained virtually unknown outside the United States. A handful of European investors, such as some who invested in TA Associates' early funds, knew enough about the success of venture capital in the United States to have begun investing in this asset class. Yet none of these investors thought about venture capital in a European context. In Asia, where Japan's managed economy and keiretsu system were still achieving spectacular economic growth, and the countries that would one day be known as the East Asian tigers were still trying to lift themselves out of poverty by developing their industrial sectors, venture capital had no relevance at all to existing economic conditions.

The first person to see the logic and potential of venture capital becoming a global business was the founder of the modern venture capital industry itself, Georges Doriot. In the early 1960s, Doriot conceived the idea of establishing an international community of venture capitalists. The General advised a group of British investors who established Technical Development Capital (which grew out of the British government-founded Industrial and Commercial Financial Corporation, or ICFC) in Britain in 1962. He also helped establish two venture capital firms modeled on ARD and intended, as he said, "to be of constructive help to companies on either side of the Atlantic who wish to develop their activities across the ocean": the Canadian Enterprise Development Corporation (or CED, founded in 1961) and the European Enterprise Development Company (or EED, founded in 1963).[1] Doriot faced obstacles in trying to implant venture capital in a European setting, as he knew he would. Neither the capital markets, legal systems, nor attitudes toward entrepreneurship in Europe in the 1960s made for a favorable climate for venture investing. For example, as recently as the years just after World War II, the concept of investing in the common stock of private companies had been virtually unknown outside the United States. Various institutions had been established in Europe after the war to provide loan capital to small businesses, but equity investments in such enterprises were still almost unheard of. By 1976 (four years after ARD was acquired by Textron in the United States), Doriot's EED had failed.[2]

Although General Doriot's plan for bringing venture capital to Europe did not succeed, General Marshall's plan for stimulating economic development on the continent had worked spectacularly well in Western Europe by the early 1970s. The countries that received Marshall Plan aid rebuilt themselves economically in the 1950s and '60s. Meanwhile, from its modest beginnings in the European Coal and Steel Community, founded in 1951, the process of European economic integration had progressed to the establishment in 1957 of the European Economic Community; by 1973, the EEC had expanded beyond its six original members — France, West Germany, Italy, and the Benelux countries — to include the United Kingdom, Ireland, and Denmark. Yet European industry had spent most of the years since the end of the war catching up with the United States in such basic industries as primary metals and automobiles. Stimulating the development of new technologies, companies, and industries was not yet on the agenda in most countries.

In 1971, however, when I was barely into my forties and still struggling to get my first venture capital organization, TA Associates, on firm footing, I was becoming interested in the applicability of foreign technology to U.S. markets and how TA Associates might benefit from transferring that technology here. I figured that there had to be some interesting technology being developed elsewhere that could be exploited in the United States. We still had a very limited budget at TA Associates, but I was not going to let this stop me from pursuing any opportunities we might uncover. As I was about to begin investigating what these opportunities might be, I was approached by the consulting firm Arthur D. Little and asked to help out with a project. ADL was under contract to the French Ministry of Industry to study the forces that were creating innovative enterprises in the Boston area. The project was named the Route 128 Study, after the "technology highway" encircling the city and its inner suburbs. I was asked to write a section of the report describing the role venture capital was playing in the development of the region's technology firms. The French government, which had begun an effort to modernize the nation's industry in the mid-1960s, was curious about how venture capital could become a tool for economic development, and I discovered that I was curious about whether what venture capitalists were doing in the United States could be replicated in Europe.

In the process of writing my section of the report and presenting it to the visiting delegation from France, I met a young deputy minister, Christian Marbach. He quickly recognized the pivotal role of venture capital in the development of innovative companies in the United States, and believed that it could play a similar role in France. He also believed that since the private sector in France had not created a venture capital industry there, the government needed to do so. Marbach's thinking represented a departure from French postwar industrial policy up to that point, which, like that of the other Western European countries, had emphasized simply catching up with U.S. technology and industry by copying existing technology and supporting national champions rather than fostering the development of new technologies, firms, and industries.

Soon after our meeting in Boston, Marbach invited me to Paris to present my ideas about how venture capital could be applied to create innovative companies in France. I flew to Paris and made my presentation to Marbach and Antoine Dupont-Fauville, the chairman of the government-controlled lending institution Crédit National. Dupont-Fauville was also open to new approaches to modernizing France's economy, having served as the top aide to Michel Debré while the latter was minister of economics and finance from 1966 to 1968 and launched an initiative to revitalize French industry and open up the economy to more foreign investment and technology. After our meeting, I walked from the Ministry of Industry along the right bank of the Seine to my hotel, the Plaza Athénée, just two blocks down the avenue Montaigne from the Champs-Elysées. It was a beautiful late April afternoon, with the chestnuts in bloom along the river. And to be honest, it was the vision of doing business in that beautiful city, as much as my curiosity about whether the French would embrace venture capital, that convinced me that I wanted to push forward.

The enthusiasm of my two French colleagues, Marbach and Dupont-Fauville, was the other critical factor in my decision to try to introduce venture capital into France. Marbach was an unusual person. In terms of background, he was a typical product of the *dirigiste* system that France had adopted after World War II: a polytechnic graduate and a member of the civil service, steeped in the ways of the French government bureaucracy. At the same time, however, he was a real entrepreneur. He understood the venture capital business much better than most Europeans did in the early 1970s and, like any good venture capitalist, was an excellent judge of people. Dupont-Fauville, for his part, liked the idea of creating a venture capital fund concentrating on innovative companies in France. The fund, which was sponsored by Crédit National, the Ministry of Industry, and TA Associates, would be called Sofinnova. The name was derived from *société financière d'innovation*, which is the French term for what in English we call a venture capital firm. That same year, 1971, the French government had made provision for the creation of *sociétés financières d'innovation*, with investors able to write off their investments and pay a capital gains rate of only 15 percent. Dupont-Fauville became chairman of Sofinnova's board of directors, on which Marbach and I also served.

The investors in Sofinnova, which was officially launched in 1972 with a fund of 22 million francs, were a combination of financial institutions — including private and national banks and insurance companies — and individuals who had been corralled by Marbach and Dupont-Fauville, with a lot of arm-twisting along the way. Part of the attraction for these investors was the opportunity to participate in venture capital investment in the United States, since besides establishing Sofinnova in France, Christian Marbach formed two small investment funds — Sofinnova International and Innova, both to be comanaged by TA Associates and Sofinnova — that invested in the United States. I assume that Dupont-Fauville did not tell any of the investors he courted about his first impression of TA Associates, which he had visited while the firm was still located in some rather shabby quarters at 84 State Street in Boston — a far cry from his magnificent office in Paris, which was all marble and fine fabrics. The day he came to our offices for the first time, I introduced him to my young associates and gave him a brief introduction to the firm, after which he excused himself and was shown the bathroom. After a rather long delay I followed him, only to find that he had become locked in the bathroom, where the toilet had overflowed. It was not exactly the kind of reception that the chairman of Crédit National expected, but my wife Anne saved the day with an elegant dinner party at our home that night, and Antoine and I went on to become fast friends.

Finding investors willing to put money into our fund was just one of the challenges we faced in trying to launch a venture capital concern in France. Staffing the management company was another. Venture capital was not a business that young Frenchmen were stampeding into in those days, but we were lucky enough to find some very talented people for Sofinnova's management company. Jean Deléage was the first investment manager hired by Marbach, and he was a good one. With a cigarette with a long ash always hanging out of his mouth, Deléage looked more like a French movie detective than a venture capitalist, and with his intelligence and determination he would have made a good sleuth. He was a smart, instinctive investor who did not easily accept a "no" from an investment committee — in fact, I have seldom met anyone who was so determined to succeed. He was also a true venture capitalist, someone who was never risk-averse.[3]

Jean-Bernard Schmidt was another member of the first group of investment managers in the firm. Schmidt, who has an MBA from Columbia, recalls being intrigued by the idea of venture capital when he heard Christian Marbach speak about it at a dinner for French alumni of Columbia Business School in 1972. He was so intrigued, in fact, that he called Marbach the next day to express interest in working for him, even though he feared that all the other Columbia MBAs who had heard Marbach's talk must have beaten him to the punch. He needn't have worried, because no one else had called. The two men met, and Marbach offered Schmidt a job at Sofinnova. When Jean Deléage left Boston, where he had come to train with TAA, to join Sofinnova's new West Coast subsidiary in 1976, Jean-Bernard Schmidt and Christian Cleiftie joined us in Boston for their training.

Because Sofinnova's investors were so unfamiliar with venture capital and the managers were young and untried, the board, on which all the investors were represented, wanted to maintain tight control over management. A formal investment-review structure was established, and the French tendency to bureaucracy complicated management's performance. Jean-Bernard Schmidt recalls that because all the large investors in the fund were represented on the investment committee, making presentations to them was a daunting experience. All the investors were curious about how this strange activity of venture investing would work, but they were also more than a little frightened of it. Despite its size and inexperience with venture capital, however, the investment committee rarely turned down an investment that Schmidt and his fellow managers recommended to it.

Those managers had to be as enterprising as we were at TA Associates in those days just to find good investments. Schmidt and his colleagues at Sofinnova pored over local newspapers and knocked on the doors of banks, lawyers, accountants, and chambers of commerce looking for leads, much as I was still doing at TAA. As those who followed their lead in later years would also find, it took considerable resourcefulness and tact to convince Europeans that cold calling — a routine practice in America, and one that we had to teach our European managers — was not rude. Under these circumstances, Sofinnova's portfolio, in the early years, resembled those of the first three Advent funds; it was a grab bag of small and medium-size companies in every kind of industry, from machine tools to restaurant chains to services for pet owners. Two of Sofinnova's more successful investments were in Foraco, now a leading supplier of drilling services to the mining and water industries on five continents, and a computer systems company, TITN, which was later sold to Alcatel and now forms part of Alcatel-Lucent's wholly owned computer and engineering and consulting subsidiary Answare. Not until after Jean-Bernard Schmidt had spent six years in Soffinova's office in San Francisco and, in 1987, returned to Paris to take charge of the firm did Sofinnova become the first venture capital firm in France to focus on technology and start-ups, which has been its business ever since.

Despite the obstacles it faced, Sofinnova progressed in the early days, mainly because Dupont-Fauville sheltered management from the investors' tendency to meddle, and because Marbach was a smart, dedicated leader who worked well with his chairman and assembled a good staff. My own role was primarily to provide training and advice for the management team. To help with this, I brought over a young man from TA Associates, John Wright, who had been a Mormon missionary in Marseille and was fluent in French, to serve as a Paris-based adviser to the firm. I also brought Sofinnova's investment managers over to Boston, two at a time, to spend six months to a year learning the ropes of venture capital investing from my colleagues and me at TA Associates. Meanwhile, I traveled to Paris five or six times a year during the period that Sofinnova was being launched, and I would spend a week of each visit with the portfolio managers of the Sofinnova team.

My own work with the Sofinnova managers was an important part of the development of Sofinnova itself, because the management team there, though talented, still lacked the management skills necessary to help build small companies. Sofinnova's managers appreciated new technology but didn't, at first, understand the process of converting technology into products that could be sold profitably by a business enterprise. Managing a technology-based company is a difficult thing. It was difficult to learn to do in the United States, as I had learned from my experience with the early spin-offs from MIT in the 1950s and '60s. In any case, with the realization that the main challenge at Sofinnova was to provide effective managerial assistance to its portfolio companies, we staffed the management company not just with people with financial expertise but also with managers who had operational experience, people who could advise the portfolio companies not just about strategy but about all the functional disciplines. (Christian Marbach, who had a technical background, was helpful in finding such individuals.) In this respect, Sofinnova was ahead of TA Associates, all of whose managers at the time came from financial rather than operating backgrounds.

In the meantime, Marbach, as I have said, provided excellent leadership for Sofinnova. When Dupont-Fauville left Crédit National in the late 1970s and relinquished his seat on the board, however, the protective shield he had provided for Marbach was removed. Dupont-Fauville was replaced as chairman by a capable but cautious bureaucratic type from the bank who did not believe in the idea of venture capital and wanted to convert Sofinnova from an equity source into a lending organization. Sofinnova would survive and eventually prosper, but meanwhile it had only secured a beachhead for venture capital in France and in Europe. The French deserved great credit, however, for introducing such a novel idea as venture capital at a time when, in most of Europe, it was completely unknown. Their ability to look outside France for new ideas, to incorporate these ideas in an economic development plan, and to form a company to realize them was unique in Europe at that time.

The relationship between Sofinnova and TA Associates in the 1970s was close and collegial, the investment results were good in France and superior in the United States, and TA Associates had procured a base on the continent from which it could offer a gateway to Europe to corporate clients such as INCO and Xerox and monitor what was happening throughout the continent. After this successful first step, I soon began thinking about creating a network of venture capital firms across Western Europe. Jean Monnet and Robert Schuman, the visionaries behind the creation of the European Coal and Steel Community and the European Economic Community, had already foreseen that trade and investment across national boundaries would be critical to the economic future of the continent. I thought that venture capital, if it was to succeed in Europe, would have to be adapted to the particular strengths and limitations of various national environments. But a network of venture capital firms in many different European countries, with member firms sharing informa-tion about best practices, could help stimulate investments, technology transfer, and learning both within Europe and between Europe and the United States.

In thinking in terms of a network rather than a pan-European venture capital operation, I was consciously taking a different approach to launch-ing venture capital in Europe from the one that Georges Doriot had used. Doriot's European Enterprise Development Company had invested throughout Europe, for General Doriot shared the Schuman-Monnet vi-sion of a united Europe dominated by the French. When I began to think about how to make venture capital work in Europe, however, I did not feel that a pan-European approach would succeed. I believed that postwar Eu-rope was going to rebuild itself country by country, that individual coun-tries still wanted to concentrate on building their own national assets. Doriot and I talked at length about our different approaches to venture capital in Europe, and I remember saying to him at one point, "I would not expect the Deutsche Bank to give the very best deals in Germany to a pan-European investor. It seems to me they would give you something at the bottom of the pile." The united Europe that Doriot, Schuman, and Monnet envisioned would come later, of course, but perhaps the General was too far ahead of his time in this respect.[4]

In any case, my visits to Paris in the years that TA Associates worked with Sofinnova became jumping-off points for my own "missionary work," as I traveled throughout Western Europe talking about venture capital to people I met and encouraging them to try it in their own countries. Un-fortunately, the encouragement fell mostly on deaf ears in the 1970s. I met advocates of venture capital who were convinced that it had a place in their countries, but who believed that the route to this end for their clients was success in the U.S. market. As mentioned in chapter 2, TA Associates had raised capital in Europe in the late 1960s and the 1970s for its U.S. funds. Sofinnova's positive experience investing in the United States attracted other investors in France, and the performance of American firms with international reach, such as TA Associates and Hambrecht & Quist, attracted investors from Great Britain and Switzerland, but only for investment in the States.[5] Interesting European investors in venture capital in their own countries was another matter.

There were some exceptions in addition to the investors in Sofinnova. In the mid-1970s, for example, I talked with Deutsche Bank at a time when it was forming a venture capital company, somewhat on the model of Sofinnova, called Wagnisfinanzierung Gesellschaft (WFG). (In contrast to Sofinnova, this was a purely private-sector effort — in fact, the German government has shown no interest in venture capital until quite recently.) Deutsche Bank itself and other commercial banks in Germany were investing in WFG, as were some of the regional savings banks. WFG had hired a managing director who had developed a strategy of investing in small, technology-based businesses. I met for lunch with the officials involved in establishing WFG, who I assumed were interested in learning from my experience with Sofinnova in France.

The conversation was an eye-opener for me. For one thing, I was startled to find that the Deutsche Bank people had done little research to determine whether small, technology-based companies could actually survive in Germany, with its industrial culture of large, hierarchically structured companies. Nor were they particularly interested in learning about my experience with venture capital in the United States or in France, even though I tried to tell them about the mistakes we had made with Sofinnova — for example, its failure to focus on selected sectors that the managers actually understood. What's more, I foresaw real challenges for the development of small entrepreneurial enterprises in Germany. Amazingly, however, my hosts from Deutsche Bank did not seem to have asked themselves any questions about such matters. They thought that venture capital investing was simply a matter of supplying capital to small, innovative companies, and failed to understand that management development was the key to success. They seemed to think that the concept of venture capital was interesting and that if the French were trying it, they should try it too. They went ahead with their half-formed plans and had cause to regret it in later years, for WFG proved a failure.

As this story suggests, in most of Europe in the 1970s venture capital was looked upon — to the extent that people thought about it at all — as a laboratory curiosity, not a serious way to vitalize an economy. Nor were overall conditions in Europe conducive to its success at this time. In the 1970s, Western Europe was in a state of economic torpor. Socialist governments, whose economic policies were based on full employment even in industries that were made redundant by foreign competition, had created a rigid system in which change was virtually impossible. And yet change — whether in markets and products or in entire economic structures — is the only condition that interests venture capitalists, or in which they can thrive. Even in France, which had center-right governments throughout the 1970s, economic policy moved increasingly to the left as the governing parties sought to usurp the positions of the Communists and Socialists, whose gathering strength eventually led to the election of a Socialist government in France in 1981. Another obstacle in the way of venture capital at this time was the prevailing view in Europe that individual enterprise and small business had little to do with innovation, which was thought to occur only within the laboratories of large private corporations or public research institutes.

Germany was actually trying to break out of this mold in the 1970s, although the difficulty it encountered provides a good illustration of the cultural obstacles to venture capital in Western Europe at the time. In the '70s, the West German government and German industry were actually beginning to take steps to improve the country's ability to commercialize innovation. Government-funded research organizations such as the Fraunhofer-Gesellschaft and the Max-Planck-Gesellschaft, both founded after World War II, have long produced outstanding research in the full range of scientific disciplines. Beginning in the late 1970s, at the instigation of both government and industry, scientists at many of these research organizations started to be given incentives to bring in funding from both large corporations and small and medium-size enterprises. The idea was not only to promote research with potential commercial applications but also to familiarize researchers with the commercial sector and give them experience managing collaborations with industry. German universities began to follow suit soon afterward by accepting research funding from corporations.

These were all steps in the right direction. But the gap between producing world-class research and being able to commercialize the resulting technology successfully is a large one. It takes time to develop the mechanisms for transferring innovation from the laboratory into the hands of capable entrepreneurs, and it takes time to develop the entrepreneurs. This is not just a matter of institutional structures and incentives. Having all the right structures and incentives in place will do little to promote entrepreneurship without a culture that encourages creativity, adaptability, and risk taking. Such a culture did not exist in Germany or anywhere else in Europe in the 1970s.

By the end of the decade, however, the bankruptcy of socialist economic policy was becoming obvious even to many of its most ardent supporters, as the subsidization of unproductive unemployment grew to unmanageable proportions. The economic policies of the socialist governments were exposed for what they truly were — demotivating and productive only of stagnation. Meanwhile, the widening technological gap between Europe, on one hand, and the United States and Japan, on the other, made Europeans question for the first time whether collective research was really the only route to innovation — possibly the individual entrepreneur did have a role to play.

The questioning of old policies, systems, and structures gave way to action when the Conservative Party took power in Great Britain in 1979 under the leadership of Margaret Thatcher. Mrs. Thatcher argued that nationalized industries should be privatized and that individuals should be motivated to manage and work more productively. She believed that to hide behind the shield of collective mediocrity was wrong and that to stand accountable was right. This was pretty heady stuff after years of socialist hand-holding. What it meant was change. The new prime minister not only believed in change; she forced it through the system. As a result of the changes in government policy and, just as important, in attitudes that Mrs. Thatcher brought about, the technology sector in Britain became much more productive. Fortuitous economic circumstances also contributed to this development: for example, rising oil prices in the 1980s would make the exploitation of Britain's North Sea oil fields more economically feasible than it had been in the preceding decade, creating demand for new technologies to extract these reserves, clean up spills, and facilitate other related activities.

It is hard to describe how quickly attitudes changed in Britain in the wake of the Thatcher revolution. It was as if an oppressive shroud had been removed. The country, at least those within it who wanted to do something, looked more hopefully at the world. Instead of looking for protection against competition, industry sought ways to become more efficient and effective. Challenges were looked upon positively, not with fear.[6] This created a much more auspicious climate for venture capital than had existed in Britain before.

Great Britain, like Massachusetts, is a place with a long history of industrial innovation. The idea of stimulating economic development by private investment in promising new enterprises, or existing ones in need of improvement, had first been considered in Britain at least as far back as the 1930s, when the Charterhouse Industrial Development Co., Ltd., was founded. Charterhouse took minority positions in companies and worked with existing management to improve performance, an approach it used successfully for many years.

By the time Mrs. Thatcher took power, there were only a few organizations besides Charterhouse trying to promote venture capital in Britain. Technical Development Capital, founded in 1962, invested mostly in the areas of electronics and scientific instruments. The Industrial and Commercial Financial Corporation, which the British government had established in 1945 to provide risk capital — in the form of debt, not equity — to growing companies, was owned equally by the four major British commercial banks (each with 20 percent), the Bank of England, and the Bank of Scotland (with 10 percent apiece). In effect, this made the ICFC virtually the only game in town. Spey Investments, Ltd., founded in the late 1960s, was another early entrant in the venture capital field in Britain. In 1968, the merchant bank N. M. Rothschild & Sons established New Court & Partners in London to build on Rothschild's existing venture capital activity in the United States. Rothschild, the ultimate relationship bank, proved unsuccessful at running a focused venture capital fund, and in 1972, with Rothschild's sponsorship, one of New Court's founders and principals, John Incledon, banded together with two colleagues to form the venture capital firm IDJ.

Innovation languished in Britain, however, from the years just following World War II until the 1970s, by which time British industry generally had a justified reputation for poor management in private as well as publicly owned enterprises. In 1977, John Incledon and I joined forces to try to stimulate further growth and development in the fledgling venture capital industry in Britain and to help Britain close the gap between it and the United States in the development of new technology. John, a very enterprising individual, is a former RAF pilot who got his MBA at Harvard Business School, worked in the United States as a management consultant for four years, then returned to Britain and became a founding director of New Court & Partners. He and I formed a company, the Trans-Atlantic Business Growth Fund, based in the British Virgin Islands.

Trans-Atlantic was to be a vehicle for two main purposes: to work with TA Associates to bring its venture capital know-how to Britain, and to channel investment capital from British institutions into American ventures that TAA was financing. We saw two ways in which encouraging British investment in the TAA portfolio could benefit the technology industry in Britain. For established American technology companies with products that were ready to enter international markets, but whose managements were absorbed in domestic expansion, Trans-Atlantic would invest in their U.K. subsidiaries and help open doors for expansion in Europe via a base in the U.K. For newer technology companies that were not yet ready to think about international expansion, we would identify technologies that could be licensed to British companies or arrange joint ventures for the exploitation of these technologies. These would both be ways of giving TAA portfolio companies a rapid introduction to the European market, allowing them to build market share ahead of their competition. Today it is not uncommon for venture capitalists to help their portfolio companies to enter international markets, even at a relatively early stage of their existence, but in the 1970s this was a quite novel idea.

John and I faced a problem, however. Britain had exchange controls at the time, which had kept many of the U.K. financial institutions, particularly the life insurance companies and pension funds, from investing in venture capital in the United States. Our task was to try to persuade the Bank of England to find a way for British institutions to make such investments without having to purchase investment currency. In the end, after spending £35,000 on legal fees without obtaining a final ruling from the Bank of England on whether investment in U.S. venture capital funds could be deemed a direct investment (which would have dealt with the exchange control problem) rather than a portfolio investment, John and I had to abandon our effort.

When the Thatcher government came to power in 1979, however, it not only abolished exchange controls but quickly improved the environment for venture capital within Britain by taking two steps. First, it cut the top tax rate on income from 83 percent to 60 percent (and eventually to 40 percent), while investment income — which had previously been taxed at 15 percent on top of the rate for ordinary income, making the top rate on investment income effectively 98 percent — was now taxed only once and at the same rate as ordinary income. Second, it introduced the limited partnership structure for venture capital funds, which provided additional tax advantages for investors. At the same time, the London Stock Exchange created a second board, the Unlisted Securities Market, for trading small companies, which had previously found it difficult to be listed because of a requirement that a company show five unbroken years of increasing profits before its shares could be publicly traded. Taken together, these changes swiftly eliminated the most significant legal and structural barriers to venture capital investment in Britain.[7]

At this point, as would soon happen elsewhere in Europe, I was able to take advantage of a connection I had made with another of those few Europeans who were interested in venture capital and what it could do for their own countries. I had met David J. S. Cooksey in 1978 through a TA Associates investor, Philip Weld, a successful entrepreneur who had founded a chain of local newspapers in the Boston area (where he developed prototypes for computer typesetting and computer-based editorial systems) that he later sold to Dow Jones & Co. Weld was a friend of Cooksey and sailed with him. Once when they were sailing together in the "Round Britain" yacht race and were becalmed off the Hebrides in Scotland, Phil talked with David about venture capital and what I was doing with it in the United States. Weld introduced me to David in the backyard of my undergraduate club at Harvard, the Owl Club, when I was in Cambridge for commencement in June 1978.

David, a doctor's son like me, had grown up in London and studied metallurgy at Oxford. He was a very entrepreneurial fellow who had spent many years as an industrial engineer and head of manufacturing operations at Formica International, a company owned by the Scottish conglomerate De La Rue, then led a management buyout — something that was completely unheard of in Britain at the time — of a Formica subsidiary in 1971. David was an ambitious man, but his ambition was constructive because he was ambitious for his country. I believe that he saw a way to identify himself with the venture capital movement and to lead the development of it in the U.K. We began talking about venture capital seriously in 1979, when he said that the environment in Britain had changed so much under Thatcher that we should think about starting a venture capital operation there.

After a series of false starts, David and I were encouraged by an investment banking firm in Scotland, Noble Grossart, to raise a fund. The bankers there advised us to add another member to the management and introduced us to Michael Moran, a very successful electronics entrepreneur in Scotland, who became our partner. It wasn't until the winter of 1980 that we homed in on an ownership structure. David, Michael, and I decided to divide the equity of the management company equally and to reduce our ownership to 25 percent each, reserving the remaining 25 percent for others who would join the team, as a way of motivating them. My interest in the management company was assigned to TA Associates. Cooksey became the managing director of the management company, Advent Ltd.—the first venture capital firm in Europe built on the U.S. limited-partnership model—when it opened its doors in 1981.

We had a very competent board of directors at Advent Ltd. Our chairman, Douglas MacDonald, was the head of the newspaper-distributing organization John Menzies. Douglas was a colorful character whose entrepreneurial management style was admired by his colleagues on the board. He was also a hard-drinking Scot who felt that great things were hidden in the last dram of the bottle. Probably few venture capitalists today drink anything stronger than Diet Coke on the job, but most of our decision making on the Advent Ltd. board was accomplished over a bottle of scotch at Denzler's restaurant in Edinburgh; led by MacDonald, we were a boisterous lot and were often turned out of Denzler's well after closing time.[8] We were doing something no one else was doing and having fun at it. Venture capital, by and large, is still a boys' club, but Douglas could show young venture capitalists today a thing or two about being macho. Once while we were driving to Edinburgh from his home, he reminisced about his time in the Special Forces during the insurgency in the Malay Peninsula. I asked him if it had been dangerous, and he replied that he had done his share of killing. He went on to say that it had been a long time since he had killed a man, but that he could get used to it again.

Our first investors, mostly investment trusts and insurance companies located in Edinburgh's Charlotte Square, were interested in investing with Advent Ltd. because they had found ways of investing in venture capital in the United States and enjoyed success. Given the new economic environment in Britain, all of them were excited about trying out this new investment model there, and many would subsequently move into the venture capital business themselves. Cooksey recalls that one institution in Britain that did not welcome the arrival of Advent Ltd. was the ICFC, which, by the time Advent arrived on the scene, made no equity-only investments.[9] The Bank of England, on the other hand, strongly supported our efforts to introduce a new model of small-company financing into the U.K.

Our goal was to raise £10 million ($17 million at that time) for our first fund, Advent Technology. This was a small amount compared with the $70 million Advent IV fund that TA Associates closed in 1979, but large for a U.K. fund at the time. The purpose of Advent Technology was to invest in British technology-based companies and in U.S. companies whose technology could be transferred to Britain for product development, manufacture, and entry into Europe. The idea was that Advent Ltd. would recognize emerging technologies in Great Britain that had application in the United States, and TA Associates would recognize emerging technologies in the United States that had application in Britain and Europe. One of Advent Ltd.'s key management personnel, John Littlechild, was assigned to the States to aid in the transfer process.

We had planned to raise £5 million in Edinburgh and £5 million in London, but in a matter of days the fund was virtually fully subscribed from investors in Edinburgh who hoped to replicate the success of venture capital in the United States. They invested with the proviso, however, that our main office be in Edinburgh. We decided to take the money and run with it. Yet it turned out that, just as with TA Associates' early funds in the United States, the £10 million we had raised for Advent Technology wasn't enough money with which to operate. This forced us to go back to investors the following year for another £10 million for a second fund, Advent Eurofund. Hamish Glen, the managing director of the Scottish Investment Trust (an investor in Advent Technology), was upset that we had raised more money, so we tried to explain to him that we had to have more management fee income to cover the costs of carrying out our mission: the business and technology-transfer costs, when added to the normal costs of running a venture investment operation, were more than could be covered from the management fees from one £10 million fund. Hamish, a flinty Scot, never bought into our explanation, but did not stand in our way. He sensed that, with the introduction of this new fund, the Scots would be losing their influence over Advent Ltd., and he was right. Although Edinburgh, where Mike Moran stayed on, remained the main office at first, David Cooksey opened a branch in London within a year of Advent Ltd.'s founding, and it was soon clear that the center of power had moved south. David realized that there was more opportunity in the south of England, and the London branch office had become the main office by the time we started Advent Eurofund.

Advent Eurofund featured an important new element, a corporate investor that became the sponsor of this new fund. The corporate investor, Monsanto, was already a successful venture capital investor in the United States and wished to use the TA Associates network of relationships in Europe to access technologies of strategic interest. Costas Anagnostopoulos, the head of Monsanto's European organization, was assigned the responsibility of monitoring the performance of Advent Eurofund and of identifying sectors of interest to the parent company. Monsanto took a 50 percent interest in this £10 million fund, in which it was the lone strategic investor, and began a long and successful relationship with TA Associates and, eventually, Advent International Corporation.

With the establishment in 1985 of Advent Capital, the successor fund to Advent Technology and Advent Eurofund, Advent Ltd. would become the leading venture capital management company in the U.K. and Europe. David Cooksey had gathered a hard-hitting group of managers who were energetic and clearly focused. Finding entrepreneurial managers to run the portfolio companies could be a real challenge, and Cooksey and his managers spent an enormous amount of time working with these companies — much more than a venture capital firm typically would in the United States. Advent Ltd. made some very successful investments in technology-based companies in its early years, however. One such company was Filtronic, which provides an interesting parallel with some of the technology companies formed in the Boston area by MIT professors in the 1950s and '60s. Founded in 1977 by David Rhodes, a professor of electronic and electrical engineering at Leeds University, Filtronic provided research and development services to the British government. It specialized in radar and waveguide technology for the military, and one of its contracts involved the development of a compound that proved crucial to the success of an antimissile system that the British used against Exocet missiles in the Falklands War. Ten years later, the compound proved to have a use in cell phones, and on the strength of this conversion from military to civilian applications the company went public and Advent Ltd. was richly rewarded for its patient, long-term investment. Filtronic is now a world leader in the design and manufacture of components and sub-systems for wireless communications equipment, electronic defense systems, and point-to-point communications.

The early success of Advent Ltd. became widely known in Europe, and as TA Associates was still one of the few proponents and practitioners of venture capital there, many financial institutions became interested in working with us. After establishing a foothold in a country — France — where the conditions were relatively difficult, I had found a much more congenial environment in Britain. These two early achievements, along with my sense that the economic and cultural tides in Europe were shifting in my favor, now buoyed my hopes. Looking back toward the Continent, I decided to see if I could replicate my success with Sofinnova and Advent Ltd. and build the network of European venture capital firms of which I dreamed.

CHAPTER 4

# THE BEGINNINGS OF
# A GLOBAL NETWORK
## WESTERN EUROPE AND
## SOUTHEAST ASIA

· · ·

The new spirit of optimism and enterprise that Margaret Thatcher unleashed in Britain when she came to power at the end of the 1970s quickly
spread to the rest of Western Europe. Suddenly everyone — investment
institutions, corporations, and governments — wanted to know how venture capital could spur technological innovation and create dynamic new
companies. People came to believe that venture capital could change the
face of industrial Europe: Germany's Ruhr Valley, once a region of coal
mines and steel factories, was going to become the next Silicon Valley,
while Western Europe generally was going to join the United States at the
forefront of the high-tech revolution.

   In what suddenly seemed a promising environment for venture capital, TA Associates continued to benefit from the connections I had made
in the 1970s with some of the few people in Europe who were interested
in venture capital at this time. There were a handful of other venture
groups from the United States active in Europe at the end of the 1970s
and very beginning of the 1980s: Alan Patricof and Ronald Cohen, for example, had started a £10 million fund in Britain six months after Advent
Ltd. was launched, and Citicorp Venture Capital, led by John Botts, had
set up operations in London (although it was making very few investments). However, the relationships I had established would enable us to
get off the mark in Europe sooner and with more force than any other
venture group.

The expansion of the network to the continent of Europe involved two major players, David Cooksey and Piet van de Ven. I had met van de Ven in the mid-1970s. Tucker Anthony and R. L. Day had an office in Amsterdam by this time, and the manager there mentioned van de Ven to me as someone whose firm, Buvermo, might be interested in venture capital in the United States. I vividly remember my first meeting with Piet in his office in 's-Hertogenbosch, which was filled with paintings of the old Dutch masters of the seventeenth century. Two very important things happened at that meeting: I found a venture capital soul mate — or so I thought at the time — and began the fascination with seventeenth-century Dutch art that eventually led to my collection of painters including van Goyen, van Huysum, Salomon van Ruysdael, Esias van der Velde, Adriaen van Ostade, and many more. I became interested in these artists because they expressed, in their work, the energy and vitality of a small nation that had become a great economic power through resourcefulness and determination. The Dutch in their golden age were true venture capitalists. They had won their independence from Spain and became rivals of the English and the French on the seas and in colonization. Their drive and ability created a great trading nation — rather unbelievable, when you think of it, for a small country hemmed in by neighbors with greater resources. All this vitality is expressed in their art. It seemed to me that a country that had shown so much inventive capacity in the past would be receptive to venture capital, and in Piet van de Ven I had found the person who could investigate that possibility with me.

Buvermo, of which van de Ven was managing director, was an investment advisory firm established by the Teulings family to manage its wealth and that of other Dutch families. One of Buvermo's clients was the Orange Nassau Group in The Hague. Orange Nassau was a wholly owned subsidiary of the French group CGIP. It had been engaged solely in coal mining in the south of Holland, but when the mines became uneconomical after the war, they were sold to the government and the proceeds invested in North Sea oil and gas. Piet van de Ven was later recruited away from Buvermo by Orange Nassau to help diversify its asset base and eventually became the company's managing director. Van de Ven became interested in venture capital while at Buvermo, and Orange Nassau later established accounts with TA Associates to participate in venture investing in the United States. What's more, van de Ven became intrigued with the concept of a network of European venture capital firms, invested in Advent

Technology in Britain, and took an active role in expanding the network on the Continent. TA Associates never established a fund in Holland,[1] yet van de Ven played a crucial role in the establishment of our second true network member, Advent Belgium.

In 1978, before I had collaborated with David Cooksey to found Advent Ltd. in Britain, van de Ven introduced me and TA Associates to an Orange Nassau client in Belgium, Sofina. Part of the Société Générale de Belgique group, Sofina invested in real estate and what we now call alternative assets, among many other activities. Its chief investment officer was Leo Deschuyteneer, a wonderful fellow to whom I instinctively related and for whom I developed a deep affection.

My relationship with Deschuyteneer and the way it figured in the establishment of Advent Belgium exemplified my strategy for expanding TAA's network in Western Europe generally. My goal was always, first of all, to have a champion within each country, a leading financial institution or corporation that was a national opinion leader, such as Crédit National in France when we founded Sofinnova. Then, alongside high-level representatives from these institutions, I would make the rounds of likely investors. The key to the success of these fund-raisings was my relationship with the key people in these "champion" institutions. These were close personal friendships built upon a shared belief that venture capital could play an important part in the economic development of their countries.

The entry point of my relationship with Leo Deschuyteneer was an investment by Sofina in TA Associates' Advent III fund in the United States, a fund that produced excellent results. This experience made Sofina amenable to a suggestion from van de Ven and me that we establish a fund in Belgium based on the Advent Ltd. model. Advent Belgium was formed in 1982. It pursued a different course than its British cousin, providing expansion capital for rapidly growing companies rather than early-stage capital for new technology businesses. This strategy for private equity investment, as we would now call it, fit the skills of the firm's managers, Paul de Vree and Luc Van de Plas, whose backgrounds were in industry and banking, respectively.

The strategy also fit the needs of the country. Belgium required expansion capital for small, growing businesses. Although technology was often used to improve operations in Belgian companies, innovative technology, competitive on a global basis, was not one of the country's strong suits. Belgium is a small country whose French- and Dutch-speaking parts have their own separate institutions. While there are a few centers of excellence, such as the Université catholique de Louvain for the Walloons and the Katholieke Universiteit Leuven for the Flemish, these institutions do not have the critical mass to produce cutting-edge technology. Thus the country was not producing enough pure technology companies to justify a concentration in that area for Advent Belgium. Our approach to creating a venture capital organization in Belgium became our standard one as we moved throughout Western Europe. We identified the need in a particular country—be it for investment in technology and start-ups, expansion capital, or restructuring—developed a strategy to respond to the need, and then found the people with the requisite skills to execute the strategy.

Sofina was a good partner due to the support of Yves de Boël, its chairman, and Deschuyteneer, who, with his ever-present cigar, smoothed the way in the early days. He made sure that the managers stayed on the same page, and when they did not, he moved quickly to take corrective action. The ownership structure of the management company was somewhat similar to that of Advent Ltd., with 25 percent owned by each of the sponsors (Sofina, TA Associates, and Orange Nassau) and the remaining 25 percent held by the management. The investment results, while not spectacular, were good enough to prove that capital linked with management advice could make a difference in Belgium.

Most of the European investors who backed organizations such as Advent Ltd. and Advent Belgium, as I have said, first became interested in venture capital as a result of successful venture capital investments in the United States. This was also true in Germany, where the next member of TA Associates' European network was formed in the early 1980s.

In 1976, I was introduced to Count Albrecht Matuschka, the cofounder, with Rolf Dienst, of the Matuschka Group, by International Nickel Company, whose relationship with TA Associates I have described in chapter 2 and which was interested in using our network to identify investment opportunities in Europe. The scion of an aristocratic German family from Bohemia, Matuschka was crippled by polio at a young age and walked with two canes. He was clearly driven by an ambition to succeed and to prove something to the world. Since starting his firm in 1968, he had developed a simple but very effective strategy. His goal was to perform just a little bit better than the Deutsche Bank, and to give his wealthy clients excellent service. Matuschka picked the best of breed managers in the various asset classes long before this strategy became popular. The results of his strategy were gratifying for his company, for it produced a steady growth in wealthy clients for the firm.

When I explained my interest in seeing if venture capital could work in Germany, the count was very polite but let me know he had no interest in exposing his clients to anything as risky as venture capital. Only a couple of years later, however, it was becoming apparent that venture capital in the United States was producing interesting returns, and that a forward-looking firm had to at least have an opinion about this asset class. At my suggestion, Matuschka's partner, Rolf Dienst, came to Boston for a meeting in 1978. Dienst's job was to sort out and make sense of Matuschka's many enthusiasms, some of which were good and some bad. Rolf himself, meanwhile, had all the verve of a true pioneer. He was flamboyant, a great schmoozer, a man who truly loved life, whether he was conducting a band at Oktoberfest or discoursing enthusiastically about opera (about which he actually knew nothing). In any case, Rolf became sold on the idea of investing in venture capital in the United States. The result was a $15 million fund—minuscule by today's standards, but accounting for about 20 percent of the capital under management by TA Associates at the time—that produced excellent returns. This led to a much larger fund of $100 million in 1980, which also produced good returns.

Given these results, I asked Matuschka why venture capital should not at least be tried in Germany. His answer was, "No, my clients would not understand this diversion from our strategy." This was his attitude until, during a lunch in Munich in 1983, he suddenly changed his mind. One of those attending that lunch—and sitting next to me, in fact—was Jochen Mackenrodt, a senior officer of Siemens who was in charge of mergers and acquisitions and relationships with Siemens subsidiaries worldwide. Mackenrodt, who was a very capable, well-regarded, and entrepreneurial person, had studied the venture capital industry in the United States and was curious as to why TA Associates had succeeded. "We've never been able to invest successfully in the United States the way you have," he said. "Obviously you've been doing it the wrong way," I replied. "Could be— tell me more," Mackenrodt responded. So we started talking about venture capital in America. Then I turned the tables on him and said, "You know, you really ought to think about doing this in Germany. Siemens would be the perfect investor to try to kick this thing off." Matuschka— who was sitting nearby and had heard this—was horrified that I had made these comments to someone from Siemens. After all, the purpose of this lunch was to attract venture capital investment to the United States, not to divert it to Germany. But Mackenrodt turned to Matuschka and said, "You know, it would be wonderful to do something like this." Matuschka, always the opportunist, replied, "Of course!" We had found our champion — Jochen Mackenrodt of Siemens — and another suddenly willing partner, Count Matuschka, in Germany.

The upshot was a firm called TVM Technoventures. When we decided to launch TVM with TA Associates, Siemens AG, and the Matuschka Group as its cosponsors, Mackenrodt and his driver picked up my wife and me one evening and took us out to his house for drinks. On the way out in the car, he turned around from the front seat and asked me, "Why do we need Matuschka and Dienst in this thing?" "They're my partners," I said, "and I don't abandon a partner. What their contribution will be, I don't know, but if I'm in this, they're in this." I'm sure Mackenrodt was testing me, and I made it clear that I wasn't going to throw away a relationship for the sake of financial advantage. I had never operated like that in the United States, and I wasn't about to start doing so abroad, where I understood that a reputation for trustworthiness would be essential for success.

I became chairman of TVM and kept that position until Mackenrodt succeeded me in the late 1990s. The organizational model, like that of Advent Belgium, involved each of the sponsors owning 25 percent of the company and the management owning the remaining 25 percent. Mackenrodt designed the program with thoughtfulness and pragmatism. Part of the capital would be invested in the United States by TA Associates and other successful venture capital managers; the remainder would be invested in Germany under the management of the TVM staff. If the experiment in Germany failed, the positive results from the U.S. investments (if history was a guide) would more than offset the losses in Germany. If the whole program tanked, Mackenrodt explained to me, the results would not be known until he was well into retirement from Siemens.

Even with the name Siemens behind him, Mackenrodt needed all his powers of persuasion to recruit a roster of investors for TVM, just as Christian Marbach and Antoine Dupont-Fauville had to do in France when lining up investors for Sofinnova. The German banks were the hardest to convince, because they had so little comprehension of venture capital that they couldn't understand how it was any different from the kinds of financing they were already providing. The large industrial concerns, for their part, were convinced that no small company could hope to match their own innovative capabilities. At Siemens, indeed, Mackenrodt had presented his move into venture capital as a purely financial play, because he knew the technical people in the company would have no interest in it.[2] Mackenrodt finally succeeded, however, in lining up a group of investors that included Bayer, Mannesman, and the Deutsche Bank. The first TVM fund, unlike the first Belgian venture capital fund, was large for its time: DM 120 million ($60 million).

As had been the case with Advent Ltd. and Advent Belgium, at TVM the face of the management company was the face of the country in which it invested. This represented a departure from the organizational model that General Doriot had employed with his European Enterprise Development Company. Although EED employed managers from the various European countries, the imprint was definitely French. EED was headquartered in Paris and led by a very effective Frenchman, Arnaud de Vitry. Here, as with his pan-European approach to investment, Doriot was following the lead of his contemporaries, Monnet and Schuman, who believed deeply in the European Community and also in its domination by France. The problem with this approach, it seemed to me, was that it flew in the face of history. The various European countries had no intention of being dominated by what appeared, on the surface, to be a French concern. Thus when I organized the members of what became the Advent network, I recognized national differences. Each network member was staffed and led by nationals of its country; each network member was provided funds to manage by institutions within its country; each worked with governmental and financial institutions within its country to establish its own national identity and to succeed as the national expression of venture capital. Although TA Associates trained the staff and owned a piece of each of these network members, it was a minority interest, and we were not overtly visible. Both David Cooksey and I sat on the investment committees of both Advent Belgium and TVM, for example, but TA Associates had no permanent presence in their offices.

The reason for staffing the network members with nationals of the country where they were located was simple. They knew the language; they knew the local players and scene; they frequented the bistros where business was discussed; they heard the local scuttlebutt about who was good and who wasn't. An expatriate would never know these things, and would not even know where to start learning them. Besides, my goal in taking venture capital abroad was to help people in other countries learn to manage their own economic affairs more effectively. TA Associates would transfer its operating model and experience and provide counsel and advice to its affiliates. But in the long run it was up to the locals to make venture capital work in their own countries.

Not surprisingly, I ran into some obstacles as I pushed ahead with this particular experiment. TVM provides a good example. Although we managed to recruit a team of investment managers who, with training and experience, proved able to do a competent job, we had a very difficult time finding the right managing director. It took us a good ten years before we had the right senior management team in place, after a long process of trial and error. We ran the firm by committee to begin with. Later on we tried people with technical, marketing, and operational backgrounds, but none of them worked out. Then we put one of the younger people in the firm in charge because we didn't know what else to do. He stabilized things for a while, and two people eventually emerged from his management group who then became the leaders of the company. We were lucky, amid all this turmoil, to be able to keep the game going. One thing that helped us was having Meyer Barel, a very hard-driving and competent Israeli, as a manager on the TVM team. He understood technology and invested in a few Israeli companies that he linked with our German portfolio and that were quite successful. When a couple of those companies went public, it gave us enough firepower to be able to raise additional capital.

Why did it take us so long to find competent management? One explanation is that we had a meager talent pool from which to recruit. We were unable to locate anyone in Germany with venture capital experience, let alone the ability to manage a venture capital organization. Moreover, it was difficult to find talented people who were interested in working for a small company like TVM. In Germany in those days, most talented German university graduates wanted to work for Siemens, Bayer, Daimler-Benz, or one of the other large, prestigious German companies. If you wanted to join a small entrepreneurial company, people thought there was something wrong with you.

Needless to say, this aspect of German culture also made it difficult to recruit talent for portfolio companies. A second challenge TVM faced in finding young, entrepreneurial companies in Germany and managers capable of running them was the managerial culture of Germany's large corporations. German companies such as Siemens, Mannesman, and Bayer had many brilliant researchers in their R&D organizations. Yet their researchers were isolated within their own silos, with no chance to develop any understanding of marketing, manufacturing, or other functions crucial to the development of successful new products. The same held true for managers in these other functions. Such managers were very literate within their own functional areas but quite illiterate outside them. This was a major structural difference between German companies and American ones. In large American companies, managers were given product-line experience with responsibility for all functions. As a result, they understood something about all the different factors involved in designing, manufacturing, and marketing a product. Even though the large German corporations managed to produce successful innovations, they did not produce managers with the broad range of knowledge and skills necessary to manage small, entrepreneurial, technology-based companies. Such knowledge and skills do not come naturally to even the most gifted technologists, as my experience with MIT entrepreneurs in the 1950s and '60s had taught me.

TVM had one major success in the portfolio of its first fund, TVM I, which offset what otherwise was a string of failures. In 1985, TVM invested in Qiagen, a provider of innovative sample and assay technologies and products for the life sciences. TVM's CFO, Peter Kaleschke, guided Qiagen through a long gestation period and remained on the board through the company's IPO. When Qiagen became the first German company to go public on NASDAQ in 1996, TVM realized the current equivalent of €89.4 million on what had been an investment of €1.8 million. Qiagen now employs over 2,600 people in thirty locations around the world, is still growing rapidly, and is projecting revenues of between $875 million and $905 million for 2008. The Qiagen deal made up for disasters like TVM's 1985 investment, alongside Advent Ltd., in European Silicon Structures. ES2, as it was called, was an ambitious — some might say foolish — stab at creating the first European-based designer and developer of integrated circuits at a time when a worldwide glut of silicon chips was wreaking havoc with the industry. ES2's new chip design and much-touted rapid production process did not bring success in the marketplace, and the company was sold at a fraction of what its investors had paid for it.

It would be ten years after the founding of TVM before Germany developed any real ecosystem for venture capital. The Ruhr Valley did not turn to silicon just because there were German venture capitalists on the scene. Indeed—as would become apparent over time—Europe itself did not offer nearly as conducive an environment for early-stage venture capital as I had hoped it would. Meanwhile, however, knowledge of the Advent network was spreading rapidly, especially among those who had a global perspective. As I was launching Advent Ltd. in Britain, Advent Belgium, and TVM Technoventures in Germany in the early 1980s, I had begun to form the ambition of building a "global" venture capital network. Yet I was so busy with my activities in Europe that I'd hardly really thought about the rest of the world.

Late in 1981, however, I was approached by David Gill, the head of the capital markets group at the International Finance Corporation (IFC), the arm of the World Bank that engages in private-sector investment. David, who had been a successful merchant banker in Canada prior to joining the IFC, knew how to get things done. He had hired a very capable team that included Antoine van Agtmael and Michael Barth, who were to go on to great futures at Emerging Markets Management and FMO (the Dutch development bank), respectively.[3] When I met David, the IFC had recently begun to promote and invest in venture capital funds in the emerging markets of Spain[4] and Brazil. It would soon invest in new funds in Kenya and South Korea. David, in the meantime, had been convinced by one of his bright young officers, a Chinese Filipino named Augustin (Toti) Que, that the IFC should encourage the development of venture capital in Southeast Asia, and he asked me if I was interested in taking part in such an exercise. My first reaction was to say, "David, why the hell are you bringing this up now? I've got my hands full." He replied, "Well, just go down to Singapore and see what you think."

Today, when China and India are attracting significant amounts of venture capital and, along with other parts of Asia, are also becoming increasingly popular markets for private equity, it is worth recalling that in Asia twenty-five years ago, as in Europe just a bit further back, venture capital and private equity were virtually unknown. When I went to Singapore on my exploratory mission, however, I was intrigued. Along with the other "East Asian tigers"—Taiwan, Hong Kong, and South Korea—Singapore had been growing rapidly since the early 1960s through a policy of export-driven industrialization. At the beginning of the 1980s, the government of Prime Minister Lee Kuan Yew had embarked on an effort to move from the labor-intensive, low-value-added industries it had promoted in previous decades to more high-tech, science-based, and knowledge-intensive ones. In the process, Singapore had created much of the infrastructure that a venture capitalist would need in order to succeed there — or so it appeared to me at the time.[5]

Elsewhere in the region on that first trip, I saw how far some of the other countries there lagged behind Singapore. In Malaysia, a dirt road led from the Kuala Lumpur airport past colonial-era buildings to the center of the city, where there was hardly a modern building in sight. My wife and I were taken to visit "industrial estates" in the countryside that consisted of Quonset huts housing businesses such as a "scorpion factory" that made glass penholders, paperweights, and so on with scorpions encased inside. Even so, I could see that countries such as Malaysia, Thailand, and Indonesia, which were now trying to follow in the footsteps of Singapore and the other East Asian tigers, were poised for growth in the years just ahead.

I was drawn to the idea of introducing venture capital into Southeast Asia, but I knew that a project like this would involve an immense effort. Toti Que, who had determined that he wanted to be a venture capitalist and, furthermore, that he wanted to work under the wing of TA Associates, knew the region well, was convinced of its long-term growth potential, and was ready to devote his considerable talents and energy to the project. Raising capital from institutional and corporate investors for a venture capital fund in a relatively unfamiliar part of the world, however, would be a formidable challenge. Moreover, I was beginning to have reason to doubt that my partners at TA Associates would want to cover the costs of launching a Southeast Asian fund, which I estimated at $1.5 million for legal and administrative expenses, Toti Que's salary, and travel. While I had been able to tap the TA Associates partnership for the establishment of affiliates in Europe, the costs of this were manageable, and there was always the promise that these European affiliates would prove to be new sources of capital for TAA to manage in the United States. There was no such promise in Southeast Asia.

Despite these obstacles, however, I became convinced that the region was the growth area of the future, that its potential was untapped, and that by moving quickly TA Associates could establish a proprietary position.

There are times when it is necessary to stake out your ground and then figure out how to build on it later. This was a lesson I had learned when I started TA Associates, and experience would reaffirm it for me many times in later years. Auditing the strengths of the various ASEAN countries (at the time, these were Indonesia, Malaysia, the Philippines, Singapore, and Thailand), I found that Singapore was the most logical nation in which to be based. Located on a major sea-lane between Europe, Africa, the Middle East, and India to its west, and China and Japan to its east, Singapore was an entrepôt for the Malay Peninsula, Indochina, Thailand, and South China. It was a service center for the region serving the rapidly growing economy of Indonesia. Its people were well educated and well trained, hardworking and adaptable, with formidable skills in manufacturing and trading. The country was politically stable with an efficient government civil service, and a system of law and regulations left by the British and familiar to us. While not yet a center of high technology, Singapore was home to corporations and a population that could readily accept technology, upgrade it, and apply it to its own and the region's needs. My colleagues and I decided we would make Singapore our base and see if we could use it as a springboard to the rest of Southeast Asia.

The process we adopted in analyzing the opportunities in Southeast Asia, I should add, is critical for any venture capital or private equity organization thinking of entering a foreign market. What makes investing domestically different from investing internationally is the requirement that the manager approach the market from a cultural, historic, and geographic as well as an economic perspective. One needs to ask a lot of different questions: What comparative advantages does the country or region have over its neighbors and competitors as a result of geography, history, or culture? Are these advantages in location, in natural resources, in low-cost labor, in technological or manufacturing skills? What historical experiences and cultural traits influence the attitudes of the business community and the country or region at large? Answering this last question requires investment managers to have a presence on the ground and to work closely with local partners over the period of time it takes to acquire deep knowledge of the local culture.

In any case, the first challenge I faced in expanding into Southeast Asia was the increasing reservations my TA Associates partners were expressing, albeit indirectly, about financing my international activities. This made it necessary that I find a partner who could share the expenses. I found one, fortunately, in my old friend from Orange Nassau, Piet van de Ven. Given the history of the Dutch in what is now Indonesia, van de Ven had always been interested in the region. When I spoke to him about my newly awakened interest and asked him what he thought, he said, "I think this would be very interesting to some of the Dutch institutions." Piet shared my view not only of Southeast Asia's growth potential but also of the wisdom of establishing a proprietary position there. While I realized that, in soliciting his help, I was inviting a potential competitor into the picture, I needed financial support for the job of establishing an affiliate nine thousand miles away. I was steadily accumulating costs of which my partners at TA Associates were unaware, and had built up a head of steam. With van de Ven's agreement to absorb half the costs, I was finally able to convince my partners at TA Associates to shoulder the other half.

The second person who proved critical to the effort in Southeast Asia was Henry Huntley (Tony) Haight IV, a native Californian who had migrated to the Boston area. Tony comes from adventuresome stock: one of his ancestors, Henry Huntley Haight I, was a native easterner who went to San Francisco during the gold rush to practice law and later became governor of California. (Haight Street in San Francisco is named for him.) Tony had been in the timber business in New Guinea and Malaysia, not with any spectacular success. But he knew the region and was excited by the prospect of doing business there. He was also willing to live in Singapore, which not many Americans would have been willing to do in those days. Tony was a central-casting version of the Great White Hunter. You could envision him coming off a Chinese junk and up to the Long Bar at the old Raffles Hotel in Singapore for one of its famous Singapore Slings, with Hoagy Carmichael at the piano. He loved Asia — the people, the food, the customs — and wanted to live as the locals did, renting an apartment without air conditioning, for example. (He did allow himself a red pickup truck that he bought in Singapore shortly after arriving there and, to confuse the local authorities, drove using a Massachusetts license.) Although Tony was irrepressible and difficult to control, he would prove to be just what I needed for running a venture capital management company in Southeast Asia.

The fund-raising for what became the Southeast Asia Venture Investment Company (SEAVIC) began in earnest at the beginning of 1983. It was an immense job. Toti Que traveled Asia, Europe, and the United States in search of investors. Some were identified and recruited by me, such as the First National Bank of Boston, American Can Company, and my old client Monsanto, whose representative, Costas Anagnostopoulos, had invested in Advent Ltd.'s Advent Eurofund in Britain and never lost faith in the network concept. Piet van de Ven also identified a number of investors from France and Holland through Orange Nassau and its French parent company, CGIP.

Assembling this group of international investors was not enough, however. My strategy in Europe of finding a local champion in each new country we entered had served us well there, and I was not prepared to move into Southeast Asia without local representation. Even with the sponsorship of the IFC, however, we were not succeeding in finding such a champion or developing a core group of investors within the region. I had made several trips to Southeast Asia in the first few months of 1983. These early visits to institutional and corporate investors had been promising, and by late spring I was fairly confident that we were well on our way. In June, however, it became obvious that the early indications of interest I had received were not maturing into commitments, and that we were far from our goal.

In retrospect, I can see that the lack of sponsorship from a local champion, such as Sofina had been for us in Belgium or Siemens in Germany, was the reason for the reluctance of these potential investors. Our mistake in raising capital from Singapore and Malaysian institutions was fundamental: we were using as an agent a capable, but not local, merchant bank, Morgan Grenfell, which had raised capital in Europe for TA Associates. Unfortunately, it did not have the leverage to succeed in Southeast Asia. I was ready to admit defeat and to cut the expense drain. My last telephone call before I planned to pull the plug was to Ang Kong Hua, the president of National Iron and Steel (NIS) of Singapore, the only local company that had committed to the program.

It was a fortuitous call. Kong Hua was a very visible, well-connected person in the Singapore establishment. He was also an iconoclast — which is unusual for a Singaporean — and a real believer in venture capital. Like many of the early investors in TA Associates' European affiliates and their funds, Kong Hua was very much aware of Silicon Valley and Route 128 and the gains that were being made there, having invested in the United States himself. He was also technology-oriented and wanted to diversify his company along these lines.[6] Kong Hua told me that if I cleared the decks by dismissing Morgan Grenfell, he would convince the

Development Bank of Singapore (DBS)—where he had worked from 1968 to 1974, establishing the bank's investment banking division, and which was a big shareholder in NIS—to take the job and get it done.

This was confirmation, if I ever needed it, of the wisdom of proceeding in a region as an insider, not an outsider. I said yes, and by October we had the necessary commitments from Singaporean and Malaysian investors (many of the Singaporean entities were public companies that were clients of DBS) to satisfy our U.S. and European investors that the fund would have sufficient support from the power structure of both countries. TA Associates was about to become the first U.S. venture capital firm with a presence in Asia—if only my TAA partners had been interested in taking advantage of this opportunity.

The early 1980s, when fundamental changes in the global political economy appeared to be getting under way, was an exciting time to be expanding overseas in a business like venture capital. The new spirit of economic optimism unleashed in Western Europe was reviving the dream of European economic integration. In what was then called Eastern Europe, Pope John Paul II's visit to Poland in 1979 and the founding of Solidarity there a year later had suggested that Soviet control of the Warsaw Pact nations was weakening. Also in 1980, the Chinese government promulgated regulations for a "Special Economic Zone" in Guangdong Province and created an SEZ in the city of Shenzhen. Meanwhile, the economies of the East Asian "tigers" were booming, and international trade and capital markets were expanding. Amid these changes, I began to see opportunities both to help finance new enterprises and to assist more established companies in expanding their operations and reaching new markets. I visualized taking advantage of these opportunities by developing TA Associates into a global enterprise with strengths in venture capital, in what would soon become known as private equity, in real estate (in which TAA had begun investing at the beginning of the 1980s), and in international outreach.

My partners at TA Associates turned out to have other ideas, however. They had been willing to indulge my vision of a global venture capital firm—most likely a fantasy to them—by funding the start-up of network affiliates in Europe. Yet they had done so somewhat grudgingly, with a certain amount of grumbling to the effect of "What is Brooke doing this time?" My European activity was tolerated because Kevin Landry kept a lid on the criticism and because I brought back considerable capital for TAA to manage from groups such as the investors of Sofinnova in France, Orange Nassau in Holland, and the Matuschka Group in Germany. My partners were not interested in the evolution of the venture capital industry in Europe, but they were happy to manage the capital generated by these connections. While they funded the start-up of the European affiliates Sofinnova, Advent Ltd., Advent Belgium, and TVM, they were less willing to cover the operating expenses of network members. This was occasionally necessary, since these firms were at first undercapitalized. To become economically self-sufficient, they would need to have more capital under management than they could raise at the start.

When I began to think about expanding into Southeast Asia, my partners were willing to assume half the start-up costs because Piet van de Ven, who had agreed to assume the other half of the costs of setting up operations in the region, had brought in capital from Holland and Belgium for TAA to manage. Soon afterward, however, I began to realize that I had pushed the envelope at TAA as far as I could.

This first became apparent in December 1982, when I was discussing the budget for the coming year with Kevin Landry and David Croll. I had made Landry and Croll managing partners earlier that year, while I became the senior managing partner devoting most of my time to the network of international affiliates. When we went over the budget for 1983, Kevin and David asked me, "Well, how much money are you going to spend developing the network and international business?" At that point we were about to make a lot of money, because in 1982 we had launched the $165 million Advent V fund; at a rate of 2.5 percent, Advent V would yield over $4 million in management fees, thus increasing the cash flow of our business dramatically. Moreover, everything we had spent on international expansion up to that point had been recovered in revenue; when I started Advent Ltd. in London, for example, I charged the new firm for my management time. I thought there was a good case for pressing ahead with TAA's international activity, and I told Landry and Croll that to build out the network, as I now planned to do, I would need $1 million for the next year. I said I believed that I could eventually recover those expenses, but that was what it was going to cost to roll out an expansion into Asia and fund our ongoing activities in Europe.

There was a lot of hemming and hawing from my two partners. So finally I said, "OK, here's what I'm going to do. I'm going to find a way to finance this operation so that it will never have an impact on the budget of TA Associates." Although I didn't realize it at the time, this decision marked the beginning of the end of my dreams for the firm I had founded. Within little more than a year, TA Associates' domestic operations would split into three separate entities — TA Realty, TA Communications Partners (later renamed Media/Communications Partners), and TA Associates itself — while my fledgling international operation became the new firm Advent International.

When the breakup of TA Associates began to occur in 1983, it had been fifteen years since I had achieved the dream of establishing my own venture capital firm. After starting out with a $6 million fund we had raised four more, including the $165 million Advent V. Despite losing good people such as Bill Egan and Craig Burr, we had built a first-rate team of investors under the leadership of one of the best, Kevin Landry, and our third fund, Advent III, would soon come in with an IRR of nearly 40 percent. As I have said, I had envisioned TA Associates as a global enterprise with strengths in venture capital, private equity, real estate, and international outreach. The various units were all in a strong position in 1983 and would raise close to $1 billion among them in the mid-1980s — a lot of money at that time. Had we managed to keep the company together, we clearly would have had a jump on firms such as Carlyle and Blackstone. Yet I was not successful in convincing my partners that following my vision would, in the end, create more value to them than going it alone.

My partners' reaction to my desire to build out TA Associates' international network surprised as well as disappointed me — not only because of the hopes I had nurtured for TAA as an organization but also because of what it meant for my vision of making venture capital a global business. I was disappointed by both my partners' lack of enthusiasm for my global ambitions and their focus on how much pursuing these ambitions would cost. I hadn't succeeded in getting TAA going in the first place by worrying about what I spent. More fundamentally, for me, there was an issue here of what venture capital was all about. Our industry was supposed to anticipate change, to thrive on change, and to be the agent of change. And yet here were my partners failing to recognize and respond to a basic shift in the balance of economic power in the world that would create a wealth of new opportunities for ourselves and for others. Were they being shortsighted? Or — as I now have to ask myself — was I expecting them to buy into my own dream without knowing what was in it for them?

One of my TA Associates colleagues, Steve Woodsum, has recounted how my vision looked to him when he interviewed for a job at TAA, early in 1980, as a twenty-six-year-old working as an analyst for the First Chicago Investment Corporation:

> I met with Peter . . . and he was talking about VC [venture capital] activities that were going on in Europe, and how he likened it to how America was at the time that he got started. I was just trying to find a way to make a few good investments, and I just couldn't believe that Peter was so focused on building this great big network. . . . I found it very entertaining that I was supposed to be interviewing with this guy and all he wanted to talk about was this big international network he envisioned. He didn't want to talk about what it took to make a good investment. We were clearly worlds apart in terms of where we were in terms of the whole grand cycle of venture capital. . . . It just seemed that there were so many opportunities in the United States, and I didn't see the business appeal to it at all. I think most people in the industry felt the same way—that Peter was kind of involved in this wild goose chase. Not that he wouldn't be successful (because I think we thought he would be able to pull it off), but it was just that, why would you want to do that? Most of us thought there was plenty of business in the United States, and it was certainly hard to figure out non-U.S. investments, whether it be the currency or the economics or the going public rules or the investment banking rules, it was just that the VC business wasn't easy in the United States, and doing it outside the United States made it just that much more complex.[7]

Thinking about Steve's reaction, I understand more about why a vision that inspired me so much almost thirty years ago might not have had the same appeal to other American venture capitalists, actual or aspiring. As Steve's comments imply, whether or not venture capital could succeed outside the United States was a very big unknown twenty-five years ago. It is important to recall that when I began my network building in Western Europe and Southeast Asia in the early 1980s, venture capital on the East Coast was just coming into its own, thirty-five years after Georges Doriot started American Research & Development.[8] When ARD and other early venture capitalists in the region, including myself, began investing in innovative enterprises back in the 1950s and '60s, it wasn't at all clear whether this type of investment would succeed. I don't mean whether many or most of our individual investments would succeed, but whether venture capital itself was economically viable as a sustained activity. ARD took almost ten years to show any significant profits from its investments, and the firm's storied investment in Digital Equipment would be the only "home run" it hit in the twenty-seven years between its founding and its acquisition (in 1972) by the conglomerate Textron.

The venture capital industry as a whole — just getting on its feet on both the East and West coasts in the mid-1960s — would go through a difficult period in the 1970s as a result of an increased capital gains tax and the general economic malaise of that decade. In my own case, it took twelve years (from 1968 until 1980) before TA Associates made significant money through its share of the profits from the firm's investments. So Steve Woodsum was right when he observed that venture capital was still challenging enough in the United States, without throwing in the added complexity of going international. Given the focus required to invest profitably in the domestic market, the success my partners at TAA were beginning to enjoy, and the opportunities they could foresee, I can understand their reluctance to spend time and money on anything as apparently quixotic as spreading venture capital outside the United States. Even today, indeed, when venture capital and private equity have become profitable pursuits in many parts of Europe, Asia, and Latin America, returns on venture capital investment in the rest of the world — except for Israel — have never been as high as they have during the most profitable periods for venture capital in the United States. (Private equity in Europe, however, is another story. Since 1986, when comparisons between Europe and the United States began to be made by Venture Economics, upper-quartile performance for buyouts in Europe has actually been equal to, if not a bit better than, that in the United States.)

Meanwhile, my TAA partners, all at least fifteen years younger than I, still had young families and were less willing to take the financial risks that I could afford. (I would turn fifty-four in 1983.) They were making a handsome income investing domestically, with plenty of opportunities to go on doing so. Was it reasonable for me to ask them to forgo high returns in the short term for highly uncertain ones over the longer term, no matter how fervently I believed in my vision? Probably not. I had to show them that my plan was workable and how they would benefit. I was asking them to take a lot on faith. There were many reasons why it might have been difficult to convince them that my plan would work: for example, we were in a very new environment with a high degree of uncertainty, some of the European affiliates were struggling, and there were costs associated with further expansion that could not be quantified. In any case, too much of my vision remained just a sketch to my partners.

I had still had the vision, however. With the beginnings of a network in Western Europe and a foothold in Southeast Asia, I felt that I had made a promising start. My progress to date, along with the many significant changes taking place in the world, told me that the time was indeed right for a global approach to venture investing. The only important questions now were about means, not objectives. Even if TA Associates was not going to remain the vehicle for pursuing my vision of a global venture capital organization, there was no question in my mind but that I would do so.

# CHAPTER 5

# PUSHING AHEAD

## ADVENT INTERNATIONAL
## AND EXPANSION IN ASIA

· · ·

When my partners at TA Associates made it clear that they were no longer interested in financing the expansion of the firm's international activities, it soon became obvious to me that I would have to pursue my dream
outside the orbit of TAA. My interests and those of my partners had simply diverged too much. This realization represented a considerable setback for me. TAA's experience, relationships, and deal flow in the United
States had been an indispensable asset as I began forming a network of
affiliates in Europe and Asia. Being unable to continue to leverage these
resources would make my job of forming a global organization that much
more difficult.

By the winter of 1983–84—a year after my budget discussion with Kevin
Landry and David Croll, and after having established network affiliates in
Britain, Belgium, Germany, and Singapore as well as one in Japan[1]—it
was also becoming clear to me that I would need a considerable amount
of capital to finance my plans for further international expansion. Building
a company that would establish new affiliates in Europe, Asia, and perhaps
elsewhere, integrate them into a global network, and—as I originally intended—provide them and their portfolio companies with services was
going to be an expensive proposition. It did not take me long, therefore,
to realize that pursuing my vision was going to require capital from outside shareholders.

Fortunately there were a number of TA Associates clients in Europe
who were interested in my vision of a global company. However, bringing

in outside shareholders would mean that TAA, whose international assets I wished to acquire, would have to be satisfied with a relatively small share of the new entity. The solution we arrived at was an exchange of the international assets — that is, the network relationships — in return for a 15 percent interest for TAA in the new company, Advent International Corporation. The outside shareholders would receive 25 percent for their capital contribution, the employees 25 percent (an option pool was also available for Advent employees), and the Brooke family the remaining 35 percent. All the voting stock resided with me. I set things up this way partly because I wanted to have control of the firm during its formative years. When Advent began to receive carried interest — the portion of the capital gains, usually 20 percent, from a venture capital or private equity investment that is retained by the managers as opposed to the limited partners — I decided that 25 percent of the carry would go to the corporation. I made this arrangement because I wanted to retain capital for projects such as financing the establishment of new network members, building a mergers and acquisitions activity, or building a technology and business transfer capacity. I also wanted to have money in reserve against any economic downturn.

I did, at first, hope that TA Associates would be the Advent network member in the United States, which would mean that Advent could share investments with TAA in the States and spend its own time and effort monitoring and managing what happened abroad. I had no interest in rebuilding a U.S. venture capital group. The relationship between Advent International and TA Associates, however, was tense for the first few years. No one at TA Associates did me any favors when I started Advent. As a matter of fact, my former partners probably did as much as they could to make it difficult, even though they were substantial shareholders in the new company. There was a lot of paranoia about me leaving and starting something new. Kevin Landry and the other partners had never raised money on their own, and I had the reputation of being a master fundraiser. Some also worried that by raising money for its affiliates, some of whom had "Advent" in their name, Advent International would create confusion in the marketplace, since TAA's funds also carried the Advent label. Finally, some of the partners in TA Associates thought that we could become a difficult competitor. Kevin didn't care about that, however. He figured that the world was full of competitors and had no fear about competing with Advent or anyone else.

While there was an understandable amount of anxiety when I left TA Associates, it dissipated rapidly. The team there was well trained and led by a very able man. It regained its confidence quickly and has proceeded, under Kevin's leadership, to build an enviable record.[2] During this period of anxiety, however, TAA declined to become an Advent network member. I was therefore forced to build a new team of venture capitalists in the United States, which was unfortunate. It meant that I could not leverage the experience and deal flow of TA Associates. It meant that I would have to replicate what I had done before. On top of all this there was, for me, the trauma of separation from a firm that I had founded, built, and led for fifteen years. But there was nothing to do now but push ahead as best I could.

Fortunately, my investor base for Advent International was a strong one. The outside investors in Advent were families and institutions in Europe for whom I had made successful venture investments in the United States. The Bembergs, a venerable old French family that had been prosperous for generations before Otto Bemberg went to Argentina during World War II to make a new fortune for himself in breweries and finance, were the lead investor. Indeed, given TA Associates' success in managing the funds that the Bembergs had invested with the firm (beginning with Advent II), they would have provided all the money I needed. However, I thought it wise to include two other groups who had been useful in assembling the network, Sofina in Belgium and Orange Nassau in the Netherlands. The Bemberg-controlled industrial and financial company Entreprises Quilmes invested $5 million, and Sofina and Orange Nassau $1.75 million between them. The idea was to use that money to build out the network, to add new programs, and to be a backup if we needed it. Meanwhile we would live off consulting arrangements with our affiliates and the fees these would generate, as well as carried interest that we received from the affiliates' investments.

When I founded TA Associates in 1968, American Research & Development Corporation had been in business for over twenty years and Greylock Partners, an ARD offspring, had recently been established. By contrast, when I started Advent International with the intention from the start of creating a global organization, I had virtually no models. The lone venture capital organization with international operations at the time was

Apax Partners, which had grown out of Patricof & Co. in 1977. Apax managed separate funds through separate management companies in the U.K., France, Germany, and the United States. This was a different model from that later employed by Advent International, where investment operations, by the end of the 1980s, would be centrally controlled.

When I founded Advent, however, I envisioned it not as a venture capital firm making its own investments but rather as an organization that would provide advisory services to members of the international network of venture capital firms that I had assembled and planned to expand, as well as to their portfolio companies. These services would be in the areas of strategic planning, technology transfer, marketing, manufacturing, mergers and acquisitions, and investment (for that portion of the network members' funds — usually 25 percent — that was invested in the United States). Advent would also link the network members together and be the catalyst for an exchange of ideas and information that could help them improve their portfolio companies and give those companies access to international markets. On top of all this, Advent would manage corporate venture capital programs (similar to TA Associates' program for INCO), serve as an adviser to companies with international ambitions, and provide international merger and acquisition services. For all these services Advent International would be paid a fee. Advent International's investment activity at the beginning was limited to the advice it gave to its network members when they made strategic investments in the United States. My original design for Advent was partly pragmatic: even if I had originally conceived of Advent as a global investment organization, no one would have given me the money to start such a firm in those days.

For the first few years of the new company's life, I would have to focus on securing the network and staffing Advent International with people I felt could execute the strategy I had described to the investors. Even though I had some resources at my disposal, as I had when I founded TA Associates, I would need to build the new firm on relatively modest foundations. Holed up on the fourth floor of TA Associates' offices at 45 Milk Street in Boston's financial district (we would not have our own office space until 1988), my new partners and I set out to build a new type of global organization that would continue my mission of spreading venture capital around the world.

The nucleus of the new company consisted of myself, COO Tom Armstrong, John Littlechild (who joined us from Advent Ltd. in London),

Clint Harris, and Tony Haight. None of us, except for Littlechild and myself, had any experience in venture capital, although each member of the team possessed his own skills. Armstrong came to Advent from the Allen Group, where he was vice president for international operations, with an operating background as well as international experience. Harris had a strategic planning background from his seven years as a consultant and partner at Bain & Co. Haight had extensive operating experience in Southeast Asia. In all it was a motley group, interested in the concept of a global service company but hardly what you would call distinguished. But as a regrettable secretary of defense has said, you go to war with the army you have.

Advent International was actually still on the drawing board when, in December 1983, SEAVIC — the first venture capital firm in Southeast Asia — began operations. The SEAVIC story is worth delving into in some detail because it offers an especially good illustration of the challenges — some stemming from the novelty of venture capital in the settings into which I was introducing it, others from economic conditions, still others from cultural factors — involved in my quest to take venture capital abroad in the 1980s.

SEAVIC was launched with the international sponsorship of TA Associates, Orange Nassau, and the IFC, and the regional sponsorship of National Iron and Steel Mills of Singapore, the Development Bank of Singapore (DBS), and the Arab-Malaysian Bank in Malaysia. Another prominent investor was the Yeo Hiap Seng Group, a major international food and beverage distributor whose chairman was Alan Yeo. The Singapore-born grandson of the founder of Yeo Hiap Seng (which was established in Zhangzhou, China, in 1900), Alan took over as managing director of the company when it was first listed on the Singapore and Malaysian stock exchanges in 1969. He would play a key role in building it into one of the major food and beverage companies in Southeast Asia in the course of the 1980s (at which point the company acquired the bottling franchise for Pepsi-Cola in Singapore and Malaysia). During that period he also became chairman of Yeo Hiap Seng and of Singapore's Trade Development Board. Alan served on other government entities and was highly regarded by both the Economic Development Board and DBS. At the suggestion of DBS, we asked Yeo to serve as chairman of SEAVIC. He still serves in that capacity today. The personal friendship that developed between our two families was one of many such relationships that were critical to the extension of the TAA and Advent networks into Asia.

The first year of operation at SEAVIC was not easy. For one thing, despite the strong relationships I had formed with people like Alan Yeo and Ang Kong Hua, I had no prior personal experience with the cultures of Southeast Asia. I had one remote personal connection with the region, but it was not one I would have chosen to trumpet: I shared a family crest (though no blood connection) with Sir James Brooke. Sir James, who lived from 1803 to 1868, was an English soldier and adventurer who helped the sultan of Brunei put down an uprising among the Dayak people of Borneo in 1839–40. In recognition of this service, the sultan named him Rajah of Sarawak in 1841, and the Brooke dynasty of White Rajahs (Sir James was succeeded by his nephew Sir Charles Anthony Johnson-Brooke, who in turn was succeeded by his son Sir Charles Vyner deWindt Brooke) continued to rule the kingdom of Sarawak until 1946, when it became part of British Malaya.

As I say, I would have preferred to keep this particular connection to the region to myself. It surfaced, however, when my wife Anne and I, the investors in SEAVIC's first Southeast Asia fund, and members of SEAVIC's management team visited our partners in Malaysia, the Arab-Malaysian Bank. Alan Yeo arranged for the chairman of the Arab-Malaysian Bank, Tan Sri Dato' Azman Hashim, to have us all for dinner at his country villa outside Kuala Lumpur. After I had drunk about three quarts of mango juice before dinner (no alcohol in a Muslim gathering), we sat down to what proved a long and arduous meal. Conversation was a chore, although Anne seemed to be handling the situation better than I. At one point I noticed her leaning toward the Dato' Azman, whom she was sitting next to, as if confiding something.

On our way back to the hotel after dinner, I asked Anne what she had said, and she told me that she had been explaining my obscure relation to the White Rajahs. I was aghast. "Oh my God, now they're going to think that I'm a colonialist returning to exploit their country," I told her. After a few stiff martinis at the hotel bar, I went to bed wondering how I was going to face my Malaysian partners in the morning. I needn't have worried, however. When I arrived at the bank's board meeting the next day, one of the Malaysians rushed up to me, squeezed my hand, and said admiringly, "You're related to the White Raj!" I learned that my new partners regarded the White Rajahs as enlightened men who had governed the Dayaks fairly. Thanks to Anne's introduction, I received high marks with the Malaysians, and thus began a wonderful and productive relationship. Yet it was a lesson in the unpredictability of things in a culture that was new to me.[3]

Meanwhile, SEAVIC itself faced a significant challenge as it became clear that Toti Que's considerable skills in fund-raising were not the same skills required to comanage a venture capital program. Some people possess both, but he was not one of them. He did not understand the venture process — the search for investments, the due diligence required, and the need to develop a focus for a fund. Tony Haight did understand the process, but was new to managing a venture team. The result was a slapdash approach to investing, a rather cavalier approach, that did not promise success. There was a cultural issue here as well. Aspects of Que's personality clashed with the conservative ways of the Singaporeans, to whom he seemed overly fond of life after dark. By mutual agreement, Que left us early in 1985 for a career in merchant banking. He had devoted himself to the formation of SEAVIC, and it was unfortunate that he was not around to see it succeed.

When Que left the company, we needed to replace him with someone who would bring stability to the organization. Tony Haight hired an executive search firm to find Que's successor as comanager of SEAVIC. The search firm fortunately found Tan Keng Boon. Keng Boon was a native Singaporean who had studied engineering and business administration at the University of Singapore, taken his first job with Esso, then gone on to work for DBS, where he rose to become vice president of the National Banking Group. In 1979, he had cofounded a semiconductor manufacturing firm, Semicon Industries, where he served as director and general manager until the company was sold in 1985. His combination of financial and operational backgrounds, not to mention his experience as an entrepreneur, were good qualifications for running a venture capital firm. Keng Boon was Singaporean, and his connection with DBS was a credential that made him acceptable to the local establishment. He was organized, well mannered, fastidious, controlled, and possessed a sense of command. We needed someone like him for SEAVIC to be well regarded locally.

Fortunately, by the time Keng Boon arrived at SEAVIC, Tony Haight had already assembled a strong team. He had recruited two very capable managers who were also Singaporean, Derrick Lee and Koh Lee Boon. Derrick and Tan Keng Boon had actually been classmates in secondary school. Keng Boon went on to university while Derrick went to London to study at the Chartered Association of Certified Accountants. After working as an accountant for Hertz in London, Derrick had returned to Singapore to work as an auditor with Coopers & Lybrand, then joined a leading dairy products manufacturer based in New Zealand. Although Derrick eventually became the company's financial controller, he wanted broader responsibilities and moved over into general management, serving as de facto COO for seven years. He was looking for new challenges when the executive search arm of Deloitte and Touche, which Tony Haight had employed in his search for a CFO, contacted him about working for SEAVIC. Although he didn't at first know what venture capital was, Derrick quickly got excited about the business. He told Tony that he thought SEAVIC was too small an organization to need a CFO, and that once he had the accounting set up he wanted to be able to spend time doing deals. Derrick may have been new to venture capital, but he certainly had the right attitude to succeed at it.

The other member of the original SEAVIC team, Koh Lee Boon, was recruited by Tony Haight only a month after Derrick Lee joined the company. Coming from a family of "Straits Chinese" (descendants of the earliest Chinese immigrants to the Malay lands of Southeast Asia), Lee Boon earned a degree in electrical engineering from the University of Malaya, then went to work for the Economic Development Board of Singapore after graduation. He later accumulated thirteen years of managerial experience with two companies in the electronics manufacturing industry, one of them an American multinational in which he rose to general management.

The SEAVIC team was a good one once Tan Keng Boon came on board to serve as co–managing director with Tony Haight. Tony spent every other month in the region, and he was a valuable person to have on the ground there. It takes a guy like Tony, who is intuitive and resourceful, to operate in the Far East. He could move quickly on a deal. He had good instincts and a lot of energy. His traits matched those of the Chinese societies in which he operated. He was a risk taker, as are the Chinese. There was tension, however, between Tony and Keng Boon, who, in Tony's view, had a typically Singaporean preference for hierarchy and didn't like sharing the managing director's role. Derrick Lee, on the other hand, enjoyed being free of the bureaucracy and politics of a large company. He thrived in the atmosphere of a small, entrepreneurial organization where flexibility and initiative would be rewarded. He respected Keng Boon as a leader, as did Koh Lee Boon, and together the three Singaporeans struck a good balance between focus and opportunism for the new venture capital organization.

In establishing TA Associates' affiliates in Western Europe, as I have explained, my partners and I identified the needs of the particular countries and developed strategies for responding to them. My SEAVIC colleagues and I took the same approach. Singapore had unique strengths: manufacturing companies whose productivity was unmatched anywhere in the world, as well as, we believed, the capacity to exploit technologies that were applicable to the country's needs and skills. Southeast Asia generally in the early 1980s was becoming a place not just where Western manufacturers could find low-cost labor but also where growing local markets were creating an opening for new, locally based businesses. Thus we devised a twofold strategy for SEAVIC. We planned to invest 50 percent of the capital raised for SEAVIC in technology and manufacturing transfers from the United States and Europe, and 50 percent in new companies in the region or more mature companies that required expansion capital. To execute this strategy, SEAVIC actually raised and managed three separate funds: a S$14 million fund for Singapore, Venture Investment Singapore (VIS I), which was organized by NIS and DBS and had six other local investors; a US$28 million regional fund, SEAVI, whose investors included companies outside the region (such as the First National Bank of Boston and Monsanto) and which would invest both in Singapore and in other ASEAN countries; and a S$16 million Malaysian fund, Malaysian Ventures Sdn. Bhd., whose sponsor was the Arab-Malaysian Bank.

In devising our strategy for SEAVIC we used the phrase "technology and manufacturing transfers," although I realize, in retrospect, that we were using the term *technology transfer* rather loosely. The deals we actually sought out and completed were manufacturing transfers. Tony Haight originally had the idea of setting up SEAVIC as an international procurement office that could help American manufacturers obtain low-cost components for use in their U.S. factories. Koh Lee Boon saw a problem with this strategy, however: the American firms that SEAVIC would be targeting would not likely have the volume to realize significant cost savings from lower-cost components. Lee Boon thought that a better strategy would be to identify American companies whose managements knew that they could reduce costs by going offshore but hesitated to do so because they lacked the capability to effect such a transfer. SEAVIC would be the mechanism that would overcome the lack of confidence and trust felt by U.S. companies contemplating a move into Southeast Asia and, eventually, China. It would provide everything from technical assistance in setting up manufacturing facilities to advice and contacts for navigating the legal and financial aspects of the transfer process.

This strategy seemed sound, but we encountered a number of problems with it from the outset. For one thing, the decision to transfer operations offshore had to move up through at least two levels in the typical American manufacturing company. The first level, the manufacturing department, had to be convinced that an American (Tony Haight) could lead the company through the complexities of doing business in Asia. Remember this was in the early 1980s, when establishing manufacturing operations in Asia had not yet become old hat for Americans. Once the head of manufacturing was convinced, he would have to convince top management, a laborious exercise that carried risks for the manufacturing manager if the project failed.

Structuring the transactions for manufacturing transfers proved complicated as well. The standard structure was an offshore subsidiary of a U.S. or European corporation funded by SEAVIC, owned 50 percent by the U.S. or European corporation and 50 percent by SEAVIC. Performance goals were set in advance of operations. If these goals were met, the 50 percent share owned by SEAVIC would be exchanged for a predetermined number of shares in the parent. The structure was imaginative for its time, but had its weaknesses. If the shares of the parent had declined during the execution period, then SEAVIC would not have received the gain that it deserved for achieving the performance goals. While adjustment in the number of shares was the answer to this dilemma, the management of the U.S. or European corporation would cap the number of shares it was willing to exchange. SEAVIC did have a few successes with its manufacturing-transfer strategy: for example, Unitrode Electronics Singapore, established in 1986, a deal in which I leveraged a relationship with the parent company in the United States that went back to my days at Bessemer Securities. In most cases, however, the complexity of helping young companies (our targets) organize and transfer part of their manufacturing operations to Asia proved overwhelming, and our occasional successes did not cover the costs of providing the transfer services.

While pursuing the manufacturing-transfer strategy, however, we also planned to invest the remaining 50 percent of SEAVIC's capital in new companies in the region or more established companies that required expansion capital, and these local deals proved more successful. Although Tony Haight would sometimes go prospecting for companies with members of the Singapore team, on the whole he relied on them to find and negotiate the deals themselves. Cold calling, which went against the social grain of the investment managers we trained in Western Europe, proved even harder to do in Southeast Asia — in fact it simply didn't work. Relationships were everything in looking for deals in the region, as remains true in Asia as well as a region like Latin America today. Occasionally potential deals would come in over the transom, while others came through Ang Kong Hua or his contacts at DBS. The rest, however, came through the contacts of SEAVIC's own people. Different members of the team had their own industry expertise, but SEAVIC would invest in any opportunity that looked promising, regardless of sector. In the beginning, Tony Haight, Tan Keng Boon, and the rest of the team looked at all potential deals together. As Tony developed confidence in Keng Boon and the other Singaporeans, however, he left the review and the decisions to them.

SEAVIC's first investment, in 1984, was actually in a start-up: Venture Manufacturing Singapore (VMS), which SEAVIC founded and in which it invested US$1.7 million. This would prove to be a great deal, although not one that SEAVIC found it easy to replicate or build upon. A contract manufacturer of electronics components, VMS, like other such companies SEAVIC would finance, provided a way around the problems with manufacturing transfer that Koh Lee Boon anticipated and that would soon materialize. Singapore, as I have mentioned, already excelled in manufacturing, and managerial and technical know-how for electronics manufacturing was not hard to come by for the new company. As a result, VMS got off to a good start and was moderately profitable at a relatively early stage.

Despite this early success, however, the SEAVIC team could see that VMS would have trouble expanding if it continued to rely on contract manufacturing for its customer base. Its American clients, which were early-stage companies, could not produce enough volume, and their products were not fully engineered and were constantly being modified. As a consequence, VMS's margins were squeezed. Management agreed that the company had to develop its own business in the region and embarked on this course. SEAVIC, meanwhile, urged VMS to pursue an even more aggressive growth strategy—for example, by moving much of its production into Malaysia to take advantage of labor costs that were lower than Singapore's. SEAVIC and the original VMS management found themselves increasingly at odds and finally parted ways in the late 1980s. It was at this point that SEAVIC engineered a merger that brought in a new management team including Wong Ngit Liong, the present chairman and CEO of the company (which is now called Venture Corporation Ltd.). In 1992, VMS went public at a market capitalization of S$25 million on Singapore's SESDAQ. It is now a S$3.9 billion global electronics services provider. Koh Lee Boon still serves on its board.

While representing a significant achievement for SEAVIC, VMS proved to be a notable exception, however, as a successful Southeast Asian company built from scratch with early-stage venture investment. As we began to discover, the region simply did not have either the capacity for technological innovation or the cultural and institutional support for entrepreneurship necessary for early-stage investment to succeed. There were no MITs or Stanfords, there were few successful entrepreneurs to serve as models for others, and there was little understanding of what it takes to successfully commercialize a new technology. This was true even in Singapore, where, as I have noted, the government was making significant investment in trying to jump-start a high-tech sector. In other countries in the region, where this public investment was lacking, early-stage investment was even less feasible than in Singapore. In sum, Southeast Asia in the 1980s was not amenable to venture capital. Given these conditions, SEAVIC quickly focused on a strategy of providing expansion capital for existing companies in the region rather than investing in start-ups.

The lesson my SEAVIC colleagues and I learned in Southeast Asia was one that would be repeated when I turned my attention to Hong Kong and China. Using the model I had employed in Europe after the founding of Sofinnova in the early 1970s, I made Singapore and SEAVIC the base from which I spread my missionary message of venture capital to other regions in Asia. In 1983, while on my way to Singapore from Taiwan (where I had met with government officials and private companies to discuss venture capital), I stopped in Hong Kong to address the Young Presidents Organization in Hong Kong at the request of its president, Victor Fung. Victor's grandfather, Fung Pakliu, had cofounded Li & Fung, a trading company dealing in Chinese exports, in Guangzhou in 1906. When I met Victor, he and his brother William Kwok Lun Fung were in the process of building the family company into a powerful Asian multinational group of companies active in export trading, retailing and distribution, and global supply chain management. Victor has degrees in electrical engineering from MIT and a Ph.D. in business economics from Harvard Business School. I do not think I have ever met anyone who understands economics, politics, and trends as well as he, and I have known few people with his energy and drive. When I met him in 1983, he was interested in entrepreneurship and venture capital, and four years later he would found the Hong Kong Venture Capital Association.

Early in 1984, shortly after my address to the Young Presidents Organization, Victor visited me in Boston, and we decided to introduce a venture capital fund in Hong Kong. In a strategy analogous to SEAVIC's, the fund would invest in companies in the United States and Europe that were interested in transferring their technology to Hong Kong and China, and in companies indigenous to the region. We hoped to capitalize on one of the major developments then taking place there: China had begun to liberalize its rules of engagement for foreign investors as part of a conscious policy, launched in 1980, to let South China, especially Guangdong Province, establish relationships with the international community. There were restraints on trade and the free movement of capital, but business could be done. The fund that Victor and I cochaired, the Hong Kong Venture Investment Trust (HKVIT), began investment activity in 1985, shortly after the formation of Advent International. The management company Techno Ventures Hong Kong was the first network member to be formed under the aegis of Advent International rather than TA Associates.

The anchor investors in HKVIT, a $22.3 million fund, were Hancock Venture Partners (formed in 1982 and the precursor to today's Harbour-Vest Partners), Prudential Life Insurance Company, and Touche Remnant; other investors included the Bemberg family, the Campari family, Harvard University, and Bank Boston. Victor brought in an MIT classmate who was also from Hong Kong, Chris Leong, to run the management company; on paper, HKVIT was comanaged by Leong and Tony Haight, but it was really Leong who ran the show. To work with Leong, Victor later hired a family friend who also had an MIT degree, Martin Tang, who had worked for Bank of America in San Francisco and Taiwan and as an executive for a textile manufacturing company in Hong Kong and Indonesia. When Tang left the management company in 1988, Tony Haight recruited Simon Wong, a young man with a background in both banking and the electronics industry who became a valuable member of the management team.

Both Victor Fung and Chris Leong had technology backgrounds and were interested in bringing technology to Asia to boost economic development in the region. Like SEAVIC in trying to execute its manufacturing-transfer strategy, Techno Ventures ran up against some fundamental problems with its plans for technology transfer. The major difficulty it encountered was that most of the U.S. companies in which Advent was investing for its corporate clients, the companies Chris targeted for transferring technology to Asia, were not ready to do so; they were either start-ups or more established companies that were still preoccupied with the challenges of growth in the U.S. market. However, Techno Ventures did invest in two technology-transfer deals that worked out very well. One was in Aspen Technology, founded in 1981 by Larry Evans, a chemical engineering professor at MIT, to commercialize modeling software for process design in the chemical industry. AspenTech was selling in Asia in the mid-1980s but needed local support. In 1987, Techno Ventures invested in and helped set up AspenTech Asia, which AspenTech acquired outright after it went public in 1994.[4] A second successful technology-transfer deal came through Victor Fung's connection with Roy Vagelos, who became CEO of Merck in 1985 and with whom Victor sat on the board of Prudential Asia. Merck, which had established a Hong Kong subsidiary back in 1957, was interested in entering China even though Vagelos clearly understood the risks. Victor sold him on the idea of creating a joint venture — which Merck was given an option to buy back if it was successful — and Techno Ventures set up the Chinese company (originally called TTV) that Merck licensed to sell its products in China. This joint venture became the germ of Merck's direct presence in China today.[5]

Techno Ventures made one foray into contract manufacturing, with a company called Advent Industrial Holdings set up as a sister organization to Venture Manufacturing Singapore. It did not turn out well. For one thing, the small American start-ups that Techno Ventures targeted as candidates for offshoring did not have the scale to provide work that could be performed economically by an Asian contract manufacturer. (This was the same problem VMS in Singapore had encountered in its early days.)

For another, the prototyping process in manufacturing requires hands-on attention, and Tony Haight, who was heavily involved with SEAVIC, was stretched too thin to provide the necessary help. In all, contract manufacturing, at which Venture Manufacturing (Singapore) proved to be so successful, turned out to be a lot more complicated than Victor and Chris anticipated.

Techno Ventures Hong Kong then focused most of its attention on local deals in Hong Kong, Taiwan, and southern China. About half of its investments involved early-stage capital, while the rest provided expansion capital for more mature, already profitable companies. Most of these portfolio companies were manufacturers of low-tech goods for export. HKVIT's most successful investment, however, was in a technology-based company, a contract manufacturer named Multitech, founded in Taiwan in 1976 by Stan Shih. Multitech eventually spun off everything but its core computer manufacturing business, was renamed Acer in 1987, and had a successful IPO on the Taiwan Stock Exchange in 1988. It has since gone on to become one of the most successful PC manufacturers in the world.

Despite the success of this early-stage investment (one in which Techno Ventures was allowed to participate essentially as a favor to Victor), Victor and Chris were disappointed, on the whole, to find technology investing so difficult to accomplish in Hong Kong. It turned out that the Hong Kong government's laissez-faire approach to fostering a technology sector and a local venture capital industry was no more successful than the more interventionist approach taken in Singapore. Hong Kong joined the lengthening list of places around the world where, I was discovering, early-stage venture investing of the kind that had succeeded in the United States could not be easily replicated.

With an IRR of 10 percent, HKVIT did well for a first fund — and a first fund in a new market, at that — and Chris Leong deserves credit for its success. But some of the differences between Techno Ventures and SEAVIC, and between Advent's relationships with each of these firms, illustrate the challenges Advent faced in managing a network of venture capital firms. There was never as collegial a relationship between Advent and Techno Ventures, as there was between Advent and SEAVIC. Much of this had to do with the fact that Tan Keng Boon, SEAVIC's Asian codirector, was a focused, disciplined manager and a team player, whereas Chris Leong tended to be independent and headstrong and didn't necessarily like receiving advice from Tony Haight. Tony, the American codirector of both SEAVIC and HKVIT, was also more at home in Singapore and could add more value for SEAVIC than he could for Techno Ventures. Yet that doesn't explain the differences between his relationships with our two Asian affiliates. The fact that Tony was able to pick his own team in Singapore, while Victor hired the Techno Ventures team in Hong Kong, was probably more of a factor. The crucial point, however, is that the success Advent's network depended a great deal on the leadership of the individual network members, and our team in Singapore was better suited for the job than was Chris Leong in Hong Kong.

In all, Advent International's record in Asia in the early 1980s was decidedly mixed. The combination of successes and failures the firm encountered is illustrated in rather dramatic form by Advent's two other forays in the Asia-Pacific region in this period — one in Australia and the other in Japan — where the results differed significantly. The contrast between the relatively receptive environment for venture capital that we found in Australia and the significant obstacles that we encountered in Japan suggests both the diversity of the Asia-Pacific region and my own underestimation of the challenges involved in my plan to implant venture capital there twenty-five years ago.

In the early 1980s, as venture capital was establishing roots in Western Europe, Southeast Asia, and greater China, the Australian government launched its own initiative, modeled on the SBIC program in the United States,[6] to promote the creation of a venture capital sector. Not long after taking office in 1983, the Labor government of Prime Minister Bob Hawke passed laws providing for the creation of Australia's first venture capital funds and tax breaks for investors in them. In May 1984, one of the first seven licenses to run a venture capital fund in Australia was granted to a new firm named Western Pacific, founded by an aspiring venture capitalist named Nick Callinan. Nick was a civil engineer by training who had earned an MBA at the University of Melbourne, then been recruited by Cummins Engine as a marketing manager. Energetic and hard-driving, he quickly worked his way up to become CEO of Cummins's Australian subsidiary. At Cummins, Nick was one of many engineers with MBAs. When one of his friends at the company left in the early 1980s to join Sutter Hill Ventures, the Silicon Valley venture capital firm, Nick soon became convinced that venture capital was something he wanted to pursue. He formed Western Pacific and set out to learn the business.

Within a month of receiving his license to start Western Pacific, Nick had raised his first fund, which totaled $7.5 million. In the fall of 1984, on a stop in Boston on his way to Europe from the West Coast, Nick paid a visit to Advent's first office on the fourth floor of TA Associates' headquarters at 45 Milk Street. Nick had been told by people he had met on the West Coast that Peter Brooke in Boston was more interested in international venture capital than anyone else around. So when he arrived at Logan Airport he placed a cold call to Advent and was invited to come in and talk. At Advent, Nick met Clint Harris, Tom Armstrong, and John Littlechild (I was over in Asia at the time), who suggested that he look up David Cooksey in London. Nick did pay a visit to Cooksey, who then called on Nick in Australia in the spring of 1985 to see firsthand what he was doing with Western Pacific. Cooksey was impressed, and subsequently came to Boston and suggested to me that Advent and Western Pacific collaborate in some way. This resulted in Nick's firm becoming Advent's affiliate in Australia when we raised an AU$26 million fund named Advent Western Pacific.

Advent Western Pacific (AWP) closed in 1986 with investments from leading Australian industrial companies and financial institutions. As TA Associates had done with its new European affiliates at the beginning of the 1980s, Advent took a 25 percent interest in the Australian management company. The fund downloaded 60 percent of its capital to Advent International and TA Associates for investment in the United States, an arrangement that proved to be the cement that held the relationship with Advent together. Advent, which was barely two years old and sorely needed the revenue, benefited from the management fees it received for investing its portion of AWP's capital. AWP, in turn, benefited from the prestige it received in Australia from reporting deals done by Advent and TAA. Nick Callinan also found three corporate investors in Australia for the corporate programs Clint Harris was managing for Advent.

AWP performed well with both early-stage and expansion capital investments in both technology and industrial firms. After Nick sold his interest in Western Pacific to his partners in the early 1990s and moved to London to head up Advent International's expansion into central Europe,[7] several of its funds were merged into a new publicly listed entity, Advent Ltd. Today Advent Private Capital, the management company descended from Advent Western Pacific, is a leading midmarket private equity firm in the Australasia region. The successful introduction of venture capital in Australia must be credited to the government but also, in no small measure, to Callinan's persuasiveness and drive to form the first venture capital management company in that country.

Perhaps it is not surprising that Australia, with its frontier heritage, proved to be a place where venture capital took root relatively easily. I found much less fertile ground in Japan, which was the site of one of my least successful attempts to introduce venture capital to a foreign market.[8] In 1982, a fortuitous circumstance had exposed me to someone who eventually became my partner in Japan and whose company became the Japanese affiliate of the Advent network. I was asked to give a speech to the USA-Japan Society and shared the podium with Dr. Yaichi Ayukawa, the head of a firm, Techno-Venture, he had founded to transfer technology between Japan and the United States.

In a way, it was not such an accident that we happened to meet when we did. Tom Armstrong—whom I did not yet know but for whom Dr. Ayukawa was working as a consultant—had heard from people he knew at Monsanto about my work in international venture capital and was trying to arrange on his own for Ayukawa and me to meet. In any event, I was introduced to Dr. Ayukawa on the podium at the USA-Japan Society by Dr. Jerome Wiesner, the recently retired president of MIT and former science adviser to President Kennedy. Wiesner and Ayukawa knew each other well, because Ayukawa (who had three degrees from MIT) had been a member of the MIT board of trustees and various visiting committees at the school since the mid-1970s. Jerry Wiesner always had a great feeling for relationships and felt that a Brooke–Ayukawa connection would be interesting and produce something of value.

Yaichi Ayukawa had an interesting background. His father, Yoshisuke Ayukawa, was an entrepreneur who had helped to build the Nissan Holding Company prior to World War II. In 1952 he established a firm called the Small Business Promotion Company, the predecessor to Yaichi's firm Techno-Venture. Yaichi, a graduate of Tokyo Imperial University, had received his second bachelor's degree from MIT, followed by a master's in food technology and a Ph.D. in food technology and industrial management. At Techno-Venture, which he founded in 1975, Yaichi had developed a company based on aquaculture and shrimp-packaging technology that he had invented. His wife, Masako, was of the Toyota family, and her father had served with distinction as the Japanese ambassador to France and as chamberlain to Emperor Hirohito. Masako Ayukawa and my wife Anne would become good friends, and the Ayukawas' son, when he came to the United States for college, would also become close to our family.

Yaichi was a visionary with a deep belief in the necessity of friendship between Japan and the United States. He had come to America alone just after the end of World War II and hardly knew what to expect from his country's recent enemy. Upon arriving at MIT he was assigned a course adviser, Professor Sam Goldblith. Goldblith had been captured by the Japanese in the war and survived the Bataan Death March. One might have expected him to harbor a deep resentment toward the Japanese. However, he and Yaichi became close friends, and Sam became the godfather of the Ayukawas' son. Yaichi later ran the Japanese office of MIT's industrial liaison program, where his U.S. counterpart was Sam Goldblith. I have always felt that this was one of the great stories of reconciliation and postwar U.S.-Japanese relations.

In any case, Yaichi and I developed a relationship that led to the formation of the first venture capital fund in Japan based on the U.S. model, Advent Techno-Venture, in 1984. Capital for this fund came from institutional and corporate investors in Japan, Europe, and the United States, investors who were attracted by the growth of technology-based companies in Japan. They were interested, as were we, to see if venture capital could succeed in a country whose industrial companies were making serious inroads in markets around the world.

Advent International comanaged Advent Techno-Venture and shared in the override and in the revenues generated from the program, but did not have an ownership share in the management company. Tony Haight tried to identify companies in Japan where U.S. technology might apply, and Techno-Venture made investments in the hope that technology transfer would occur. Only occasionally did this happen, however. The lion's share of the monitoring of these investments was on my shoulders due to my close relationship with Yaichi—boss dealing with boss, in the Japanese manner. Yet oversight proved difficult. Yaichi would decide what to do based on his knowledge of the local scene and, despite my role as a member of the investment committee, pretty much did what he wanted. We did not have the kind of productive working relationship that I had with my colleagues in Singapore, the language barrier in Japan being virtually insurmountable.

All this might have been overcome if Yaichi had understood the venture capital process as practiced in the United States, which he did not. However, Techno-Venture's problems extended far beyond its founder's limitations as a venture capitalist. When Advent did poorly in one of its international programs, it was usually because of poor fund management or, as we would see in Southeast Asia in the 1990s, changing economic conditions. In Japan, we failed because the structure of Japanese industry and fundamental aspects of Japanese culture were hostile to individual entrepreneurship.

As for the industrial structure, three factors stand out in my mind as having particularly hindered our success in Japan. First, as in Germany, managers were illiterate outside their own functional specialties. The structure of Japanese companies did not give managers the experience in the different disciplines necessary to successfully manage a small, entrepreneurial company. Second, large Japanese companies dominated their suppliers, and even the successful ones were taken over by their larger customers. There was no chance for the smaller fish to grow before they were eaten by the larger ones. Third, exit routes were predetermined by the zaibatsus. If you were part of the Nomura Group, you could exit, but if you were independent, you could not. These three conditions all conspired to make early-stage investing a quixotic undertaking in Japan. Even buyouts proved to be difficult there, since noncore businesses offered for sale by the Japanese conglomerates often had the least competent managers.

In addition to these structural impediments, cultural factors played a large role in limiting the prospects for venture capital in Japan in the 1980s. Germany again provides a parallel, for just as the brightest university graduates there all wanted to work for one of the big German companies like Siemens or Bayer, the best students from the University of Tokyo wanted to work for Hitachi or Sony. Going to work for a small company would have been considered a sign of failure. The team that Yaichi Ayukawa assembled at Techno-Venture reflected the same difficulty in recruiting people for the management company that we had in identifying promising entrepreneurs or managers for the portfolio companies. The Techno-Venture crew consisted of some very nice fellows whom Tony Haight described as "semi-capable." The most memorable of these was a fireplug of a guy who simply keeled over in a restaurant one night toward the end of a dinner after a good deal of drinking.

The investment process in Japan was skewed by another cultural phenomenon. When Techno-Venture had made its initial investment in a company, other investors would be brought in at subsequent stages for social rather than business reasons. Finally, the cultural prohibitions in Japan against frank, direct communication — the necessity, in other words, of never criticizing others and always allowing them to save face — made for too great a cultural divide for the American venture capital model to succeed. The core of our approach is rigorous due diligence in which tough questions are asked. This was not acceptable to our Japanese partners. For example, a Techno-Venture manager who clearly failed to grasp the requirements of the due diligence process once reported to me that a particular portfolio company had gone "suddenly bankrupt." I, in turn, caused him to lose face when I informed him — somewhat abruptly, I am afraid — that companies did not go "suddenly bankrupt," and that it was his job to see problems like this coming before it was too late.

Techno-Venture in Japan was a notable failure, and Advent International's relationship with its Japanese affiliate ended after Techno-Venture's first fund was invested. Advent would have no presence in Japan for the next twenty years. When we did return, our investment strategy had changed significantly and, based on what we had learned in Asia in the early 1980s, was directed to buyouts and control transactions.

Meanwhile, my experience in both Europe and Asia in the early 1980s had shown me that my dream of transplanting venture capital from the United States to other countries around the world was not going to be realized quickly, easily, or without some shifts in strategy and tactics along the way. I had believed from the start that for venture capital to succeed in new environments, it would have to be adapted to local conditions. I realized early on that I would need local champions to help recruit local investors, that I would have to find and train venture capital managers in the countries where we set up funds, and that the investment strategies of the funds would have to be geared to the local or regional economy. Yet I hadn't understood the specific challenges I would face in these markets — for instance, the challenge of raising funds from Southeast Asian investors — or seen the difficulties that TVM in Germany and Techno-Venture in Japan would have in recruiting capable managers, or found that SEAVIC's original investment strategy required radical adjustment.

Such difficulties were to be expected, however, and by the mid-1980s — with new venture capital operations up and running in Britain, Belgium, Germany, Singapore, and Hong Kong—I thought I had learned a lot of the basics. With the beginnings of a European network in place and affiliates established in Southeast Asia and greater China, I was ready to continue building out my platform for global expansion of venture capital. In Western Europe, Southeast Asia, and greater China beginning in the mid- to late 1980s, my vision for venture capital would continue to be tested and transformed by events, as I relate in the next chapter.

CHAPTER 6

# TRIAL AND ERROR IN
# EUROPE AND ASIA

· · ·

In 1984, when I founded Advent International, the new firm inherited all
the affiliate programs that had been the property of TA Associates, so that
the existing international network survived the transition intact. Shortly
after Advent International began operations, I received a surprise when we
acquired an interest in a venture capital firm in the last country in Western
Europe where I would have expected venture capital to take root. If I had
been too optimistic about the prospects for venture capital in Germany,
Southeast Asia, and Japan in the early 1980s, in at least one case it turned
out that I had been too pessimistic.

While I was still at TA Associates, in the early 1980s, and helping to
launch Advent Ltd. in Britain, Advent Belgium, and TVM in Germany,
word of our network reached Sweden. I was already somewhat familiar
with Sweden due to a relationship with Perstorp, a Swedish industrial company that had established a subsidiary, Pernovo, for venture investing in
areas of strategic interest back in the 1970s. In fact there were four or five
such captive venture capital organizations in Sweden (including one within
Investor, the Wallenbergs' holding company) at the time. I had also been
introduced to Bertil Agdur, an important figure in technical circles there,
who had the temerity to criticize the Swedish financial establishment for its
unwillingness to provide equity capital for small, technology-based companies. Agdur had attempted to establish a venture capital fund but failed,
mainly because of his frontal attack on the powers-that-were. Between the
conservatism of the Swedish financial establishment and the socialist policies that then reigned in that country, I would not have expected much
from any subsequent attempt to introduce venture capital there.

Despite these obstacles, however, two gentlemen at the Swedish Investment Bank had pioneered venture capital, with some success, beginning in the mid-1970s. Lars-Olof Gustavsson and Gösta Oscarsson had never heard the term *venture capital* when they started their program for investing in small, innovative companies at the bank, but this did not prevent them from becoming venture capitalists. In 1983 they established their own venture capital company, Four Seasons AB, which was financed by institutional investors and one large corporation (Alpha Laval) in Sweden with the objective of financing and advising small companies.

Gustavsson and Oscarsson were entrepreneurs in the truest sense. Both came from working-class backgrounds and were proud of it. They already knew a lot about venture capital when they founded Four Seasons, had their own ideas, and were fiercely independent. Gustavsson had met Norman Fast, an American entrepreneur and investor who cofounded Venture Economics, and it was from Fast that I learned about them. I found it difficult to believe that venture capital could succeed in a country like Sweden, but Fast urged me to meet with these two mavericks. In 1983, as I was about to leave for Paris and fly from there to Bangkok on a fundraising trip for SEAVIC, the Swedes suggested that we meet briefly at the airport in Copenhagen. The meeting was indeed brief. Gustavsson and Oscarsson said that they had heard about what I was doing and wanted to join the network. However, they first wanted to let me know about their humble beginnings, their work ethic, and their investment philosophy. They also wanted to assure themselves that TA Associates was not a stodgy organization populated by banker types but was actually interested, as they were, in taking risks. I was not interviewing them, they were interviewing me; but I had no problem answering their questions, and we established a good rapport.

In mid-August of that year, Lars-Olof and Gösta came to Boston for a negotiating session and agreed to membership in the network in September 1983. The agreement was formalized upon a visit I made to Stockholm a month later. The ownership relationship with Four Seasons differed from the arrangements with other network members. In every other case, as we have seen, TA Associates, in return for its effort in establishing the network member, was awarded an ownership stake (usually 25 percent) for a nominal amount. In the case of Four Seasons, Advent International (which I had founded by the time we completed the transaction) actually purchased a 10 percent interest in Four Seasons for $405,000. Four

Seasons was an already established fund with real value, while the other network members were newly minted and yet to prove themselves. In addition to their investment skills, Gustavsson and Oscarsson were good strategic thinkers and organized a new member of the network, Four Seasons Norway, as part of their Scandinavian strategy.

I mention the fierce independence of Gustavsson and Oscarsson. Their fund was designed for Swedish investors and differed markedly from the limited partnership structure that we employed. They were not particularly interested in adjusting the structure of this fund for investors from abroad. Nor were they particularly interested in talking to their investors, whom they considered to be necessary evils. They were perfectly happy to just accept their money and be done with them. Gösta observed that investors were rather tiresome, asked irrelevant questions, and were difficult to communicate with, all of which had led him to the conclusion that it would be better for him and Lars-Olof to invest on a deal-by-deal basis and forget the task of servicing investors. They felt that their results were good, and that this should be enough.

To my knowledge, Lars-Olof and Gösta were not able to raise funds outside Sweden, which was hardly surprising given both the structure of their funds and their attitude toward investors. I had not encountered this attitude anywhere else in my travels. Every other network member was very attentive to the requirements of investors, whether in structuring a relationship, reporting results, or providing other information. I had also established an operating process for network members that included sector focus, proactive deal sourcing, and due diligence and monitoring procedures. Since the network members that we established were new to the venture capital game, they needed this process. Four Seasons was not a new player and had its own way of doing things — whatever process Lars-Olof and Gösta employed was intuitive and known only to them.

I wished that I could integrate Four Seasons into the network more closely than proved possible, because other people could have learned from the instincts and intuitions of these very independent people. However, there was no way to organize this, because Gustavsson and Oscarsson were too committed to doing things their own way. I have always adhered to the old adage, "If it ain't broke, don't fix it," and these two guys knew what they were doing. Moreover, in building the network, I was always conscious of the strengths and weaknesses of the individual members. I had a playbook for their development, but if the playbook didn't apply in a particular case, I did not try to use it. In the case of Four Seasons, Gustavsson and Oscarsson used me when they needed me, for advice on expansion of the portfolio companies and contacts with those who could add value to their investments. They made money for their investors, contributed to the Swedish economy, and were a lot of fun the way they were.

After Advent's acquisition of a share in Four Seasons, the next member to be added to the European network was Alpha Associés in France. Advent International had no existing network member in France, as TA Associates' relationship with Sofinnova had come to an end in 1979 after Jean Deléage left the firm to join Bill Egan and Craig Burr in what became Burr, Egan, Deleage, and brought the relationship with Sofinnova with him. Alpha Associés was the idea of Piet van de Ven, who by this time was working for Orange Nassau. Orange Nassau, as I have mentioned, was a wholly owned subsidiary of the CGIP group, a large industrial holding company in France. Van de Ven convinced CGIP to establish a venture capital fund in France, which it did in 1985 with the assistance of Lazard Frères. Two years later, Advent International was asked to participate in Alpha as an investor through Advent's first fund, the International Network Fund,[1] and to share in the capital structure of the management company.

I was anxious to participate in Alpha in order to establish a presence for Advent in France. It seemed to me, however, that CGIP accepted the invitation to establish Alpha rather reluctantly. The group's CEO, Ernest-Antoine Seillière, was a graduate of the Ecole Nationale d'Administration who had spent ten years in the French diplomatic corps in the 1960s and '70s. In 1976 he joined the three-hundred-year-old French industrial concern the Wendel Group, eventually leading the company through the divestment of its steel-manufacturing activities and its transformation into Wendel Investissement, where he is now chairman of the firm's supervisory board. He was an operating man — a brilliant one at that — and wanted to control the companies in which he invested. It was obvious that he was not comfortable with minority investments. I well remember the first annual meeting of Alpha Associés, with Seillière nervously looking around the room, wondering what he had been talked into.[2]

As if to confirm Seillière's doubts, Alpha had some rocky moments in the early years, as a struggle developed over investment philosophy and direction among the supervisory board, investors, and managers. But when it hired three very competent managers — Alain Blanc-Brude, Dominique Peninon, and Nicolas ver Hulst (a member of the family that controlled CGIP)[3] — and changed from a venture capital to a private equity firm, Alpha's fortunes improved markedly. Seillière and his designee on the Alpha board, Guy de Wouters, suddenly became quite engaged. I remember clearly the first indication of this that I received, at a dinner at the Hotel Crillon where de Wouters, whom I always thought a nasty piece of work, "explained" to me that the equal coinvestment agreement that had been drawn up by CGIP, Lazard Frères, and Advent did not really give Advent equal status. When Alpha proceeded to raise capital for its third fund and Advent was not in a position to participate, I was informed that its presence was no longer required.

This was pretty hard to take, but it was an interesting lesson. Alpha had been formed by van de Ven, not by me, and I did not have the close personal relationship with Seillière and de Wouters that I had with Antoine Dupont-Fauville and Christian Marbach at Sofinnova, with Jochen Mackenrodt at TVM, and with Leo Deschuyteneer at Advent Belgium. In addition, Alpha was a captive of the CGIP group. It was not an independent management company and answered to de Wouters and Seillière. This was not the case with any of the other affiliates. For instance, when Albrecht Matuschka tried at one point to wrest control of TVM from me and my other partner, Siemens, and make it his own venture capital management company, Mackenrodt and I succeeded in thwarting him, ensuring that the company remained independent. As I have said, the Alpha experience was a good lesson. After receiving notice of our dismissal, I requested that Advent's shares in the management company be redeemed, thus ending the relationship with this network member in France. After going through its initial period of turmoil, Alpha Associés would eventually emerge as one of the most successful venture and developmental capital organizations there.

I had been fortunate enough, until my experience with Alpha, to find reliable partners with whom to work in constructing a network of venture capital firms in Europe. As I continued to expand the network, however, I found some new partners who were competent and trustworthy, and others who were not. One of the best people I found was in Austria, where I turned my attention after forming the relationship with Alpha and also establishing a new firm, called Innovent, in Switzerland.

In the early days of TVM in Germany, a young Austrian, Franz Krejs, had applied for a job as an analyst. Krejs's ultimate objective was to establish a venture capital company in Austria. He hoped to get the instruction he would need to lead his own firm from Rolf Dienst, and Dienst agreed to bring him on board as an apprentice. While at TVM, Krejs approached Dr. Helmut Haschek, the chairman of the Österreichische Kontrolbank. Haschek was a man of considerable attainment, politically savvy and well positioned to interest others in an innovative concept. He was regarded as an agent of change, and succeeded in attracting both public and private institutions to the new venture capital fund, Horizonte, that was established in 1985.

Krejs, who firmly believed in venture capital as an economic development tool, was a diligent leader working in what was a difficult environment for venture capital given the socialist politics in Austria at the time. I especially appreciated having him as a partner, because it was difficult to tout the economic development benefits of venture capital in those days when there was not much empirical data to point to. In the early days of Advent International, we conducted research of our own on this subject and found that it was usually not for several years, when successful new enterprises began to grow geometrically, that their economic impact became dramatic. Thus I had to ask people to take a lot on faith. I was occasionally fortunate enough to meet a government official who got the point that using venture capital as a means of economic development was not an effort that would necessarily pay off in the short term but was still worth trying. Franz Vranitzky, the minister of finance (in the mid-1980s) and later the chancellor of Austria (1986–1997), was one such individual, as was Christian Marbach of the French Ministry of Industry in the 1970s. I was also sometimes lucky enough to find people in banking or industry who got the idea and were prepared to run with it, people such as Helmut Haschek in Austria, for example, or Jochen Mackenrodt of Siemens in Germany.

After Austria, in any case, we moved on to Spain and Italy, where I would not be so wise or so lucky in my choice of partners. Advent España was added as a network member in 1987 and Itavent (Italy) in 1989, the former with the sponsorship of the Bank Bilbao Vizcaya Group[4] and the leadership of a young industrialist, Jose Creixell, and the latter with the sponsorship and leadership of Guido Cefalu of the CFI Group. Neither of these affiliates was successful. Itavent had neither enough capital to build

a well-balanced management team nor a well-defined investment strategy.
It had no sector focus and spread its investments across an overly broad
range of companies. Given this approach, it was not able to add value to
its investments. In addition, Cefalu was a mercurial character with whom
I found it difficult to communicate. He had his own idea of what the venture business was all about, took whatever guidance from us he thought
useful, but never followed the playbook—not unusual behavior for an
Italian entrepreneur, in my experience. I could also be accused of not having given him enough time, as I was stretched too thin overseeing a European network that included nine members by this time.

Advent España was another story. It did have a sufficient amount of
capital under management (provided by the Bank Bilbao Vizcaya, one of
the largest commercial banks in Spain, and the March Group, the country's leading merchant bank) to build a well-rounded team, and focused
its investment activity in the industrial sector. However, there was a conflict between the personal interests of Creixell, who had substantial industrial holdings, and his role as manager of the fund. In once instance, a
company in which Creixell had a substantial interest was allowed to bid
on an investment of the fund. My Advent colleague Doug Brown, who
was managing our European activity at the time, became concerned about
this conflict of interest and employed Ernst and Young to investigate this
transaction and others as well. The investigation was inconclusive, but the
audit trail led to many questions about the propriety of Creixell's decisions. Creixell also tried to shift responsibility for some of his poor decisions onto his chief investment officer, Juan Carlos Torres, a person
in whom I had complete confidence (and whom I would be fortunate
enough to recruit for Advent International when we expanded into Latin
America in the mid-1990s). While the board members continued to support Creixell, I said that I could not and resigned. This was a painful situation, caused by a structure that allowed Creixell to make a personal profit
at the expense of the fund, and by the board's lack of diligence in policing
the fund's manager.

The additions of network members in Switzerland, Austria, Spain, and
Italy between 1985 and 1989 completed Advent International's network
building in Western Europe. In the meantime, however, our very success
in building out the platform for Advent's activity in the region led to the

first of what would prove to be some fundamental changes in the nature of that activity and, ultimately, in Advent itself.

As I have explained, I had originally envisioned Advent not as an investment firm but rather as a company providing advisory services to its network members and their portfolio companies, services for which we would be paid fees. There was one big problem with this vision, however. Even though all agreed that Advent's services in areas such as strategic planning, technology and manufacturing transfer, and mergers and acquisition were valuable, the network members were all relatively young concerns with limited financial resources with which to compensate Advent for its services. Their portfolio companies, which were small, had the same limitation. As a result, Advent needed to find other sources of revenue.

We developed one such source through the efforts of Clint Harris, one of my first hires at Advent and the most innovative partner in the firm's history. Clint, who had spent seven years as a consultant at Bain & Co. specializing in corporate strategy, devised a number of corporate venturing programs for Advent clients that eventually included Nabisco (U.S.), Alcoa (U.S.), Asea Brown Boveri (Switzerland and Sweden), Hoffman LaRoche (Switzerland), Broken Hill Proprietary (Australia), Western Mining and Lend Lease Corporation (Australia), Nippon Steel Corporation and Nippon Telephone and Telegraph (Japan), Monsanto Chemical (U.S.), and Apple (Europe). These corporations were looking for ways to access new technology-based companies with which they could establish strategic partnering relationships. Advent developed separate, focused programs for each of these firms targeting investments in sectors and companies of strategic interest. Advent then assisted these corporations in arranging joint ventures and partnering arrangements in research, development, and distribution. The focused programs were real partnerships between the industrial company and Advent. Personnel from the industrial company were encouraged to locate in Advent's offices in Boston and London and to become an integral part of the analysis and decision-making process. Such close interaction between manager and client is a rarity in the venture community, and we found that it benefited us as much as it did our corporate clients, eventually making Advent International the undisputed leader in corporate venture capital.[5]

Advent's corporate programs quickly became another important part of our activity, but other new forms of opportunity soon presented themselves as well. As the network in Western Europe expanded in the mid-1980s, it began to become apparent that it was a source of increasing numbers of interesting investment opportunities. It was also becoming clear that Advent International was in a unique position to make these opportunities available not only to its corporate clients — who were now approaching Advent to see if its network could be used to identify foreign technologies and companies of strategic interest — but also to a number of financial institutions that had taken note of the deal flow being developed by our network members. Institutional investors in the United States had begun participating in foreign equities in the late 1970s and early 1980s. By 1986, when passage of the Single European Act created the legal framework for a single European market to be established by 1992, these investors were beginning to see attractive opportunities in the private markets as Europe began restructuring in anticipation of tighter economic integration. At the same time, current and prospective portfolio companies of the network members, although often unable to afford the fees for Advent's advisory services, were often willing to part with shares in exchange for these services, often at favorable prices.

As I began to take such new possibilities into account, it dawned on me that what we had at Advent International was the makings of a global merchant bank for the 1990s and beyond, but with a notable difference. Advent International, the merchant bank, would be rewarded for its services not by transaction fees that were unrelated to the ultimate success of the transaction but by a share of the profits of the company for which the transaction was made. By investing clients' capital in a company, by adding value to that company through strategic planning, technology transfer, marketing and manufacturing, and mergers and acquisitions services, and by sharing in the profits that would be enhanced by these services, Advent would be aligning its interests with those of its investors. This was nothing radically different from what venture capitalists had done in the past in their own domestic markets. However, Advent in this case would be providing the services with managers who had operating experience in a number of disciplines such as manufacturing and marketing, and would be doing it globally. A reporter for *Fortune* magazine described my aspiration perfectly when he wrote that "unlike the banks of Florentine Italy that financed the movement of raw materials, Advent would finance the movement of technology and ideas."[6] In 1986, the convergence of all these factors led to the formation of Advent International's first fund, which was also the first global venture capital/private equity fund in the world: the International Network Fund (INF).

Even with the interest we had from corporate and institutional investors, raising capital for the INF presented challenges. One of Advent's board members at the time was Julio Nuñez, who was CEO of Entreprises Quilmes, the Bemberg-controlled industrial and financial company.[7] Nuñez thought that Lehmann Bros/American Express would be the ideal people to raise capital for the INF, and Henry Kissinger, whom Nuñez knew, was on the American Express board. Nuñez arranged for Kissinger to come with us to American Express and help us make our pitch. I went down to New York, and when it was time to leave Nuñez's office for the meeting with Kissinger and American Express, I was told that the limousine was waiting downstairs. "What the hell do we need a limousine for?" I asked. "We could take a cab downtown." No, not for Henry, Julio said. We had to go with a limousine. So we took the limousine to pick up Kissinger, who got into the jump seat with his bodyguard, and we rode down to Wall Street. Julio was sitting right across from Kissinger, and he said, "Henry, we're going down there to make a sale. I don't want any bullshit about the Russians. Don't talk about the Russians. We're there to get an order from American Express to underwrite this fund." Kissinger said something to Nuñez, and then Julio turned to me and said, "Listen, Peter, after you make your pitch, and after they've agreed to raise the capital, you turn to Henry and thank him."

It was the funniest episode. We went down to the American Express office to meet with the chairman and CEO, Jim Robinson, whom I already knew. We made our pitch, and Robinson agreed to raise the money. I thanked Dr. Kissinger, of course. As the solicitation for the INF proceeded, however, it became quite obvious to me that American Express didn't have the faintest idea of how to raise a venture capital fund. I finally called up Robinson and said, "Look, Jim, this isn't working. I know so much more about how to raise this money than your guys do." "Well, what do you want to do?" Robinson asked. "I think it's just best to cut the thing off, and I'll go out and do it myself," I replied. Robinson agreed, but did decide to have American Express invest in the INF for its own account, and persuaded Coca-Cola (where he was on the board) to do the same. In the end, then, we came away from the whole exercise with two pretty good investors for our first fund, which closed in 1987.[8]

Besides American Express and Coca-Cola, the investors in the INF were the Equitable Life Insurance Society, the Rockefeller Foundation, Yale University, the Howard Hughes Medical Foundation, the Delta Airlines Retirement Trust, New York Life, the Aetna Casualty Company, Washington University, the United Technologies Retirement Trust, and many other prestigious institutions. Capitalized at $225 million, the fund downloaded $65 million of this capital to its network members and co-invested the remaining $160 million with them in situations where Advent —which still did not have a seasoned investment team of its own— could add value. I had hoped that TA Associates would provide that expertise, but it chose not to participate in Advent International's investment activity. Advent was represented on the investment committee of each affiliate and had the right to veto any deal that was put forward. Advent was not involved in the due diligence process, however.

The many weaknesses of this structure, in which Advent had a role that stopped short of the involvement that a venture capital firm would have in managing a conventional fund, soon made themselves apparent. For one thing, Advent's ability to veto investments recommended by the network members without having participated in the due diligence process often caused friction. The network members felt, with some justification, that Advent was simply disregarding their work on deals and rejecting them without sufficient understanding of the specifics. The reason Advent sometimes had to veto deals, however, was that the due diligence process had not always been carried out with sufficient rigor. Many of the network members were still new to the venture capital game and needed analytical support.

Another major weakness of the INF structure was that there was no common investment strategy among the network members. Some aimed to invest in early-stage technology-based companies, others in mature companies requiring expansion capital, and still others in buyouts. Sector focus, which would become a part of Advent's strategy in subsequent years, was also impossible given the lack of coordination in investment strategies. Looking back at the INF portfolio, one is struck by its "grab bag" nature: the fund invested in everything from technology companies to a vacuum cleaner manufacturer to a chain of party supply stores, in Europe, Asia, and North America. That we were able to achieve any returns at all—the fund made about 5 percent—was due more to the INF's diversification than to good execution by the network members or the Advent staff.

We learned a lot from the INF, and what we learned persuaded me that, having made the transition from a service provider to an investment organization, Advent International had to make other changes as well. I now understood the necessity for control of the investment process, for common standards of due diligence, and for concentration on sectors that we found particularly attractive. This would require a different way of managing the relationships with our network members than we had so far employed. By 1989, the European network consisted of nine members, all reporting to Boston. It was becoming obvious that such a large and diverse group could be better served by connecting to an Advent International presence somewhere in Europe, where communications and travel, so necessary to the success of the business, would be easier. Moreover, given the structural weaknesses that were causing the INF to underperform, we realized that we needed to better coordinate our network members and establish better quality control — two purposes that a direct presence in Europe would also serve.

Because Advent Ltd. had been our first European affiliate, London was the obvious location for an office in Europe. And because he had led Advent Ltd. and had been one of my key partners in Europe since the end of the 1970s, David Cooksey was the logical choice to lead Advent International's operations there. I had brought David into Advent International as a founding director in 1985, and then as vice chairman in 1989, the year I turned sixty. My intention was to have him comanage the firm along with our COO, Tom Armstrong, and Victor Fung (who I hoped would lead Advent's activity in the Far East) after I retired. Cooksey had been an energetic and reliable partner in the establishment of the European network and was founding chairman of the British Venture Capital Association when that organization was launched in 1983.

Cooksey's tenure as head of Advent's European operations would prove to be short, however. A key part of his new job was to assemble a staff for Advent International's new London office, but we had trouble finding people who would work with him. Part of the difficulty was that Advent Ltd., which Cooksey had headed since its inception, was underperforming and under strain at the end of the 1980s. This was a problem for Advent International because it had allocated considerable capital from the INF for Advent Ltd. to manage, and also because it called Cooksey's leadership qualities into question in a very visible way. The real problem, however, was that David was acquiring a reputation in the industry as someone who had too many outside interests. While he will dispute this, I believe that his attention was diverted from his job at Advent Ltd., and then from what were supposed to be his new responsibilities with Advent International, by his role as chairman of the British government's Audit Commission (which he had assumed in 1986) and by other activities. While David had enormous energy and capacity, I believe that his plate was too full.

In the meantime — this was the end of 1989 — we were in a pickle. We had raised $230 million for Advent's second international fund, the European Special Situations Fund (ESSF), earlier in the year and opened an office in London. But in effect we had no one managing that office, and we still had no staff. I sent John Littlefield, an Englishman who had started with Advent Ltd. and was now working for Advent International in Boston, over to London to see if he could sort things out. Yet not only was John unable to right things in London, he also managed to alienate many of the European affiliates. As a virtual last stab, I sent over one of our rising stars in the Boston office, Doug Brown, who had volunteered to go to Europe to try to help. When Brown returned at the end of January 1990, he told me that if I wanted him to run the European operation that was going nowhere under Cooksey, David himself would have to go.

I decided that Brown was the man to salvage what had become an untenable situation. The resulting split with Cooksey was very difficult, but the survival of the European network I had spent the last ten years building was at stake.[9] Brown soon began putting our European house in order, however. We downloaded 25 percent of the capital in the ESSF to John Nash and Andrew Sells, who had managed the later-stage investments in Advent Ltd.'s portfolio. Advent International would manage the remaining 75 percent itself. Meanwhile, Brown began expanding our European presence and assembling a strong investment team that included Ernest Bachrach, John Singer, Chris Neizert, and Massimo Prelz. Many of Brown's new hires were people like himself with engineering backgrounds and business experience, as opposed to investment bankers whose principal business experience consisted of discussing deals over lunch. Doug found, in fact, that having investment managers with operating experience was a key means of differentiating Advent from its competition. In 1994, Brown would also engineer the acquisition of Trinity Capital Partners. This brought into the Advent fold Trinity's cofounder John Walker — a superb investor who deftly managed Advent's European operation when

Brown moved back to the United States at the end of 1994—as well as two other competent investors, Humphrey Battcock, now a managing partner in London and cohead of our European investment activity, and Ron Sheldon.

While making these changes to give Advent International a strong European presence, Brown also designed a new strategy for Advent in Europe that had three major aspects. First, decisions on investments for the ESSF would be made by the Advent personnel in Europe who were managing the fund, not by the central office in Boston. In fact no one in Boston would sit on the on the investment committee for the fund. This shift in strategy was enabled, in turn, by the transformation of the Advent network from an affiliate-centered system to a home office–centered system, analogous to a company moving from distributors to direct sales.[10] Managing this transition was not an easy task. We did not want to damage our network members, some of whom perceived the opening of our own offices in Europe as a threat. Yet it was important that we be able to manage the investment process ourselves and not have to rely on our network members for due diligence. We thus arranged a system in which network members could participate in Advent's investments, combining their own analysis with ours to provide more comprehensive due diligence and better results for our investors.

Overall, it was a relief to move from the network investment structure to a direct investment structure. The network members had been critical to building the Advent platform. No corporate or institutional investor at the end of the 1970s, when I began putting the network together, would have put up the capital for me to build a centrally controlled global venture capital/private equity management company. Without the network members there would have been no deal flow, no funds to manage, and therefore no revenue to support their operations or compensate TA Associates and later Advent International for their services — in short, I would have had none of the assets essential for a global organization. In retrospect, the wisdom of creating and linking together a network of venture capital companies in Western Europe was clear. It addressed a reality in postwar Europe, the desire of countries to fund and support venture capital efforts within their own borders, while also creating a platform from which a pan-European direct investment operation could evolve.

Despite all these benefits of the network structure, however, managing the network had its costs for Advent as well. The relationships with network members could be volatile and had to be carefully tended. I was willing to do this, but it took patience, hand-holding, and, at times, disciplining. Doug Brown and the others who followed him would not have had the paternal, even maternal, instincts that I had as the founder of the network. For the network members in Europe, the outcome of Advent's decision to establish a direct presence throughout the region and loosen its ties with the network was about as favorable as could have been expected. The strong network members — Advent Ltd. in Britain, Alpha Associés in France, TVM in Germany, Advent Belgium, Four Seasons in Scandinavia, and Horizonte in Austria — survived. The others did not.[11]

The second important strategic change that Doug Brown initiated in Europe was to make Advent's investment strategy pan-European. This was in contrast not only to the strategy that Advent had pursued in the INF, where network members invested only within their own countries, but to almost all the other venture capital/private equity investors in Europe at the time, who managed country funds. This shift in strategy was also a reversal of my original approach to introducing venture capital to Europe, which had favored a country-by-country method over the pan-European approach championed from the start by Georges Doriot. The change had been made possible, however, by the move toward economic integration that was occurring in Europe in the late 1980s, combined with the substantial cultural similarities across most of the countries of Western Europe. I had always believed that venture capital would need to be adapted to local conditions in order to succeed outside the United States, but those conditions had altered a great deal in Europe between the time I helped establish Sofinnova in France in the early 1970s and when Advent International launched the ESSF in 1989.

The third major shift in strategy that Doug Brown initiated in Europe with the launching of the ESSF was to abandon early-stage investing and focus on what we now call private equity. In the United States, the 1970s and '80s had witnessed the rise of the leveraged buyout and an increasing differentiation between "venture capital," understood as early-stage investing, and "private equity," meaning later-stage investments and, especially, buyouts. I discuss the reasons for this differentiation in chapter 8. For now we need only note that although, by the late 1980s, venture capital had become a thriving business in the United States, conditions in Europe were very different. The mixed performance of the INF was attributable, in part, to the network members swinging for the fences and going after high-risk, early-stage ventures in their own countries. No doubt the relative inexperience of these network members influenced both their investment strategies and their performance. Yet viewing the results of the INF as well as overall conditions in Europe, Doug Brown came to believe that the environment for early-stage investing there was just too difficult. John Nash, who comanaged 25 percent of the capital in the ESSF, had long been pushing for Advent Ltd. to abandon early-stage investment and concentrate on buyouts. And so the ESSF became essentially a buyout fund. After Brown returned to the United States at the end of 1994 and became Advent's chief investment officer, he focused the firm's North American activity on buyouts as well.

Of the three major changes in strategy that Doug Brown introduced along with the ESSF, the shift to a focus on buyouts was probably the most significant. In retrospect, it is clear that Brown was right about the difficulty of the European environment for early-stage investing. Even with the improved conditions for venture capital brought about in Britain, and to some extent in the rest of Western Europe, by the Thatcher government's efforts to promote venture capital and entrepreneurship at the beginning of the 1980s, the region continued to lag far behind the United States in its capacity for successfully commercializing innovation. Cutting-edge technology remained within the laboratories of large public and private institutions, and the technologists there were reluctant to leave the cocoons of their institutions.[12] At the same time, the imminent arrival of European economic integration (the Maastricht Treaty would be signed near the beginning of 1992) and the incentives it created for overhauling or spinning off unproductive assets provided another set of opportunities for private equity investment in Western Europe. So did the recession that began in Europe in 1990, which created many opportunities for restructuring companies that had to liquidate assets in order to pay down debt accumulated during the go-go 1980s; the spin-offs these restructurings generated were of great interest to our London team as potential investment opportunities. Soon afterward, privatizations of formerly state-owned companies became yet another source of opportunity in the region — for example, in the newly united Germany. Advent played an active role in developing its portfolio companies in the ESSF.

I am sometimes asked if, given my vision for venture capital as a means of economic development, I was disappointed to have to abandon early-stage investing for a private-equity strategy.[13] When early-stage investing succeeds in commercializing revolutionary new technologies and creat-ing companies such as Digital, Intel, Google, and others like them, its ef-fects on the economy are dramatic and relatively easy to measure. Private equity, by contrast, takes mature companies and makes them more effi-cient, competitive, and capable of profitable growth. It is a more modest, less glamorous type of work than venture capital (except in boom times such as those that have just ended, when private equity titans like Stephen Schwarzman briefly became media celebrities). Helping to improve exist-ing companies, however, also contributes significantly to economic well-being, especially in times and places such as Europe in the early 1990s, when many companies were underperforming and in danger of failing in a new, more competitive global environment.

Moreover, my idea since I founded TA Associates in the 1960s was to use private capital to help companies with growth potential, whether they were new companies trying to get on their feet or more established companies that needed to improve their performance. The environment in Europe had not proven as receptive to early-stage investing as I had once imagined it would be, and so we needed to change course. Again, I had always understood that TA Associates, and then Advent Interna-tional, would have to adapt their international strategies to the realities on the ground in local markets. In addition, Advent's approach to buyouts, from the start, was focused on adding value by making operating improve-ments in its portfolio companies, not just using leverage to juice returns. In deciding how much debt to use in an acquisition, we would make pro-jections as to how much free cash flow a company would generate after expenditures for items such as research and development and marketing, then use those projections conservatively to determine what the ratio of debt to equity should be.

Meanwhile, the performance of the ESSF (in which "special situations" meant financial restructurings, corporate spin-offs, and expansion financ-ings, along with management buyouts) was vastly superior to that of the INF. The fund focused primarily on four sectors: specialty chemicals, cable and broadcast, information technology, and health-care services. The net return to investors was 17 percent, compared with 5 percent for the INF. This made the ESSF one of the top-performing European funds of its vintage. The improvement in performance over the INF was due to a number of factors besides the abandonment of early-stage investing, one of which was the excellent leadership of Doug Brown. Other key factors were the structuring of the fund with fewer participants, Advent's control of the investment process for 75 percent of the fund, and the downloading of the remaining 25 percent of the fund to very competent managers (Nash and Sells). Advent was able to build upon the success of the ESSF with subsequent funds, particularly its Global Private Equity Fund IV, which was launched in 2001 and produced an industry-leading net return to investors of 45 percent through the end of 2008. In the meantime, Western Europe has become a center for private equity investment rivaled only by the United States.

The changes in organization and strategy that Advent International undertook in Europe at the end of the 1980s and beginning of the 1990s succeeded in surmounting the major challenges the firm faced in expanding its activity in Western Europe. These challenges included taking advantage of the investment opportunities presented by the network and increasingly sought by our investors; reconfiguring the firm and its relationship with its network members when the prior form of organization showed its limitations; and responding to the conditions in Europe that favored later-stage over early-stage investment. In Asia, meanwhile, where Advent's affiliates had enjoyed only mixed success in the early to mid-1980s with their multipronged investment strategies, a continuing economic boom in Southeast Asia and greater China promised additional opportunities. However, it was clear that Advent would need all the ingenuity, flexibility, and resilience it could muster in order to take advantage of them.

For the first four or five years after the establishment of SEAVIC and HKVIT, the challenges my colleagues and I faced stemmed largely from the newness of venture capital in Southeast Asia and greater China and the need to discover which strategies made sense for tailoring venture investment to the economic conditions and needs in these regions and for individual countries within them. In this respect, my early experience in Asia was much like that in Western Europe, where venture capital was equally unknown at the time I began looking for ways to invest there. As time went by, however, it began to become apparent that Asia posed obstacles and challenges that were in many ways more formidable than those I had so far encountered in Europe. Some of these obstacles were cultural, while others arose from the turbulence to which the less developed economies of the world are subject.

By the late 1980s, as the firm gained more experience, SEAVIC had actually become an increasingly successful investor in Southeast Asian companies, mostly in Singapore. For example, in 1986 SEAVIC made a S$1.2 million investment to acquire a 22 percent stake in Teledata (Singapore) Pte Ltd. Founded in 1976, Teledata was a distributor and installer of PABX systems, dealer phone systems, key telephones, fax machines, and other telecommunication equipment for offices. When the existing management was found to be weak, SEAVIC succeeded in replacing it; Tan Keng Boon played an active role for a time as caretaker chairman and CEO and helped to turn the company around. SEAVIC also found a strategic investor for Teledata, to strengthen the shareholder base prior to a successful IPO in 1994, and helped to set up a Thai joint venture to expand Teledata's distribution network in Thailand. Also in 1986, SEAVIC invested US$1.4 million in Electro Magnetic (Singapore) Ltd., a manufacturer of video tapes and cassettes, primarily for export, that had been established in 1982 with a special five-year "pioneer" status by the Singapore Economic Development Board. SEAVIC helped expand and automate the company's manufacturing capacity, move its labor-intensive operations to Thailand and Malaysia, strengthen its management and corporate governance, and secure underwriting from the Development Bank of Singapore for a successful IPO in 1988 on the Singapore Stock Exchange.

These investments in Singapore firms made it clear that SEAVIC could add value to its portfolio companies and help them succeed. However, SEAVIC had been established with a mandate to invest not just in Singapore but throughout the region. As I have noted, Singapore, as the Southeast Asian country with the most developed infrastructure for venture capital, had been the logical choice for locating a regional venture capital firm. The trouble was that the IFC — which was not only a cosponsor of SEAVIC but also the initial force behind its founding — had a mandate to invest in the developing world. Yet by the early 1980s, when SEAVIC was founded, Singapore was no longer considered a developing country. As I have also mentioned, when SEAVIC was established in 1983 it managed three separate funds: one for Singapore (Venture Investment Singapore, or VIS, which was organized by DBS); a regional fund, SEAVI, that invested both in Singapore and in other ASEAN countries; and a $16 million Malaysian fund, Malaysian Ventures Sdn. Bhd. The IFC participated only in the second two, not in the fund focused exclusively on Singapore.

I have noted that it was only after SEAVIC and Techno Ventures Hong Kong had been in operation for a while that it began to dawn on me just how challenging an environment for venture capital Asia could be. SEAVIC's experience with its two Malaysian funds — the initial, 1983 fund and a second one that SEAVIC would raise in 1991, both overseen by Koh Lee Boon — amply demonstrates how investing in a less developed country is a much different kind of undertaking than investing in a place like Singapore or most countries in Western Europe. In Malaysia, where natural resources in rubber, tin, lumber, and palm oil are the country's great economic assets, Advent financed companies that supplied and serviced these industries as well as companies in other sectors that supplied and serviced the infrastructure of a rapidly growing country — for instance, computer applications and software for the banking industry and manufacturing support for the construction sector. Two examples of SEAVIC investments in Malaysia — one in the timber industry and another in a printing company — illustrate the kinds of hazards that the country posed for venture capitalists in the 1980s and '90s.

In its second Malaysian fund, SEAVIC invested in a company owned and operated by a Danish entrepreneur that manufactured wood products (window and door jambs, window frames, etc.) for the construction industry in Europe. The upstream end of the value chain in the timber products business is extraordinarily complex: logging, cutting and planing, fabricating the end products, and controlling for defects are all laborious processes with endless potential for snafus. This entrepreneur understood the business well, however, and when SEAVIC invested in the company it focused on one step of the value chain that posed special challenges in Malaysia. The particular difficulty was securing a reliable source of high-quality timber in a country where timber concessions are controlled by the individual state governments rather than the federal government in Kuala Lumpur, making the procurement process closely intertwined with regional politics. SEAVIC thought it had an answer to this problem because the state government of Pahang, which controlled a substantial proportion of Malaysia's timber resources, was an investor in the second Malaysian fund. SEAVIC secured a promise of a timber concession in Pahang, and the entrepreneur moved his operation from its original location just outside Kuala Lumpur (in the state of Selangor) to Kuantan (in Pahang) in order to be closer to his source of supply. Despite the promise SEAVIC had obtained from the state government, however, political factors prevented the concession from coming through, the lack of a reliable source of good-quality timber at a predictable price became a serious handicap, and the company eventually went under.

A second kind of challenge SEAVIC confronted in Malaysia—one that venture capitalists and private equity investors now face in countries like China—stemmed from a business culture in which owners were engaged in practices that are unacceptable to outside investors. In one instance, SEAVIC invested in a small printing company run by a very clever entrepreneur who had developed many new products of his own and was actually negotiating with Hallmark for the right to produce greeting cards under the Hallmark brand in Malaysia. In the end, the partnership between SEAVIC and the entrepreneur unraveled because the latter was unwilling to give up practices—such as mingling company and personal finances—that are widespread in such family-owned companies in Asia.

The IFC's strategy for introducing venture capital in the less developed countries of Southeast Asia, meanwhile, revolved around individual country funds like SEAVIC's in Malaysia rather than regional funds.[14] As it turned out, the IFC's main interest in Southeast Asia was in Thailand and Indonesia. By the end of the 1980s, David Gill was encouraging SEAVIC to extend its reach into these two countries by forming country funds there.

Gill's suggestions posed something of a quandary for me. While I was certainly interested in expanding the scope of SEAVIC's operations, country funds were not my preferred way of doing so at this point. Having seen some of the challenges posed by Malaysia, I thought that dedicated funds in countries such as Thailand and Indonesia would not provide enough of a hedge against the risks of investing in such potentially volatile places. If one could invest only in Indonesia, for example, and conditions turned sour, one would be locked into that country with no ability to reallocate capital elsewhere. In a regional fund, by contrast, capital could be allocated throughout the region wherever the economic conditions and deal flow were attractive. (In Europe, where I had originally taken a country-by-country approach, the need for more flexibility had caused Advent International to move to a regional investment strategy in its European Special Situations Fund, where Advent was free to invest wherever in Western Europe the opportunities seemed the most promising.) Despite these substantial reservations about establishing country funds for countries such as Thailand and Indonesia, however, I realized that such funds would be sources of revenue for SEAVIC as it continued trying to build a platform for all of Southeast Asia. And so we agreed to Gill's plan. December 1990 saw the establishment of two new SEAVIC funds: SEAVI Thailand, capitalized at $5 million, and SEAVI Indonesia, with $6.5 million. The IFC invested $1.5 million in each fund.[15]

The small size of the Thai and Indonesian funds reflected the difficulty of finding local sponsors for them. The Indonesian fund, for example, had only three local institutional investors, with the rest of the capital being contributed by family groups. Derrick Lee, who had contacts in Thailand, oversaw the Thai fund. The idea, as with SEAVIC's previous funds, was that SEAVIC and Advent International themselves would provide the value-added services, such as advice in strategic planning, organization, and management, to the portfolio companies. SEAVIC and Advent would also work to build the professional capabilities of the management teams of their portfolio companies, and intervene if management was not getting the job done. For this it was necessary to hire and train skilled teams of local venture capital managers, just as we had tried, often with considerable difficulty, to do in Western Europe throughout the 1980s.

In Thailand, Derrick succeeded in recruiting local professionals to manage the fund's investments, often ex-bankers who could source deals. This was necessary in Thailand, as it was in every country throughout the world. The face of the managers had to be the face of the country. Even though the country's economy was dominated by business owners of Chinese descent, one had to be able to speak Thai in order to relate to portfolio company managers and carry out the due diligence process. Unfortunately, Derrick quickly found that the local managers he hired were generally not of the caliber of the people he had found in Singapore. Cultural issues created another obstacle to success in Thailand, especially the fundamental distrust of outside investors that SEAVIC had already encountered among business owners in Malaysia. This distrust was compounded by the nationalistic attitudes of the Thais, who have never been colonized and are proud of it. As Derrick describes it, the attitude of business owners to venture capitalists and private equity investors was too often, "You guys are trying to strip me naked!" Such attitudes made it hard to get reliable financial information. SEAVIC's Thai managers were also reluctant to push entrepreneurs too hard because most of the latter were well connected politically and could harm the career of anyone who crossed them. In one case that Derrick recalls, the owner of a SEAVI Thailand portfolio company who had used SEAVIC's capital to fund one of his other businesses threatened to tie SEAVIC up in court for ten years if it tried to take any legal action.

Despite these challenges, however, SEAVI Thailand performed well in its early stages, financing companies in such diverse industries as computer applications (to supply the needs of a rapidly growing banking and commercial infrastructure) and products and services for the food industry (such as refrigeration and distribution). Unfortunately, several of the fund's portfolio companies failed to get to the IPO stage before the Asian currency crisis struck in 1997, crippling the entire regional economy.

In Indonesia, Tan Keng Boon set up a management company that also consisted mostly of former bank officers. By having the local Indonesian office work closely with SEAVIC's professionals in Singapore, Keng Boon was able to develop a credible management team, although all investment decisions were made by SEAVIC's investment committee in Singapore. The Indonesian fund targeted growth companies in sectors such as manufacturing and natural resource processing. Most of the entrepreneurs, however, were interested in bringing in outside investors only for their riskiest ventures. Moreover, in Indonesia as elsewhere in Asia, groups of companies controlled by the same family owners engaged in many related-party transactions, which meant that the SEAVIC team had to be especially careful about due diligence. Distinguishing the good entrepreneurs from the fly-by-night operators was time-consuming, as was the process of winning the trust of the good ones. The search for good investments in Indonesia was further complicated by the fact that political connections were a crucial success factor for most companies in Indonesia at the time; most of the top fifty groups of privately owned companies in the country, in fact, had connections with the family of President Suharto.

In spite of such obstacles, SEAVI Indonesia's investments performed well until the Asian currency crisis occurred. Of all the countries in Southeast Asia, it was Indonesia that experienced the effects of currency crisis most acutely. The Indonesian rupiah was devalued by 80 percent, and the Jakarta Stock Exchange simply collapsed in mid-1998. The SEAVI Indonesia portfolio was decimated: to take one example, a company listed on the Jakarta exchange late in 1996 at 300 percent of SEAVIC's investment dropped to a valuation of 5 percent of the investment by the end of 1998. The economic and social meltdown that resulted from the crisis proved to be the biggest factor in the ultimate performance of SEAVI Thailand as well.

A catastrophe like this demonstrates that, especially in emerging markets, events over which a venture capital or private equity investor has absolutely no control can defeat even a sound, well-executed strategy. Sometimes these events can be instigated by the recklessness of other financiers. Our biggest mistake in Southeast Asia in the 1980s and early 1990s, as it turned out, was to assume that the local and international banks would be more prudent than they proved to be in extending credit to companies in the region. We assumed that the banks would insist upon a responsible underpinning of equity on their customers' balance sheets. Looking back at the 10 percent annual growth that the Southeast Asian countries experienced over much of this period, it is absolutely amazing to consider how small a role equity, as opposed to debt, played in this expansion. SEAVIC and Advent were using a financial model that said that if a business had strong and predictable cash flows, the debt-to-worth ratio should be 2:1. Never in our wildest dreams did we think that the ratio should be 10:1.[16] (None of the companies we invested in before the meltdown had that kind of leverage, although some that we were investigating just before the crisis did.)

We would see more of the devastation that the currency crisis inflicted on the region when Advent made its first attempt to create a broader Asian platform in the early 1990s. Our goal in setting up SEAVIC's country funds had been to establish fully autonomous offices under SEAVIC's supervision in Malaysia, Thailand, and Indonesia. This strategy for Southeast Asia, in turn, was part of an earlier design for creating an Asian network that would include Japan and the greater China area (Hong Kong and Taiwan as well as mainland China). Although the launching of SEAVIC and HKVIT and the success enjoyed by both in the mid- to late 1980s were a good start, we encountered significant obstacles in these years as well.

One of these obstacles was the failure of Techno-Venture in Japan (described at the end of chapter 5). Another complicating factor in my effort to build Advent in Asia was the designs that Piet van de Ven had for Orange Nassau in the region. Both in Western Europe and in Asia I had been extremely reliant on the quality and loyalty of my local partners for success. In France (with Sofinnova), Britain, Germany, Singapore, Hong Kong, and other countries where I had succeeded in establishing affiliates that survived and prospered, I had managed to find partners in whose competence and honesty I could trust. In France (with Alpha), Spain, and a handful of other countries, I had failed to find such partners, and as a result the relationships soured and the connections were severed. Piet van de Ven, whom I had thought of as a soul mate when I met him in Holland, who helped me to establish Advent Belgium, and who then agreed to defray half the costs of my first foray into Asia, had been a very good partner at first.

Soon after we set up SEAVIC, however, I began to feel uneasy about van de Ven and a young associate he had brought on board, Joost Tjaden, whom I simply did not trust. I found out, for example, that first van de Ven and then Tjaden were meeting on their own with SEAVIC's chairman, Alan Yeo. Van de Ven also appeared to be currying favor with Yeo at investment committee and board meetings. This did not bother me at first. Then I discovered that van de Ven had developed a relationship with another venture capital/private equity group in Hong Kong, ChinaVest. Founded in 1981 by Bob Theleen, a former CIA sinologist, ChinaVest grew out of First Dallas Asia, a Hong Kong merchant banking subsidiary of the First National Bank in Dallas that Theleen set up with the assistance of former president George H. W. Bush. Eventually it emerged that van de Ven was competing with HKVIT through the relationship with ChinaVest.

When I then heard van de Ven refer to the Advent network as the "Orange Nassau network," I became alarmed. It was obvious that my soul mate had designs of his own. I was curious about van de Ven's strategy. Was he trying to take over sponsorship of the network? Or was he building relationships that he could later merge into the network—thereby gaining more influence in Advent International, where (through Orange Nassau) he was already a shareholder? Whatever the strategy, he was playing a pretty transparent hand. I did not confront him, feeling that it was better to keep him in the house where I could keep an eye on him. ChinaVest appeared to be an interesting play, and I thought I might want to hedge my bets with HKVIT in Hong Kong.

As it turned out, this was not a bad idea. One of those unforeseen events that can turn conditions upside down in an emerging market occurred in 1989, when the Chinese government put down the pro-democracy demonstrations in Tiananmen Square. Reacting to investors who had been shocked by the incident and were no longer interested in a China-only fund, HKVIT was forced to expand its outreach to Southeast Asia. Victor Fung and HKVIT's comanaging director, Chris Leong, established a regional fund that put HKVIT into direct competition with SEAVIC. This was a conflict that could not be resolved, and while Victor, Chris, and Advent delivered what turned out to be very good returns for the fund we had established together, our relationship ended with that fund. If Tiananmen Square had not happened, I think that we could have used HKVIT as a base and made it into an organization that could have responded to the opportunities that were opening up in China in the 1980s — particularly if, as I hoped, I could have persuaded Victor Fung to take charge of Advent's Asian activity. But it was not to be.[17]

In any event, keeping a wary eye on van de Ven, I cultivated a relationship with Bob Theleen, introducing him to members of our network, arranging speaking engagements for him at conferences in the United States and Europe, and inviting him and his wife Jenny to visit Anne and me at our house in Vermont. I was then able to incorporate ChinaVest into the Advent network system when, not long afterward, Orange Nassau's parent company, CGIP, cut van de Ven loose and Orange Nassau departed the venture capital/private equity scene. I accelerated CGIP's release of van de Ven when I learned that he had attempted to persuade Alpha Associés in France to discard Advent International as a sponsor (before Alpha had made that same decision on its own). Needless to say, we removed him from the Advent board. It was a sad ending to a relationship that had been crucial to the building of the Advent network and personally meaningful to me.

The incorporation of ChinaVest was solidified when we included it as a participant in a pan-Asian fund, the Asia-Pacific Special Situations Fund (APSSF), which was launched in 1991. The purpose of the APSSF was to fill the acute need for equity capital that we saw in the Southeast Asia and greater China regions. This fund, capitalized at $69 million, had three participants: Advent International, which managed 50 percent of the capital directly, and SEAVIC and ChinaVest, which shared the remainder equally. The APSSF was a notable failure. Each participant performed poorly, ChinaVest most poorly of all. While all the fund managers shared responsibility for this poor performance, part of it was due to circumstances in the region after the currency crisis struck in 1997.

The story of one of the biggest disasters in the APSSF portfolio illustrates the effects of the Asian meltdown not just from SEAVIC's point of view but from the standpoint of a region where I hoped SEAVIC would be a force for promoting economic and social progress. As I have mentioned, Indonesia was one of the countries hit hardest in the aftermath of the crisis. One of the APSSF's Indonesian investments was in a commercial tile manufacturer that had done extremely well amid the country's spectacular growth in the early to mid-1990s and was by far the best company in the Indonesia portfolio. It was growing at 30 percent per year, had a sound balance sheet with no debt, had a strategic plan to build its export sales, and was well run by Chinese managers who had been educated and trained in the United States.

Despite these attributes and an imaginative buyback structure devised by Keng Boon, however, the company was not able to survive the crisis. Keng Boon had secured the buyback provision in the investment contract with the company by obtaining a pledge of collateral from the owners that included stock in the company and other assets. Unfortunately this collateral had to be shared with the banks that had loaned the owners funds to diversify their holdings — not an unusual event in Indonesia during the go-go years. When the crisis hit and the loans were called, the collateral was of little value in making us whole (through the buyback provision), or the banks either, for that matter. Such failures were endemic in Indonesia and elsewhere in the region at that time.

The whole country, meanwhile, was in terrible economic, social, and political turmoil that would lead to the fall of the Suharto government in May 1998. I am not an economist, so I cannot explain all the complexities of how the Asian currency crisis arose and unfolded. The ruling political families of the time, such as the Suhartos in Indonesia and the Mahathirs in Malaysia, bear some of the blame, as do the local and international banks that over-leveraged local industry. Others responsible for the crisis included central banks, the International Monetary Fund, and emerging markets funds managed by prestigious investment houses such as Morgan Stanley and Goldman Sachs. The principal villains, however — as I stated at the time and still believe today — were George Soros and his fellow currency traders, whose reckless speculation in Asian currencies amounted to playing God with some very vulnerable societies. Anyone with any knowledge of the developing world knows that countries there have fragile institutions. I am a firm believer in economic liberalization for countries that are ready for it, but I also believe that measures such as capital controls are necessary in emerging economies, which need patient, long-term, strategic capital that adds value to its investments — capital of the kind that Advent International was providing in Southeast Asia in the 1980s and '90s. Soros and his fellow predators ignored these realities for the sake of quick profits.[18]

I was a student at Phillips Exeter Academy in 1947 when my father took me
to Harvard's commencement to hear Secretary of State George C. Marshall
announce an economic recovery plan for Europe. Little did I know what
my future would bring or how the Marshall Plan would inform
my vision for an industry.

After college, business school, and the army I joined Bank of Boston as a loan officer with a specialty in lending for economic development and expansion. One of my first big clients was Wang Laboratories, founded by Dr. An Wang. I later joined the board of the company. Pictured here: Constantine Boden, Dr. Wang, and myself in the mid-1960s.

Wang Laboratories proved one of the great success stories of "the Massachusetts miracle" of the 1970s and 1980s, when the economy shifted to a high-technology base. Pictured here: Breaking ground for Wang's new headquarters in Lowell in 1980. I'm the figure near the center wearing a tan trench coat.

In 1968 I founded TA Associates, one of the earliest
venture capital firms established in the country. Here I am
at about the time we launched.

Many of my partners and associates at TAA proved to be stars
in venture capital and private equity. Here they are in 1982: in foreground
(left to right), Roe Stamps and David Croll; in the middle, Rich Churchill, me,
Kevin Landry, and Jacqui Morby; in the back, Steve Gormley, Andy McLane,
Jeff Chambers, Steve Woodsum, and Bill Collatos.
*Photo by Béla T. Kalman.*

We were serious about growing the business, but we had a lot of fun
along the way. Pictured left to right, also in 1982: Jeff Chambers, Andy McLane,
me, Kevin Landry, Roe Stamps, Jacqui Morby, and Steve Woodsum.
*Photo by Béla T. Kalman.*

Although TAA focused on business in the United States, I was always interested in taking venture capital abroad, with the first opportunity coming in France in the early 1970s. We set up a fund called Sofinnova in 1972. Pictured here left to right: me, Antoine Dupont-Fauville, and Christian Marbach at the 35th anniversary dinner in 2007.

I also pursued opportunities in Asia, though Japan proved to be a very tough slog. Here I am in 1983 with Yaichi Ayukawa. We fared much better in Southeast Asia.

David Cooksey in the United Kingdom helped me set up Advent Limited in the early 1980s. We learned a lot from that venture that I later incorporated into the design of Advent International.

Piet van de Ven (pictured between David Cooksey and his wife Poppy and me, with Leuki van de Ven on my left at the Inverlochy Castle Hotel in Ft. William, Scotland) was another pioneer in the early days of the Advent network in Europe.

Here I am in 1986, two years after the establishment of Advent International.
*Photo by Lou Jones.*

As had happened at TAA, Advent International attracted highly talented people who helped us grow. Pictured left to right at a golf outing in 1993: Doug Brown, David Mussafer, Steve Tadler, and Tan Keng Boom.

At the same outing in 1993, two nongolfers critical to Advent's fortunes were Derrick Lee and Nick Callinan.

As these photos indicate, my success in venture capital and private equity depended on the help of many others — partners, colleagues, associates, and friends. For more than fifty years, my greatest help and greatest partner has been my wife Anne, pictured here with me at Harvard commencement in 1994.

The managing partners of Advent International in 2008 included (left to right) David McKenna, Humphrey Battcock, David Mussafer, Juan Carlos Torres, Ernest Bachrach, Steve Tadler, John Brooke (director), me (chairman), Joanna James, John Singer, Will Schmidt, Tom Lauer, and Chris Mruck. Missing from the photo are Ralf Huep and Mark Hoffman (director). *Photo by Shelley Harrison Photography.*

Anne and I are extremely proud of our three sons, John, Peter, and Sam. The youngest, John (to my immediate left) followed me into the business. Peter (to my right) is an acclaimed artist, whose work includes the dust jacket of this book, and Sam (to John's left) is a successful architect. *Photo by the Nourses, Canton, Mass.*

Throughout my career I've looked for ways to apply my skills
as a leader, manager, and financial expert in the world of not-for-profits.
One of my favorite assignments was as chair of the board of trustees of the
Boston Symphony Orchestra when we recruited James Levine as music director.
Here Anne and I are pictured with Maestro Levine in 2004.

Having invested in local companies in Asia and elsewhere around the world, moreover, I know a lot about the time, effort, and care it takes to build and nurture such firms, and about the pain that results when this kind of work is undone by economic and social crisis. The human suffering at such times is intense. Amid the desperation of those days in Indonesia, some native Indonesians began to scapegoat the country's Chinese minority. In Jakarta, where the tile factory was located, a mob burned down the plant and forced the Chinese managers to flee for their lives. This is a useful reminder of some of the risks of investing in emerging markets, but also of the need to invest responsibly there — to help people build their economies rather than exploit them for one's own gain. I might add that one interesting, and positive, result of the crisis was the impetus it gave the countries in the region to reduce their dependence on foreign direct investment and export-driven manufacturing and increase their capacity for innovation. This, in turn, has given renewed momentum to efforts to use venture capital to stimulate economic development in East and Southeast Asia.

In any case, the APSSF and the relationship with ChinaVest, as it turned out, hardly constituted a platform from which to build a direct presence for Advent in Asia, as the ESSF had been for Advent in Europe. The effects of the Asian currency crisis, moreover, represented a disappointment for my hopes of using venture capital as a tool for economic development in the region. Advent's experience in Asia in the late 1990s might have discouraged some people about the prospects for venture capital and private equity in emerging markets. However, I had a longer-term vision and believed that our setback in Asia would prove to be only temporary. Meanwhile, other opportunities beckoned. Even though early-stage investment in Western Europe had proven to be more of a challenge than I had anticipated, Advent had developed a successful strategy for buyouts there. Indeed the firm now had a chance to employ that strategy elsewhere to evolve into a truly global private equity organization. By the middle of the 1990s, in fact, Advent was launched on an expansion into emerging markets in two different regions of the world. I tell about Advent's move into central and Eastern Europe and Latin America, and about its subsequent fortunes in Asia, in the final chapter of this portion of the book.

CHAPTER 7

# MORE NEW VENTURES

## CENTRAL EUROPE, LATIN AMERICA,

### AND BEYOND

· · ·

In the early 1990s, Western Europe was beginning to experience the benefits of economic integration, Southeast Asia was undergoing a boom that
would end only with the arrival of the Asian currency crisis in 1997, and
China was continuing its construction of the "socialist market economy"
that was creating new business opportunities in the capitalist market
economies of Hong Kong and Taiwan. Economic conditions in all these
regions seemed to favor the development of private equity investment, although taking advantage of these conditions proved much easier for Advent International to do in Western Europe than it was in Southeast Asia
and greater China, for reasons explained in the preceding chapter.

Meanwhile, as Advent International sought opportunities for further
expansion in pursuit of my vision of a truly global venture capital/private
equity industry, important changes were taking place in two other regions
of the world. In central and Eastern Europe, the collapse of the Soviet empire at the end of the 1980s and beginning of the 1990s was transforming
half a continent. In the central European countries of Poland, the Czech
Republic, Slovakia, Hungary, and Romania, democratically elected governments were trying to build market economies virtually from scratch,
privatizing formerly state-owned companies, overhauling their banking systems, and opening up their economies to foreign investment and
trade with the world beyond the old Soviet bloc. At the same time, Latin
America — where the poor and middle classes had suffered greatly from
the debt crisis that swept across the developing world in the 1980s, leading

to sharp drops in living standards and investment—was undergoing its own market revolution. In countries all up and down the continent, civilian governments elected amid the disastrous conditions of the 1980s were embracing economic liberalization measures including free trade and the deregulation of financial systems.

In both central Europe and Latin America, large-scale economic transformation was creating the need for both investment capital and management assistance to aid in the process of restructuring companies for greater efficiency and future growth. It was a perfect opportunity for Advent International to leverage its experience in introducing venture capital and private equity into new environments, especially now that—in contrast to the 1980s, when Advent was entering new markets in Western Europe and the Asia-Pacific region—the firm had developed a successful private equity strategy. In the mid-1990s, Advent moved on both the central European and Latin American fronts.

As the Warsaw Pact nations escaped the embrace of the Soviet Union at the end of the 1980s and beginning of the 1990s, it became apparent to me that there was an opportunity for Advent to introduce its system of investment and economic development to central Europe. In 1992, a little more than ten years after David Gill of the International Finance Corporation had approached me about taking venture capital to Southeast Asia, I was visited by Jeff Griffin, the official at the IFC in charge of venture capital and private equity. Griffin was interested in how the IFC could participate in the renewal of the economies of formerly communist central and Eastern Europe by means of venture capital and private equity. Even before the Berlin Wall came down, the IFC had sponsored the first private equity fund in the region, in Hungary. A subsequent effort by a group of Western industrial firms, known as Euroventures and led by Phillips Electronics, did not impress Griffin (in fact it was in the process of winding down), and he thought our system—which the IFC knew well because of its success in Southeast Asia—could be useful in central and Eastern Europe.[1]

This overture from Griffin and the IFC led to the design of a regional private equity fund that would make cornerstone investments in country funds in Poland, the Czech Republic, and Hungary, managed by affiliates of Advent's choosing. When introducing venture capital to Western Europe and Southeast Asia, I had learned about the critical importance of having partners with local knowledge and connections. Central Europe in the mid-1990s had only a small number of local firms with which we could partner, but at least there were some in existence, and I did not have to get involved in building new ones from scratch. Our task was to help these affiliates develop their teams and raise their capital, and to coinvest with them in deals in their countries that Advent found particularly attractive and where its services could add value. Advent would have a small stake in their management companies and representatives on the boards of the management companies and their funds. This was a different strategy from the one that was pursued by the first outside venture firm in the region, Enterprise Investors, which concentrated at first on a single country (Poland), and from the one pursued later by the firm MidEuropa, which developed its own regional team from the outset. As had been true when I expanded into the Asia-Pacific region in the early 1980s, I thought that the combination of local knowledge and flexibility in deploying capital that a regional affiliate structure would afford provided the best means of initial expansion into central Europe. It would also help create a local venture capital/private equity industry, another of my goals for the region.

There was a major problem with this strategy, however. We did not have anyone on board with knowledge of central Europe, the desire to go there, or the skills to manage an investment program. Luckily this situation was soon remedied when Nick Callinan, the managing director of Advent Western Pacific in Australia, volunteered for duty. Nick was aware of the investment opportunities in Poland through a group of Polish émigrés he knew in Melbourne. He had advised them, as an expert on venture capital, on an acquisition of some breweries in Poland, one of which proved very successful, and was thinking of raising a fund in Poland. When I told Nick that the IFC was inquiring about Advent's interest in central Europe and asked if he might be interested in managing a program there, he said that he was. Nick was and still is the classic entrepreneur. He was interested in the world outside Australia, believed in the vision I had for Advent, and wanted to play a role in the company's expansion. He was hard-charging and always convinced he was right — just the sort of person to take on the task of creating competitive companies in what had been a command economy. He was so committed to the idea of launching a central European program for Advent that he offered to do the fund-raising on his own dime. In a testament to the saying that timing is everything, we now had the design of a program, the support of the IFC for it, and the fellow to manage it.

Despite these auspicious conditions, raising the capital for a central European fund proved to be no easy task. Our first stop when we began seeking a group of core investors in 1993 was the European Bank for Reconstruction and Development (EBRD), founded in 1991 to help build market economies in the countries of the former Soviet bloc. EBRD showed interest — despite its rivalry with the IFC — but had doubts about our ability to assemble a competent management team for the fund. Its representative, Guy de Selliers, told Callinan, Doug Brown, and me exactly what we had to do in order to get the bank's support. From that meeting we proceeded to Zurich to convince Hareb Al-Darmaki, the head of the Abu Dhabi Investment Authority (Adia),[2] that we had the key to investing in central Europe and that Adia should be our anchor investor. We succeeded in this mission and then let Nick loose on a number of other potential investors.

It required all of Nick's immense drive and persuasiveness to cobble together investors for this first regional fund for central Europe. In the end, however, everybody wanted to do *something* in the region — even though there were, as yet, few choices of vehicles in which to invest there — and Advent had a superstructure that could lend stability to its fund. We did encounter an unexpected problem with the IFC, which despite Jeff Griffin's high degree of competence and knowledge of private equity had become a bureaucratic, highly political institution since the days when I had begun working with David Gill in Southeast Asia. David was a highly motivated professional. When he was at the helm, the IFC's capital markets unit — the most important one in an organization dedicated to the introduction of investment capital to previously closed markets — was nonpolitical, with advancement based upon merit, and organized in a way that made it possible to get things done. By the mid-1990s, however, the IFC had become heavily politicized. It had a complex management structure in which the lawyers were de facto investment officers and set up roadblocks at every turn. Although the IFC was technically the sponsor of Advent's first central European fund, the EBRD effectively took on sponsorship of the fund when the IFC dithered and eventually became the last major investor to sign on.[3] Besides the EBRD, the IFC, and Adia, the eventual investors included GE Capital, the Kauffman Foundation, and FMO, the Dutch development bank. The fund, Advent Central and Eastern Europe (ACEE), closed at $58 million in 1994, at which time Nick Callinan joined Advent as director of the central European program.

Nick had other challenges besides fund-raising. For one thing, he had to assemble a management group that met with the approval of de Selliers and the other key investors. In Germany in the 1980s, TVM Technoventures had struggled to find competent managers owing to the newness of venture capital and the German presumption that only second-rate people would work for a small company. Nick faced a similar problem in central Europe in the mid-1990s: what self-respecting venture capitalist would want to join a new management company whose purpose was to invest in former socialist countries where the rules of a command economy were all that people knew? Nick succeeded in assembling a team that passed muster with the investors, but in fact it was a pretty ragtag group. How we got through those early years is anyone's guess. It takes topflight venture capital or private equity managers to succeed in emerging markets because the conditions can be so difficult. Yet with the best talent all working in private equity in Western Europe or the United States, Advent had to make do with whomever it could find to manage investments for its first central European fund.

Nick's other major task was to select and establish affiliates in each country and help them raise their capital, which eventually came from local banks. It took a very inventive person to organize and manage the affiliate structure in the fluid, frontier conditions that obtained in the region at the time. In the Czech Republic, for example, we quickly ran through two relationships before succeeding on our third try with the Genesis Capital Group, founded in 1999 by Jan Tauber, formerly the head of the Czech subsidiary of HSBC Investment Bank. Our affiliate in Poland, Copernicus Capital Management, was led by Neil Milne, a British subject residing in Warsaw who had previously worked in investment banking and private equity in the U.K., and proved to be stable. Our Hungarian affiliate, Equinox, was majority-owned by Creditanstalt Securities and led initially by Peter Kertes, an American consultant and former adviser to the State Property Agency of Hungary, and Gordon Bajnai, a young Hungarian investment banker who had worked at the EBRD.[4] This affiliate relationship was terminated by mutual agreement when Equinox decided to raise its second fund; the decision was an easy one for Advent to reach, since it had already decided to open its own hub for central Europe in Budapest.

Overall, the affiliate structure in central Europe was a movable feast, which we managed to hold together until we had our own offices in the region, our goal from the beginning. Advent had learned from its experience in Western Europe about the drawbacks of relying on an affiliate structure and the benefits of having a direct presence. Nick Callinan therefore structured the relationship with our central European affiliates from the start to give us the option of discontinuing the various affiliations when it came time to raise a second fund. Advent opened its own office in Warsaw in 1998, when it raised its second central European fund. Advent managed, however, to maintain a friendly relationship with Copernicus Capital. A Budapest office, which opened in 2000, served as Advent's hub for Hungary, the Czech Republic, and Slovakia until spring 2007, when this function was transferred to a new regional center in Prague. Genesis Capital, which Jan Tauber still leads, remains active in the Czech Republic and Slovakia. As happened in Western Europe at the beginning of the 1990s, Advent made the transition to a direct presence in central Europe after having helped several local firms in the region to develop and grow. Romania (where Advent began investing only in its second fund) was the one country in central Europe where Advent did not have an affiliate but established its own direct presence from the start; the Bucharest office now serves as a regional center covering Romania, Bulgaria, and Turkey.[5]

For all the challenges presented by the creation of the first regional private equity fund in a part of the world just being reintroduced to a market economy, central Europe in the mid-1990s presented great opportunities for private equity. In 1994, when Advent established its central European program, the region offered, in many ways, an ideal environment for the kinds of hands-on private equity investment in which the firm specialized. The former Soviet bloc countries of central Europe were undertaking major restructurings of their economies, had consumer markets with pent-up demand, and were eager to qualify for membership in the EU. The basic principles of a capitalist economy were so unfamiliar that most people did not even understand the concept of equity. However, this would actually make it easier for private equity to develop in central Europe than has been the case in some other emerging markets, since — in contrast to places such as Asia and Latin America — the region had no family-owned companies, where owners can be very reluctant to sell to outside investors. Companies in postcommunist central Europe also lacked knowledge of modern financial, managerial, and governance practices as well as the ability to formulate strategies for becoming competitive in a market

economy.[6] Amid the wealth of opportunities this created for private equity, moreover — particularly in such high-growth subsectors as mobile
phones, cable television, and IT services for business — there was no real
competition for deals.

With these circumstances in its favor, Advent's first central European
fund pursued a strategy of taking control positions, at low multiples, in
cash-generating businesses with high growth potential and was successful — despite being a first-time fund with all the uncertainties of a new,
inexperienced staff working in a volatile environment. This success bred
further opportunities when, toward the end of the investment cycle of
this first fund and before the introduction of the second central European
fund, Callinan added key members to his team including Joanna James.
Nick recruited Joanna from Kleinwort Benson, the merchant bank, and
she proved to be a ten-strike. She was an experienced investor, intelligent
and determined. The whole team that was presented to the potential investors in the second fund was considerably more qualified than the one
investors had accepted in its predecessor. This highly qualified staff and
the performance of the first fund enabled Advent to raise $181 million for
ACEE (Advent Central and Eastern Europe) II, launched in 1997. Nick
Callinan, justly proud of his accomplishment, describes the central European program as a perfect example of entry into a new regional market:
Advent started with a core activity and a group of affiliates who provided
connections and local knowledge, made the transition to a direct investment organization, and assembled a professional staff and built a leadership group that could take it well into the future.[7]

Despite the success that Advent has enjoyed in the region, it has continued to face the occasional agony there that comes with investing in
emerging markets. A recent instance in which Advent has succeeded in
particularly challenging circumstances is its investment in the Bulgarian
Telecommunications Company (BTC). For the first ten years of its central European program, Advent did not undertake any privatizations, as
the economics were generally unattractive. In February of 2004, however,
Advent, along with a consortium of investors, acquired 65 percent of BTC,
the formerly state-owned fixed-line operator in Bulgaria. Advent had actually won the tender process for the privatization of BTC in October
2002, and had contracts negotiated and initialed by the following spring.
However, certain political lobbies within the country attempted to have
Advent disqualified in favor of another bidder, and Advent was forced to

protect its interests in court. It was only a decision by Bulgaria's Supreme Administrative Court early in 2004 that found in favor of Advent and allowed the deal to go through.[8] This story illustrates the political risk sometimes facing private equity investors in emerging markets, where they may be seen as foreign predators trying to steal valuable national assets. It also shows how emerging markets offer opportunities for private equity investors with a hands-on, value-adding approach to bring about dramatic operating transformations — opportunities that also presented themselves to Advent International in Latin America in the mid-1990s.

At the same time that Advent was planning its expansion into central Europe, David Gill, who by then had left the IFC, was advising the Inter-American Development Bank on how to create a sensible private equity plan for Latin America. As Latin American countries liberalized and restructured their economies in the early 1990s, the many family-owned companies on the continent needed equity capital as well as management assistance to prepare themselves to compete in regional[9] and global markets — a perfect opportunity for using private equity as a means of improving economic performance. In 1994, Gill recommended that Advent International run a private equity program in the region.

To get us started in Latin America, Gill introduced me to an old colleague of his, Francisco (Pancho) Ravecca, the chairman of Surinvest, a consortium trade bank located in Montevideo, Uruguay. Pancho then helped me assemble a group of affiliates in the region: the banks Galicia in Argentina, Bozano Simonsen in Brazil, Probursa (a subsidiary of Banco Bilbao Vizcaya) in Mexico, and Banco Santiago in Chile. Banks were the only organizations available in Latin America at the time as vehicles for private equity activity (along with some extremely wealthy local family groups). The affiliate structure in Latin America, meanwhile, had three purposes: to share Advent's experience and expertise in private equity in exchange for the affiliates' experience and contacts in the local market; to help set up mechanisms the affiliates could use to engage in private equity transactions; and to launch local funds with each of the affiliates.

Advent would establish country funds in Argentina and Brazil with Galicia and Bozano Simonsen, respectively. In Mexico, it would coinvest with Probursa (which had its own private equity activity); in Chile, the relationship with Banco Santiago would never progress to the launching of a fund. In parallel with the country funds in Argentina and Brazil, Advent would launch its first Latin American regional fund (closed in 1996 at $187 million), which was also the first regional fund in Latin America formed by a U.S. private equity firm actually based in the region. We pursued this combination of country funds managed by affiliates and an Advent regional fund for the same purpose that we had in central Europe: to help create a venture capital/private equity sector in the region while also investing ourselves.

Ravecca, who was appointed chairman of Advent's Latin American management company, and the affiliates he had recommended gave us a set of local partners in Latin America, but we needed someone with experience in private equity management to run the operation. Early in 1995, Ernest Bachrach, an American citizen of Argentinean heritage who had joined the firm's Milan office in 1991 and now belonged to our senior investment team in London, was assigned the task of managing Advent's Latin American activity. The combination of Ravecca, a topflight relationship man, and Bachrach, a consummate private equity professional who was also on the boards of several family companies in the region, appeared to be a strong one, at least on paper. Unfortunately, they did not like each other, and a turf war broke out. Ravecca had the connections and the local clout and did not think Bachrach had the presence and the stature to manage the enterprise. Bachrach believed that he was being sent to the region as the managing director and did not want interference from someone who knew nothing about venture capital and private equity. Ravecca wrote me a long memorandum expressing his dissatisfaction with Bachrach. I shared this with Doug Brown — whom I was now grooming to succeed me as CEO of Advent — and he, for reasons I can only guess at, passed it on to Bachrach. That ended any hope of reconciliation. The result was the marginalizing and eventual elimination of Ravecca, who had become a friend, believed in the Advent concept, and had devoted his time, enthusiasm, and energy to assembling the affiliates. Yet there is no question that Bachrach should have been in charge. History has proven that he is one of the best, if not the best, private equity managers in the region, a true professional.

The year 1995, when we completed the fund-raising for Advent's first Latin American Private Equity Fund (LAPEF), turned out to be an interesting time to be expanding into the region. The effects of the Mexican peso crisis — a warm-up for the currency crisis that would roil the emerging markets of Southeast Asia and devastate SEAVIC's funds in that region only two years later—hardly created favorable conditions for Bachrach to raise a first-time fund. The investors he signed up, however—who in addition to the anchor investor, General Electric, included the Inter-American Investment Corporation (a subsidiary of the Inter-American Development Bank), the pension funds of Alcoa and Union Carbide, DEG (the German development bank), and other core Advent investors—had a long-term perspective and were confident about the prospective deals we had shown them.

In the meantime, Bachrach was building a very competent team and leading Advent's establishment of a direct presence in Latin America, beginning with the establishment of a Buenos Aires office in April 1996, followed by the opening of an office in Mexico City in June 1996 and in São Paulo in February 1997. His masterstroke was to convince Juan Carlos Torres to move from Advent's affiliate in Madrid, Advent España, to its office in Mexico City, which opened in June 1996. While in London, Bachrach had worked closely with Juan Carlos on a number of successful investments in Spain and developed a high regard for his investment skills. Juan Carlos (Charley to me) also was, and is, a great guy. He combines great ability as a schmoozer with a keen eye for the main chance, and is always a lot of fun. Chemistry is a very important ingredient in the success of a firm, and Charley brings much that is valuable to the mix.

In Latin America, as in central Europe, the first challenge Advent faced in finding potential investments was the lack of familiarity with private equity in the region. Ernest Bachrach recalls that bankers in Brazil at the time would call privately held companies and suggest they do a deal. The owner would ask the banker if he had any money, and the banker would say no, but he knew people—that is, private equity investors—who did. The owner would just hang up, thinking the banker was wasting his time. At Advent we were able to show companies that were of interest to us that we had the funds, but that was the least of our problems.

As Ernest's Latin American team scoured the region for companies in which to invest, they discovered, in fact, that introducing private equity into Latin America was more difficult, in certain ways, than it was in central Europe. In postcommunist central Europe in the mid-1990s, family ownership had been extirpated fifty years before and was not a factor in the newly privatized business of the region. In Latin America, by contrast, owners of family businesses that could have benefited from private equity investment resisted the idea of giving up control of their companies to a private equity firm. Family ownership and the commingling of business and personal interests it often entailed also made it difficult to get good information about prospective investments, a problem that is familiar to anyone who has invested in a country like China.

For these reasons, doing a deal in Latin America — from the first approach to a company till the signing of the papers — could take two or three years of intricate, parallel-track dialogues with the owner, the CEO, and the CFO. The owner needed a chance to tell a prospective buyer about the company and learn about how a private equity manager could help improve it (for example, by bringing in professional managers to replace family members in company management). The CEO, who when he was not a family member had usually worked for the family for years, had to be educated about the benefits of having an ownership stake, and thereby induced to tell the private equity firm the truth about the condition of the company. The CFO, who in a family-owned Latin American company reports to the owner rather than the CEO, had to be induced to provide the private equity firm with the financial information it could not get from either the owner or the CEO. Meeting these kinds of challenges required patience and persistence. Negotiating a deal in Latin America often requires the same elaborate choreography today.

Obviously it takes money as well as time to approach a new market in this way, and many private equity firms are unable or unwilling to commit the necessary resources. Private equity experienced a downturn in Latin American from 2001 to 2003, a period in which the Argentine peso was unpegged from the dollar and underwent a swift and severe depreciation, and many private equity firms in the region simply left.[10] Advent persevered through the difficult times and even raised a second Latin American regional fund, which has been the most successful of its three LAPEF funds to date. The firm's investment strategy of taking control positions, at low multiples, in cash-generating businesses with high growth potential was one important factor in its ability to weather these adverse conditions. Advent's global presence was another key factor. Since the Latin American team realized that most of its exits were going to come through sales to international rather than local companies, it was able to leverage Advent's global networks to find potential buyers often before deals were even completed.

Finally, the commitment of the managing directors to providing the necessary resources for the firm's Latin American activity helped Advent to strengthen the advantage it already enjoyed over competitors. While other firms were curtailing their resources in the region or getting out altogether, Advent expanded its investment capabilities there; with more than twenty investment professionals on the ground in Latin America during these years, Advent had a much larger local team than any competitor. As one result, between 2001 and 2005, Bachrach's team had screened approximately four thousand companies and met with between 200 and 250 management teams, giving it a very deep understanding of which companies were doing well and why.

As we had already learned in Europe and Southeast Asia, it is critical in any international market to have a strong local presence, with people who know the language and the local culture. In Latin America today, Advent is the only international private equity firm operating with virtually all its investment team based in the region. This local presence has proven critical to our success. Latin Americans favor face-to-face contact over e-mail and the telephone, and in Latin America, as in Asia, cultivating relationships in this way over a long period of time is absolutely essential to investment success. You are at a real disadvantage in the region if you have to fly home on Fridays, since you will not develop the social relationships that are needed to find deals and negotiate them successfully. Advent also gains advantage from the fact that, except for Chile and Uruguay (which have geographic proximity to Argentina and Brazil), it invests only in the countries in the region where it has offices.

In emerging markets like Latin America, where establishing trust is so critical to success, it is essential that private equity managers show that they can add value to their investments. Local businesspersons have to be convinced that they are not going to be exploited. In Latin America as in central Europe, adding value is often a matter of making very basic improvements in the operations of a business. In its investment in the Mexican airport operator Inmobiliaria Fumisa, for example, Advent focused on basics like cash management to turn around a company that was about to go out of business. Through its investment, alongside its portfolio company Dufry, in the Brazil-based travel retailer Brasif, Advent is helping to introduce modern retailing practices at airport duty-free shops throughout Latin America. As these examples suggest, adding value in emerging market settings is a very hands-on process. Ernest Bachrach observes that Latin American companies often need to be "untied from their past practices," and that this "requires a lot of work at different levels — with the CEO, with the finance people, with the sales people." Obviously such painstaking, face-to-face involvement requires an understanding of the local culture that managers native to a region already possess but that outsiders must acquire by immersing themselves in the local environment over a long period of time.

That said, Latin America has proven to offer outstanding private equity investment opportunities with its growing markets, now-stabilized currencies, improved regulation, strong demand for capital, and relative lack of competition for deals. Advent's first regional fund, Latin American Private Equity Fund I, was one of the top-performing private equity funds of its vintage in the region. LAPEF II, a $178 million fund that closed in 2001, was extremely successful.[11] LAPEF III, a $375 million fund, closed in 2005. Meanwhile, Advent has also made its first investments in Uruguay after concentrating its previous Latin American activity in Mexico, Brazil, and Argentina.

Most recently, Advent has raised the largest Latin American regional fund ever, its $1.3 billion LAPEF IV, which closed in 2007, expanding the firm's total capital base in the region to $2.2 billion.[12] The fund, which exceeded its target by 30 percent, is focusing its investment activity on high-growth service sectors including airport services, financial services, and business outsourcing as well as other industries experiencing regional growth or consolidation. The strategy remains the same as it has been since Advent began investing in the region thirteen years ago: taking control positions in market-leading growth companies that generate cash and providing them with hands-on management assistance for getting to the next level. With the continued economic growth in the region, the improved quality of Latin American management, the increased availability of longer-term local debt for recapitalizations and buyouts, and the rise in foreign direct investment (which improves the exit opportunities for private equity investors), Latin America is a region where, as Ernest Bachrach has said, "the stars are aligning for private equity." Moreover, given Latin America's continuing need to position itself for greater competitiveness in a global economy, the ability of a hands-on private equity investor like Advent International to add value in sectors that can advance that goal can be an important contribution to economic development in the region.[13]

Central Europe and Latin America represented two extremely successful forays into new territory for Advent International in the mid-1990s.
Meanwhile, it was time to revisit the firm's strategy for Asia. After parting ways with Victor Fung and Chris Leong's Hong Kong Venture Investment Trust at the end of the 1980s, Advent had tried and failed to build
out its platform in Asia through its relationship with another firm investing in greater China, Chinavest, and the launching of the Asia-Pacific Special Situations Fund. The early 1990s had also seen Advent's affiliate in
Southeast Asia, SEAVIC, branch out beyond its initial focus mainly on
Singapore by launching its second Malaysia fund and new country funds
in Thailand and Indonesia. As I showed in chapter 6, the APSSF and the
Thai and Indonesian funds both brought Advent face-to-face with some
of the more formidable challenges of investing in the Asia-Pacific region.
In contrast to central Europe and Latin America, where Advent had rolled
out a strategy that had proven sound from the start, Asia, it was clear, was
going to involve more of what had already been a number of adjustments
to our approach.

The job of reevaluating Advent's position in Asia would be carried out
by a new leader for the firm. I turned sixty-five in 1994, the year that Advent closed its first central and Eastern European fund and began building
a presence in Latin America. Ten years after its founding, I believed that
the company was in good shape, and I had never intended to go on running it forever. I had also identified the person who I thought would be the
best one to succeed me when it was time for me to retire, which I was now
ready to do. Doug Brown had done a superb job as an investor from the
time he joined Advent in 1985 until I put him in charge of our European
operations in 1990. As head of Advent in Europe for the next four years, he
had successfully led the firm's transition from one that provided services
to, and coinvested with, its network of European affiliates to a direct investment organization with its own offices on the continent. His decision
to make the European Special Situations Fund a pan-regional fund and to
focus the firm on later-stage investment in Europe had been the right one,
as the success of the ESSF clearly showed. He seemed to have both the
organizational and the strategic skills the firm would need to build on its
recent gains while expanding into new markets. And so in 1994 I said to
Doug, "Obviously you've done a great job with Europe. Why don't you be

my successor?" We made the transition in a two-step process, with Doug becoming Advent's chief investment officer at the end of 1994 and then succeeding me as CEO at the end of 1995. I remained as chairman.

Surveying Advent's position in Asia early in 1996, Brown saw problems with both strategy and organization. Minority investments had proven to be a problem for outside investors in the Southeast Asian environment, owing to the difficulty in obtaining reliable information about portfolio companies. SEAVIC had stayed intact by eschewing the riskier kinds of investments, which made it a stable platform. Yet in order to build off that platform, Brown believed, Advent was going to have to get SEAVIC to adopt a new strategy. Brown was also unhappy with Advent's management of the relationship with SEAVIC. Tony Haight was supervising the SEAVIC activity with a small team in the Boston office. Despite frequent trips to Singapore, Haight was not able to deliver the oversight Brown required. In addition, Brown could not tolerate Haight's loosey-goosey style, nor could Haight tolerate Brown's desire for control. I had given Tony a lot of rope — not quite enough to hang himself, but a lot. Brown tightened that rope considerably, which eventually led to the departure of my old pal.

Brown's first response to the problems he perceived was to set up a Hong Kong office for Advent. He then embarked upon a search for a new Advent man for Asia who would, in time, lead a direct investment organization in the region, independent of our affiliate SEAVIC. Doug went to Singapore with a headhunter from Spencer Stuart to interview people who might run an Advent office there. Naturally this made Tan Keng Boon quite nervous. Doug had a good relationship with Keng Boon, however, and finally asked him, "What if we bought SEAVIC and you ran Asia for Advent, investing our global private equity capital that we have targeted to Asia?" Keng Boon agreed, and Advent cut a deal to acquire SEAVIC late in 1996.[14]

With the acquisition of SEAVIC, Brown designed a strategy by which Advent would concentrate on larger, later-stage deals where it could take a controlling interest in companies that were benefiting from the rapid economic growth in the region. My son John, who had joined Advent in 1985, went over to Singapore to oversee the implementation of the new strategy. This was a job that ideally would have been performed by a local person with more intimate knowledge of the region. But we did not have such a person at Advent at the time.

John had a challenging assignment. He had to help develop an invest-ment model that was quite different from the one that SEAVIC had been using, and not only because of the changeover from smaller, minority in-vestments to larger, majority-share deals. Advent also wanted to focus on the region's future growth industries, develop profiles of the companies in those industries that would offer the most desirable investment op-portunities, and initiate a focused effort to call on those companies and sell them on our participation. This kind of "proactive deal sourcing" had been one of my specialties ever since my days at the First National Bank of Boston, and I had made it a cornerstone of the investment models of both TA Associates and Advent International. SEAVIC's practice, by contrast, had been simply to rely on the contacts of the various investment manag-ers for sourcing deals, and changing its attitudes and practices was not an easy thing to do.

Fortunately, John had a good working relationship with people he re-spected, Tan Keng Boon and Derrick Lee. Keng Boon and Derrick under-stood the investment model that Doug Brown had designed and made successful investments in established, profitable companies such as the Malaysian MasterCard issuer MBF Cards and the Singaporean contract manufacturer Speedy-Tech Electronics. Through his friendship with Vic-tor Fung, John was also able to assist a subsidiary of Li & Fung, Victor's family company, in its acquisition of Inchcape, a pan-Asian trading, logis-tics, and distribution-services company. This subsidiary, Li & Fung Trad-ing, later went public on the Hong Kong Stock Exchange at a substantial profit for SEAVIC and Advent.

Despite the success of these investments, however, the challenges posed by conditions in the region in the late 1990s proved difficult to overcome. Brown's investment model for Southeast Asia included buyouts, where Advent would acquire a control position. However, persuading family owners in the region to part with a controlling share of their companies was a difficult task. The lack of this type of opportunity, coupled with our reluctance to invest during the currency crisis, caused Brown to rethink his strategy for the region. We had a fully staffed direct presence in South-east Asia and Hong Kong, and yet we were reluctant to make investments there. The costs of maintaining this presence were high, the investment pace was slow, and the results in the region did not match those Advent was getting in Western Europe, central Europe, and Latin America. Doug Brown showed me the cost and performance numbers, and I agreed that they did not justify maintaining a fully staffed presence in Asia. Our investment strategy had worked, but only in a limited way, and it was time to scale back. In 2002, SEAVIC was spun back out to affiliate status.

When Advent made the decision to relinquish its ownership of SEAVIC, I did, however, argue for a continued presence in Asia, albeit a reduced one. Despite our having experienced another setback there, reminiscent of the failure of the Asia-Pacific Special Situations Fund in the early 1990s, I still believed that the region's growth prospects were simply too great to ignore. Perhaps I should not have been surprised that my arguments encountered opposition. The reduced investment activity following the SEAVIC acquisition had become apparent as early as 1999, and back then Doug Brown was already beginning to talk about withdrawing from Asia altogether. I was unhappy about this idea and let Brown know that I was. I also expressed my chagrin at Brown's unwillingness to have Advent participate in the new "Technopreneurship" program that the government of Singapore had just launched to stimulate and support high-tech entrepreneurship through improvements in education, infrastructure, regulation, and financing. Advent was facing other challenges at the time, as we shall see, but to me they did not justify pulling out of Asia.

Even after Doug Brown departed from Advent not long after the spin-off of SEAVIC (in circumstances I discuss in chapter 9), the managing directors resisted my continued entreaties to retain some kind of presence in Asia. With China and India emerging as new markets for private equity, and Japan showing signs of emerging from ten years of economic doldrums, I was not content with simply abandoning the field in Asia to others. I told the managing directors that I did not see how we could call ourselves a "global" private equity firm if we were not in Asia. Encountering their resistance to my arguments, I felt as if the denouement of my time at TA Associates was playing itself out all over again. Advent's success in its existing markets had made the partners inclined to stick with what they knew and reluctant to invest in new initiatives.

For quite a while my argument for moving forward fell on deaf ears. At managing directors' meetings I kept asking the questions: How can you ignore the most populous and fastest-growing regions of the world? If you do, how can you claim to be a global organization? The managing directors had reasonable responses, the most important being that we did not have an Advent person, steeped in the firm's culture, who was willing to embark for the Far East to manage an activity. Another reasonable response was that we needed to allocate income to our best performers in order to motivate them, and to others whom we wished to bring on board. After all, private equity is a competitive industry, and Advent's well-trained people are always targets for acquisition by rival firms.

As the managing directors advanced these quite reasonable arguments for staying on the sidelines in Asia, however, they for a long time overlooked the best argument for plunging back in. The case for returning to Asia became persuasive only after this team that had compiled such an impressive record in other markets began increasingly to appreciate what it had accomplished, and to feel the self-confidence that its past achievements amply justified.

As a result of their confidence in themselves, in one another, and in the firm itself, the managing directors have now made the decision to invest in future geographic expansion, a costly exercise that will reduce their remuneration. Plans for a new office and fund for Japan (with seasoned Advent professionals who have agreed to relocate there), investments in India that will lead to a permanent presence, a new office in Kiev, Ukraine, and discussion of a proposed emerging markets fund are all signs of a new willingness to take risks and to realize the full potential of the company. I believe the managing directors have realized that the value of the franchise and the investment capital the firm will attract will be enhanced by expanding the global footprint, and that they can use these added resources to achieve even greater success. Investing in infrastructure and, even more importantly, people over many years has built Advent into the firm it is today and is the key to success for any venture capital or private equity organization.

At this time I am reasonably sanguine that Advent will achieve the objectives that I set for it in the beginning, now nearly twenty-five years ago, when I set the goal for Advent International to become the most successful provider of venture capital and private equity to companies throughout the world, in both developed and emerging markets. The platform is in place, and Advent's recent success at raising $14 billion for its Global Private Equity VI, LAPEF IV, ACEE IV, and Japan funds will enable that platform to be improved and expanded. The managing directors are able and highly motivated, the units are performing at a high level, and there is a willingness to take on additional challenges. Bringing everyone to this point has not been easy, but the goal line is within reach.

Meanwhile, I have now spent over fifty years of my life trying to use venture capital and private equity to bring economic self-determination and the chance for greater prosperity everywhere from my native New England to Western Europe, central and Eastern Europe, Latin America, Southeast Asia, and beyond. Has my vision for global venture capital, inspired by the foresight and boldness of the Marshall Plan, actually been realized? Perhaps the most one can say is that it has been realized in some respects but not in others. Venture capital in what is now the usual sense of the term has spread from Boston and Silicon Valley to most countries in the developed world, although it has succeeded only in one country outside the United States — Israel — in establishing a technology sector as vibrant as that in America. Whether the same thing can happen in Europe (where industries such as biotechnology and clean energy hold out promise) or parts of Asia remains to be seen. Private equity, for its part, has found increasingly favorable conditions worldwide and has clearly just begun to reach its potential for helping companies to become more efficient and growth-oriented in today's competitive global economy.

Thus the work of using venture capital and private equity to help countries everywhere to build robust private sectors and become more prosperous and self-sufficient continues today. I take pride in having founded two successful venture capital/private equity firms, helped launch the careers of many people who have gone on to success in the industry, and contributed to constructing a global infrastructure for venture capital and private equity that will enable others, I hope, to build on what my colleagues and I have accomplished. In Part II of this book, I discuss what it will take for those who come after us to sustain this vision for venture capital.

PART II

SUSTAINING THE VISION

# CHAPTER 8

# VENTURE CAPITAL, PRIVATE EQUITY,
# AND THE ART OF ADDING VALUE

· · ·

From my days at the First National Bank of Boston in the late 1950s and early 1960s, up through the years when I founded and built TA Associates, put together the beginnings of an international network of venture capital firms, and then started Advent International, I have been motivated by a simple vision. I have always thought that by using capital and management assistance to build profitable companies that create jobs and advance prosperity, I could make a real contribution to economic well-being, first at home in New England and eventually around the world. As I learned the venture capital business and then established TA Associates, I had two goals. I wanted to help launch and build innovative companies that could become part of a new economic base for New England, and to help small established companies in the region to become more efficient and grow. Later on, I dreamed of making Advent International the catalyst for something like a global, privately directed Marshall Plan. I thought that by investing company by company, country by country, on its own or in partnership with multilateral institutions such as the International Finance Corporation, the European Bank for Reconstruction and Development, and the Inter-American Development Bank, a global investment firm like Advent could contribute to economic progress the way the Marshall Plan had assisted the recovery of postwar Europe.

My vision of venture capital and private equity as tools for stimulating economic growth and creating widespread prosperity was shared in one form or another by many early proponents and practitioners of venture capital in the United States and overseas. We wanted to make money, but we saw money as the reward for creating economic benefits that would be

shared by many others. By and large this is still the goal of venture capitalists and private equity managers today. Over the last twenty or twenty-five
years, however, the successes of venture capital and private equity have
changed these businesses in certain ways. Once an obscure cottage industry, venture capital, in the wake of the Internet boom of the 1990s, has
become famous mostly for the sizable fortunes it has created, including
those of now-famous venture capitalists such as Tom Perkins and John
Doerr. More recently, amid the buyout boom of the early 2000s, private
equity investors such as Stephen Schwarzman and David Bonderman became the new celebrities of the financial world,[1] and private equity (along
with hedge funds) was the career of choice for the brightest and most financially ambitious MBA students. While the fame and fortune that have
accrued to venture capital and private equity are no doubt welcome in
some ways, they have, however, created certain distortions both in the industries themselves and in public perceptions of them.

One such distortion has arisen from the very significant increase in the
financial rewards available to venture capital and private equity managers. I believe that the enormous sums of money that venture capital and
private equity managers were able to make in the boom years affected the
motivation of many practitioners (a subject that I take up in more detail
in the next chapter). Meanwhile, amid the fame and, sometimes, notori-
ety that venture capital and private equity managers have gained in recent
years, the public has been given a distorted view of what they actually do
when investing in a company.

Now that venture capital has become celebrated for its role in launching so many of the great technology companies of today, people often ex-
aggerate the contribution that venture capitalists make to the companies
in which they invest. In the case of private equity — a term that was unknown when I began providing growth capital to mature companies and
participating in buyouts in the 1960s — the opposite is true. In the last
twenty-five years, private equity has evolved from an obscure asset class to
a mainstream investment vehicle and a powerful force for efficiency and
growth in the global economy. Instead of being celebrated as a tool for
helping companies become more profitable and prepare themselves for
growth, however, private equity has recently met with hostility, both in
the United States and abroad. A leading German politician has called foreign private equity investors a "swarm of locusts." Trade union leaders in
Britain and the United States have equated private equity with ruthless

asset stripping, cost slashing, and job losses, and leaders of the industry have been pilloried as a new generation of robber barons. While there are legitimate grounds for criticizing the industry, to paint private equity investors as villains is just as simplistic and misguided as to celebrate venture capitalists as heroes. The real economic heroes, in my view, are the successful entrepreneurs and business leaders whom investors of both types help to succeed.

Both venture capitalists and private equity investors can and do earn handsome rewards when they do their jobs well. They deserve these rewards when they pick good companies to invest in and, especially, when they add value to their investments. Adding value is the sine qua non of both types of investment. The needs of early-stage companies differ from those of mature ones, and the difference between being a minority investor (as venture capitalists generally are) and having a control position (as private equity owners do) means that private equity managers can have a more direct impact than venture capitalists on the fortunes of their portfolio companies. Nevertheless, the ways in which venture capitalists and private equity managers add value to their portfolio companies are similar in many respects. Beyond the capital they provide, both types of investors assist companies by furnishing management advice and contacts, helping to set goals and monitor progress, and enabling companies to achieve liquidity when they have reached the next level of development. They are investors who are also problem solvers for the enterprises in which they invest.

While recognizing these similarities, however, it is important to recognize that venture capitalists do not necessarily add value to the extent that many people, including some venture capitalists themselves, believe that they do. And private equity investors — at least the good ones — add value in ways that most people today do not sufficiently appreciate. In both cases, adding value is more an art than a science, difficult to codify and mastered through hands-on experience rather than analysis and study. It is instructive to look at each type of investment in turn to see how both types add value and consider why misunderstandings have arisen about both.

## ADDING VALUE IN VENTURE INVESTING

I began my career as a banker, but when I started lending to young high-tech companies I learned that these enterprises needed more than money. They needed management help. Few of the scientists starting companies in the 1950s and 1960s in the little garages off E Street in East Cambridge knew anything about commercializing a piece of technology or running a business. Thus I discovered that my colleagues and I needed to add value in various ways, which entails a certain kind of relationship with the entrepreneur that is different from that of a lender. As a banker, you track the performance of the borrowing company because you want to get repaid, but the relationship is an arm's-length one. If the company misses a payment you get right on it, but otherwise your involvement is fairly passive. When you make an equity investment, however, you're an owner. You have a different stake in the game, so you are tracking the company much more closely and need to be involved in the major management challenges that arise.

As I have related in chapter 1, when I began finding equity investors for companies in my loan portfolio at the First National Bank of Boston and then became a full-fledged venture capitalist, I learned that entrepreneurs often resented the idea of an outsider coming in, taking a piece of their company, and having some say in how it was run in exchange for capital. We venture capitalists had to show them that we could offer real help in the form of advice, contacts, and a willingness to persevere beyond the point where a short-term investor might throw in the towel. While venture capitalists generally add value in such ways, it is important to remember, however, that even the best of them add value only at the margin. One of the finest compliments I have received as a venture capitalist came from Bill Frusztajer, the founder of Crystalonics and the BBF Group, who has written that while I provided "sound management counsel" and "useful contacts in the financial community," I was also aware of my limitations and "did not interfere in the day-to-day operations of the new company."[2]

This caveat applies especially to technology-driven companies. The claim that a venture capitalist can do a lot to help a young, technology-based company is in most cases wishful thinking. The venture capitalist is in the hands of the entrepreneur and the decisions he makes. The entrepreneur is either going to hit the market with the right product at the right time or he is going to miss it, and there is not a lot he or anyone else can do to recover if he misses the target. The technology has to work, the product that comes out of the technology has to work at the right price, and the market has to be ready for it. What really distinguishes a good venture capitalist is the ability to spot a promising company in a promising market whose management is capable of executing the business plan. Bad management can wreck a good company. Good management can save a questionable company and turn it around. A bit of luck is useful as well.

Although this is the reality, a certain mystique has grown up around venture capitalists, as if venture investing were a kind of alchemy. A lot of this mystique was created by the founder of the industry, Georges Doriot, who deserves every bit of the credit for inventing modern venture capital but who was also a bit of a showman. Doriot and his staff were very serious about all the good things they were doing for their portfolio companies. ARD's office was like a movie set, filled with earnest young men convinced that they were determining the future of American business.

The limits of what a venture capitalist can do to foster the development and success of innovative technology-based companies are evident in the overall success rate of venture investing. A venture capital firm like Kleiner Perkins is justly celebrated for having backed companies such as Google, Amazon, and Sun Microsystems, and the dream of funding the next breakout company is what motivates many venture capitalists and their limited partners. However, while it is true that venture capitalists in the top tier have produced superior returns, it must be remembered that not all managers are in the top tier, and many produced marginal returns, if that, when the Internet bubble burst. There is a wide spread between the best and the average performers in this asset class. Venture capital has played a crucial role in making the United States the most fertile breeding ground in the world for innovative technology companies. But venture capital is only part of a larger constellation in which many elements have to come together to foster innovation and its successful commercialization.

When venture capitalists do add value to early-stage technology companies, moreover, they often do so by offering the same kind of management advice, based on the venture capitalist's own business experience, that mature nontechnology companies sometimes require. In the late 1960s, when I founded TA Associates, we still used the term *venture capital* to mean investment in small companies with growth prospects, whether they were start-ups or established businesses, in technology-related or traditional industries, and worked with all kinds of companies in similar ways. The early funds managed by TA Associates included not only fledgling technology-based companies but also more mature companies in established markets that needed capital for expansion or to retire a founding shareholder. We added value to these later-stage investments in much the same way that we did for the start-ups. For example, in 1970 TAA acquired a stake in New

England Business Service (now known as NEBS), a supplier of business forms through the mail to small businesses and one of the best-managed companies in which I have ever invested. The founder of the company was selling his stock, and NEBS wanted a partner who would not interfere in the running of the business but could exercise good judgment as a board member. During the recession of the early 1970s, management wanted to increase the company's direct-mail marketing, but a couple of the directors objected. I thought it made sense to try to grab market share in the midst of an economic downturn, so I made the case for what management wanted to do and succeeded in convincing the other directors. The direct-mail campaign was successful, and NEBS significantly increased its market share. I believe that this kind of judgment is why the company wanted me on the board. What I provided was just good business sense.

There were also times when I was called upon to give advice on such essential strategic matters as acquisitions and divestitures. At Adams-Russell, a diversified company in which TA Associates invested in the late 1970s, I convinced my fellow board members to divide the operating divisions — one in cable television and the other in defense electronics — into two separate companies to better reflect the values in each division. The cable division was later sold to Cablevision and the defense division to MA/COM, a unit of Tyco Electronics, for a handsome return. As a director of the publicly listed medical-technology Damon Corporation, in which I invested for Bessemer Securities in the early 1960s,[3] I enthusiastically supported the spin-off of a subsidiary that produced monoclonal antibodies. The Damon shareholders received shares of the spin-off company, which they were free to sell, while retaining their share in the parent company. By separating the two businesses, we gave the public a clearer idea of what they owned. The shareholders of a lot of the conglomerates that were formed in the 1960s didn't really understand what they owned, and I was a big advocate of simplifying things. Little did I realize, at the time, that these kinds of strategic decisions would one day be at the center of an industry for which we did not have a term at the time but that today is known as private equity.

## ADDING VALUE IN PRIVATE EQUITY INVESTING

Private equity investment has its origins in the merchant banking business, which has been around since the Middle Ages and was instrumental in the rise of industrialism in nineteenth-century Europe and America.

The acquisition of a company with borrowed capital — known today as a leveraged buyout (LBO) — was called a "bootstrap" deal in the days of John D. Rockefeller and J. P. Morgan. Private equity in the contemporary sense, an asset class distinct from venture capital in that it makes equity investments in mature companies to bring about growth or restructuring, came to the fore in the mid-1970s when Henry Kravis and George Roberts joined Jerome Kohlberg to form Kohlberg Kravis Roberts (KKR). At about the same time my old friend Tom Lee, who had succeeded me as head of the High Technology Lending Group at the First National Bank of Boston in the early 1960s, formed Thomas H. Lee Partners in Boston to develop leveraged buyouts as an investment strategy. Other firms joined the fray in the 1970s and 1980s, including Forstmann Little, Bain Capital, the Blackstone Group, and the Carlyle Group. By the time the public woke up to this phenomenon — thanks largely to the best-seller *Barbarians at the Gate*, which chronicled KKR's $31 billion buyout of RJR Nabisco in 1988 — private equity was already a huge industry and beginning to spread beyond the United States.

As I have noted, TA Associates participated in buyouts as well as early-stage investments in the 1960s. Other early entrants into what is now called private equity followed the same strategy. Warburg Pincus, founded in 1966 and one of the pioneering firms in the asset class, provided everything from seed capital to expansion capital and also participated in buyouts. In Boston, venture capital and private equity as we now think of them began to develop into distinct industries only in the mid-1980s, as firms increasingly specialized in one or the other. One reason for this change was fund size. As managers raised more and more capital, they concentrated on larger and larger deals, taking them out of the start-up and emerging company sector. A $500 million or $1 billion fund simply could not make and monitor a series of million-dollar investments. Managers of large funds came to prefer making a few big bets on mature companies with track records to analyze rather than making a multitude of small bets on start-ups. At TA Associates, the number of struggling early-stage companies in the firm's portfolio in the late 1980s finally convinced Kevin Landry that investing in mature companies with revenues and profits was both less risky and more financially rewarding than investing in start-ups. By 1990, TAA was out of the venture business altogether.

At Advent International, which I founded in 1984, my vision of using venture capital to spark the creation of innovative, technology-based companies in Western Europe soon came up against the obstacles I have described in Part I with regard to early-stage investing in most places outside the United States. At the same time, economic conditions in both Europe and Asia were creating opportunities for successful investing in mature companies there. In Western Europe, the successful negotiation of the Maastricht Treaty had been foreseen in the 1980s by companies that knew they would have to rationalize their operations and spin off non-core businesses in order to compete within a more integrated Europe. This presented an opportunity for private equity investors who were able to provide strategic advice and management assistance as well as financial capital. We saw the opportunity in the late 1980s, and our European Special Situations Fund, raised in 1989, was invested entirely in mature companies rather than start-ups. We saw another such opportunity in the economic expansion taking place in Southeast Asia in the 1980s and early 1990s, where we observed that the extension of credit to local companies by local and international banks was approaching its limits and that equity investment would eventually be required. In responding to these opportunities, Advent effectively became a buyout firm in Europe at the beginning of the 1990s, and in Asia in the middle of the decade.

Meanwhile, private equity was acquiring a dubious reputation, inspired in part by the huge fortunes at stake in transactions such as the RJR Nabisco buyout and other speculative deals that were part of the heated merger and takeover activity of the 1980s. The approach to buyouts in that period was not always constructive. Debt from commercial banks and junk bonds sometimes overleveraged balance sheets and triggered the sale of profitable divisions that had previously been competitive in world markets. Cash flow was diverted from expenditures for R&D and product development and used to service debt.

Despite the recklessness that some LBO artists exhibited in the 1980s, however, firms such as KKR and Forstmann Little had a positive impact and helped fix many companies that needed restructuring. In the 1950s and 1960s, new antitrust legislation and the stock market's emphasis on growth in earnings per share had encouraged many corporations to diversify into a wide range of unrelated industries. Corporations did not understand many of the businesses they acquired, and investors did not understand what they were buying. As a result, many public corporations were trading at a discount to what their assets were actually worth. This created an opportunity for investors including private equity firms to acquire companies with undervalued assets, sell off the unproductive ones to owners who could run them profitably, and use the proceeds to eliminate the debt they had assumed in buying the company. Private equity firms themselves could profit handsomely, as they deserved to do, from unlocking value in this way. In sum, the leveraged buyouts of the 1970s and 1980s created much economic value through acts of what the economist Joseph Schumpeter called "creative destruction."

Today, however, private equity firms find fewer opportunities to unlock value by breaking up overly diversified firms, especially in the United States, for the simple reason that fewer of them exist. When Advent International began investing in Europe and Asia in the 1980s, both of these regions had many family-owned companies that needed to make the transition to professional management as well as public companies that had been shielded from competition and needed to become more efficient. To some extent this is still true in Western Europe and Southeast Asia today, now that global competition is forcing companies everywhere to rein in costs and use their capital as productively as possible. However, in the United States and, increasingly, in other parts of the developed world, it is not enough simply to restructure by cost cutting. Most companies are already outsourcing to regions with lower labor costs. Private equity managers have picked most of the low-hanging fruit. Moreover, today's fiercely competitive global environment also means that being a low-cost producer provides, at most, only a temporary advantage. Companies must find other, more sustainable sources of competitive advantage in order to survive and prosper. For this reason, private equity firms can generally no longer rely merely on cost cutting if they want to sell the companies in which they invest at the best possible prices. Instead, they need to be able to add value by helping their portfolio companies improve performance along many different dimensions.

The ability to add value in this way is especially important with the midmarket companies in which Advent invests. Although this segment of the private equity industry receives little attention from the business press, midmarket private equity firms perform a very valuable role in helping midsize companies to remain competitive. Such companies find it more difficult than do larger players to dominate their industries, grow market share, and absorb weaker rivals in order to achieve economies of scale and scope. They therefore need to grow or find a way to protect their markets by "locking in" customers or raising barriers to entry for new competitors through product or service differentiation. They need good strategies to achieve such goals, along with the ability to execute them. This is where the value-adding activity of private equity comes in.

Best-practice private equity investing today means a much more active style of ownership than the hands-off, financial engineering approach that produced good returns for investors in the 1970s and '80s and during the boom of the early 2000s—returns that, until recently, were enabled by a plentiful supply of inexpensive debt. During the recent buyout boom, the easy availability of debt at low rates of interest and with few restrictions on borrowers (e.g., in "covenant-lite" loans) encouraged private equity investors to increase the amounts of leverage they put on their portfolio companies, thus increasing the potential returns. Now that the days of such cheap, easily available debt are over—perhaps never to return in the lifetime of anyone now in the industry—private equity firms will no longer be able to rely on leverage, to the extent that they have in the past, in order to get the returns their investors have come to expect. To the extent that financial engineering remains an aspect of private equity investment, moreover, it has long since become a commodity. Everyone in the industry now knows the same techniques, which MBA students have learned in business school. In addition, any gains to be realized from financial engineering are known beforehand and priced into private equity firms' bids for deals, which limits their ability to realize significant gains without significantly improving a company.

Adding value in more hands-on ways, in turn, requires involvement in the messier aspects of a business that cannot be captured in off-the-shelf financial formulas. At Advent, we see the value-adding function in private equity investing as having four components: sector expertise, operational insights, exhaustive business plans, and exemplary corporate governance. Beyond these four components, our approach involves taking on challenges that others might avoid, becoming deeply involved in the hard work of transforming companies, and showing persistence.

It took a lot of persistence to pull off what turned out to be the best deal in Advent's European Special Situations Fund: the 1995 privatization of Deutsche Waggonbau AG (DWA), the Berlin-based railroad car manufacturer that was one of the last big-ticket assets that the German government sold off following the reunification of Germany in October 1990. Before the fall of the Berlin Wall and the subsequent collapse of the Soviet empire, DWA had supplied railcars to the Soviet Union and other

COMECON countries. It made the cars that ran between St. Petersburg and Vladivostok, from Baku to Arkhangelsk. It had twenty-five thousand employees when the Iron Curtain fell in 1989 and was a real socialist dinosaur. When the Soviet Union collapsed in 1991, the demand for DWA's railcars disappeared overnight, leaving the company with its twenty-five thousand employees, ten plants, and no customers.

The restructuring and privatization of the state-owned businesses of East Germany was managed by a trust fund called the Treuhandanstalt, established by the East German government in June 1990. At DWA, the Treuhand stepped in and undertook a restructuring that shut down three plants and reduced the number of employees from twenty-five thousand to about seven thousand. The dramatically downsized company put up a valiant effort to survive. While the East Germans had no experience running a business in a market economy, they had excellent skilled labor including well-trained engineers who were used to improvising. They wanted the company to succeed, and managed in just a few years to dramatically change their product portfolio, developing double-decker railcars and smaller cars for regional trains that were innovative and low cost. On the strength of this effort, they landed a few major supply contracts with Deutsche Bahn, the German national railway system.

In March 1994, the Treuhand asked Advent International to take a look at Deutsche Waggonbau because we had bought a small rail supply business the year before. It turned out that thirty-nine bidders had already looked at the company and either passed on the opportunity after seeing the due diligence results or failed to agree on terms with the Treuhand. The asking price was only about 28 percent of the revenue generated the previous year but was also roughly equal to the negative earnings before interest, taxes, depreciation, and amortization (EBITDA) for that year. The company was hemorrhaging cash — about $100 million annually — and was a disaster. A small group of West German executives had recently joined DWA and were transferring necessary commercial know-how. But when our people looked at the numbers and the considerable uncertainties the company faced, the situation did not look promising.

Nevertheless, our lead team member for the negotiations, Chris Neizert, wanted to see if a deal was possible. In a long series of conversations with officials from the Treuhand and with DWA's new CEO, Chris developed the level of confidence necessary for the long process of drawing up a restructuring plan and selling it to the various constituencies involved. Chris brought an initial plan to Doug Brown, who said that although there might be something here worth pursuing, the restructuring plan needed to be more detailed and have better cost figures. So Chris, Doug, and another Advent team member, the resourceful John Walker, spent a tremendous amount of time hammering out a restructuring plan that would reduce DWA's head count from seven thousand to three thousand employees and close two more plants. The only problem was what it was going to cost to do it. Doug finally told Chris, "I'm sorry, but even if the government gave us the company for nothing, we can't put this much money into it." It looked like that was the end of the deal.

Chris Neizert wasn't ready to give up, however. He went back to the Treuhand, showed them the restructuring plan, and convinced them to put up the money it would take to restructure the business. Advent offered to buy the company at less than 10 percent of the original asking price and split the profit from its eventual sale 50/50 with the government. It took a full year to convince the German federal government, regional and local politicians, the unions, and key decision makers in German industry to accept our plan, but in the end they agreed to it.

When Advent acquired DWA in 1995, we were lucky to be able to persuade Otto Wolff von Amerongen, whom Helmut Kohl had asked to become the chairman of the company after reunification, to stay on in that post. Whenever delicate issues arose, Wolff (who made a name for himself in postwar Germany by opening up trade relations between West Germany and the Soviet Union) was able to make a few calls to the right people. Both Wolff and DWA's CEO, Peter Witt, worked well with Chris and the rest of the Advent team. Meanwhile, DWA started focusing on its new products such as the double-decker railcars, for which there was increasing demand in Western Europe because train ridership was up and stations weren't big enough to accommodate longer trains. All of a sudden the market for double-decker railcars took off, and DWA was the market leader.

In 1997, the Canadian transportation equipment manufacturer Bombardier Inc. approached Advent about buying DWA. We had not planned to sell the company that quickly, but when Bombardier approached us we came to the conclusion that an IPO would not be the solution for DWA, given the ongoing global consolidation of the rail vehicle industry. And so we sold DWA to Bombardier in 1998, making fifteen times our original investment. This transaction was a great deal for Bombardier as well, because it bought the company — which was now debt-free, profitable, and had a large order book stretching over four years — for a price equal to the cash DWA held.

Meanwhile, the German government earned more than it had hoped from the sale. Although its share of the proceeds didn't recoup its whole investment in the DWA restructuring, the government was very happy to have achieved its objectives in backing the deal. DWA was one of very few large privatizations in East Germany that worked out very well for both the company and the government — many Western European companies in this period acquired East German firms in order to shut them down before moving on to build new low-cost facilities elsewhere. Through Advent's assistance, DWA remained as an industrial anchor in a region of Germany that would be heavily deindustrialized by the end of the privatization process. Helmut Kohl, the German chancellor at the time, was personally proud to have been part of saving DWA. Today the company has six plants in Germany (having added one since we sold the firm to Bombardier) as well as operations in the Czech Republic, Switzerland, and Russia. As for Advent, the deal not only earned us a sizable profit but firmly established our brand in the German market. During the negotiations about our restructuring plan for DWA and while we owned the company, we received strong support from the German metalworkers' union, which created a relationship between Advent and the German unions that has proved beneficial in later deals.

A hands-on approach to private equity investing that generates growth and creates jobs is also well illustrated by a second deal that Advent undertook in a postcommunist setting, this time in Romania. In 2003, Advent acquired Terapia, a manufacturer of branded generic and over-the-counter drugs. A familiar name in Romania since the 1920s, originally for its chemicals business, Terapia had been privatized in 1996 and listed on the Bucharest Stock Exchange in 1997. When Advent first looked at the company in 2002, it was profitable with just over $32 million in revenue and had become the third-largest pharmaceuticals manufacturer in Romania. The country had a rapidly growing market. Rising GDPs and purchasing power, improved health education and living standards, and higher life expectancies were increasing the demand for pharmaceuticals in formerly communist central Europe at that time. Romania had one of the lowest per capita expenditures for pharmaceuticals in the region but the potential for substantial market growth. Given Terapia's already strong reputation and the many acquisition opportunities created by a highly fragmented domestic pharmaceutical industry, this situation seemed an attractive opportunity for a private equity investor.

The major risk that an investor in Terapia would face was of a kind that would cause most to run away as fast as possible. Terapia's pharmaceuticals business was only a relatively small part of a company that had been primarily a chemicals manufacturer. Communist governments ran such businesses with absolutely no regard for environmental hazards. Not long after Terapia was privatized and then became a public company, there had been an explosion in the chemicals manufacturing facility, which the management had then simply padlocked. Whatever potential the company had, there was a large amount of negative value, as well, with a shuttered chemicals plant that clearly posed environmental problems. For most private equity investors, just the words "environmental liability" would be enough to put an end to any discussion. Our Advent team, however, led by Joanna James, the head of our central European operations, and Emma Popa-Radu from our Bucharest office, saw both an opportunity in Terapia's potential and a discount in value, given the problem with the chemicals plant. They also figured that if they took a good, hard look at the risk they could quantify and manage it.

When Joanna went to look at the company for the first time in January 2002, the CEO showed her the chemicals manufacturing facility and said that he and his management team were trying to figure out what to do with it. "Have you thought about dynamite?" Joanna asked. As our team considered its likely strategy for the company, getting out of the chemicals business seemed a fairly obvious move. However, we would still need to decommission and demolish the chemicals plant on the company's site and do the cleanup, at a cost we estimated at $10 million. Fortunately, both the potential cost of remediation and the potential liability were significantly reduced by the finding, when the site was tested, that contaminated soil was clustered mostly in isolated "hot spots."

Having satisfied itself, after two separate rounds of due diligence on the environmental issues, that the risk was manageable, Advent acquired 90.7 percent of Terapia in a tender offer to buy shares listed on the Bucharest Stock Exchange in August 2003. In February 2004 it launched a second tender offer to buy more shares and delist the company; subsequent purchases of shares from the remaining minority shareholders eventually increased Advent's stake to approximately 97 percent. Our total investment of $49.5 million was funded about 30 percent by debt and the rest by equity.[4] This was the first leveraged buyout in formerly communist central Europe.

The decommissioning and demolition of the chemicals plant went smoothly. The sale of scrap metal from the machinery removed from the facility covered the cost of the demolition work, which helped bring the cost of remediation below our $10 million estimate. Once the demolition began, Advent began receiving offers from commercial buyers for the land being cleared; the fact that the land itself had value would later help us shop Terapia to bidders, since it would help mitigate the risk for a future buyer of the company. Overall, the idea of quantifying and managing the environmental risk had proven to be a good one.

The next most important issue Joanna and Emma had to deal with was Terapia's management and governance. After the company had gone public in 1997, the Romanian investment funds that had accumulated large stakes in Terapia, and whose representatives sat on the board of directors, had removed the old communist-era management and brought in a new management team. The new managers had done a reasonably good job with the pharmaceuticals business, creating a strong sales and marketing force and developing an attractive pipeline of new products for the domestic market as well as for selected export markets, including Russia. However, Joanna soon came to believe that the CEO, whose management style was the dictatorial one of communist-era managers, was not up to the task of leading the continued change and improvement the company required.

One of the two independent directors whom Joanna had recruited for the Terapia board was Stephen Stead, an Englishman whose experience in the pharmaceuticals industry included serving as managing director of Boehringer Mannheim in the Czech Republic and later as a consultant to Valeant Pharmaceuticals. Stead had also worked for GlaxoSmithKline, where he had been responsible for countries including Russia, Romania, and Bulgaria. He had a global perspective on industry trends, valuable and extensive local knowledge, and contacts. When Joanna and Emma talked to the board about their desire to replace the CEO, Stead, to their surprise, volunteered to take on the job himself. Meanwhile, Advent's acquisition of Terapia had enabled us to dramatically improve the quality of the board by removing a group of institutional investors who had been concerned only with protecting their own interests, replacing them with our own people and a group of competent independent directors.

The strategy for Terapia developed by the new board and CEO was to de-emphasize international expansion for the time being and focus on becoming the dominant producer and supplier in the Romanian market. Competition was keen on the domestic front, both from local producers and from multinationals eager to break into this rapidly growing market. Our team made the decision to build an advantage over domestic rivals, and compete against the multinationals, by leapfrogging normal development cycles and investing to meet EU and global product standards as rapidly as possible, even though Romania had not yet joined the EU. (It would do so in 2007.)

Advent's new strategy for Terapia had three components: focusing the company on core competencies, continuing to revitalize the product portfolio, and building an even more effective commercial division. A focus on core competencies meant exiting the chemicals business, which had previously manufactured active ingredients for the company's pharmaceutical products in processes that were polluting and not cost-effective. Pharmaceuticals manufacturing would be kept in-house, but the ingredients would now be sourced from suppliers in Asia and Western Europe. The product portfolio, which was to remain focused on Terapia's four core areas of expertise (cardiovascular, respiratory and central nervous system, alimentary tract, and musculoskeletal), was improved and expanded through three means: increased investment in marketing and R&D, licensing of products from abroad, and the acquisition of two smaller generics manufacturers. To ensure that this investment resulted in the desired increase in revenues, the company increased the size of its sales team fivefold.

While executing this strategy, Terapia also carried out a number of improvements in its financial operations, including a successful effort to enforce stricter payment terms from distributors. The decision to meet EU and global best-practice criteria also reinforced Terapia's competitive advantage vis-à-vis its less credible domestic competitors. Despite the increased expenditure this entailed, Terapia maintained its cost advantages in production and distribution over foreign competitors as a result of low labor costs and shorter supply lines to local consumers. Meanwhile, by late 2005, the decommissioning and demolition of the old chemicals plant had been completed, and a broader site cleanup was well under way. Gross revenues for the year 2005 were $80 million and EBITDA was $27 million, representing approximately threefold increases in each number over the period since Advent's acquisition of the company in 2003.

In March 2006, Advent sold Terapia to Ranbaxy, the India-based multinational pharmaceuticals company, for $324 million. We consider our investment in Terapia to have been a great success not only because we made nearly ten times our money on the sale but because we added real value to the company through intensive, hands-on involvement. Of the 9.6 times our cost that we realized on our investment in Terapia, over half (5.4 times) was accounted for by organic increase in earnings over the period we owned the company, and only one-eighth came from debt paydown and refinancing. Since its acquisition of the company, Ranbaxy has been using Terapia as the base of its expansion into Europe.

Examples like Deutsche Waggonbau and Terapia show that private equity investing by responsible and forward-looking practitioners is not about financial engineering and asset stripping. It is about taking advantage of the benefits of private ownership — the ability not just to use higher levels of debt but also to focus managers on long-term strategy, help them execute the strategy, and monitor their performance closely — to improve companies' long-term prospects.[5] Competitive, growing, sustainable companies preserve and create jobs, increase tax revenues, and raise standards of living — dramatically so in emerging markets such as those of central and Eastern Europe. Private equity investors who help achieve these goals can take pride in what they do.

In the United States as well as in Europe, however, private equity investing has been criticized for practices that do deserve the scrutiny they have received. Buyouts of companies including Warner Music in the United States and the Debenhams department store group in Britain saw private equity managers take sizable amounts of money out of the acquired companies while loading them up with debt, slashing costs in ways that undermined long-term competitiveness, and, not incidentally, making significant reductions in employment and/or employee pay and benefits. In the Warner Music buyout, the private equity managers used dividend recapitalizations — a technique in which borrowed money is used to pay dividends to investors, sometimes for legitimate reasons but often prematurely. When the resulting level of debt is excessive, it restricts the ability of the company to compete and, as we have seen in the current economic downturn, can lead to bankruptcy. Meanwhile, the investors have received an early return of capital and needn't concern themselves about what happens to the company over the long term.[6]

Criticisms of such practices are legitimate, even though the virtual disappearance of the market for LBO debt has done more to root out such excesses than any amount of regulation or self-regulation could ever have achieved. Meanwhile, those who have brought disfavor to the private equity industry by stripping assets from companies in which they have invested, leveraging these companies to pay themselves and their investors exorbitant dividends, and weakening the competitive position of these firms while adding no value have done a great injustice to those of us who have worked hard and constructively to add value. Many of us who have spent a lifetime improving the efficiency and growth potential of our portfolio companies are now being lumped together with hedge fund managers. This is hard to take. To be put in the same category with computer jockeys and "quants" who have never added value to a company is the ultimate insult. My fear, in the wake of recent events, is that new regulations will ensnare those who have been investing wisely and adding value along with those who have been doing the opposite. The resulting harm will be incalculable. The skills of private equity managers who can add value to their portfolio companies are desperately needed at a time like the present, when so much financial and operating restructuring is required. These managers must not be denied the opportunity to manage our economy out of the predicament in which we now find ourselves.[7]

It is my contention, moreover, that those private equity managers who have recklessly inflicted damage on their portfolio companies to benefit themselves are a minority. Unfortunately, however, that does not mean that the majority have succeeded in improving their portfolio companies as much as they have boasted that they do. A recent study, the first of its kind, by two professors at the University of Pennsylvania's Wharton School examined 238 private equity funds raised between 1992 and 2006 and found that, on average, managers of buyout funds earned approximately twice as much in management fees as they did in carried interest. In other words, the performance of the average private equity manager's investments accounted for only a third of that manager's compensation.[8] This certainly reduces the incentives for a focus on adding value to portfolio companies. It also makes a mockery of a principle in which I have always believed, which is that the financial gains that venture capital and private equity managers realize should be the reward for helping to build profitable and sustainable enterprises, not an end in themselves.[9]

Other recent research, by the McKinsey Global Institute, has shown that only the top-quartile private equity funds outperform the public markets, while also finding that these top performers — but only they — actually improve the performance of the companies in which they invest.[10] Those private equity firms that are not top performers must therefore learn how to introduce better management into the companies in which they invest (if, indeed, these also-ran firms manage to survive the recent crash at all). Indeed the ability to add value to portfolio companies will be an increasingly important factor in the returns private equity managers can earn for their investors now that the era of cheap, easily available debt that fueled the buyout boom of 2002–2007 has ended. The use of leverage alone, even when credit becomes available again, will not yield the returns that it has in the past, because debt will be significantly more expensive. Indeed many of the best opportunities for private equity firms in the near future will come from buying companies that were overleveraged during the boom — or companies that are being sold off by their parent firms in order to raise money to pay off their debt — and then, after adding value to these acquisitions, preparing them for sale when the economy and the markets recover from the present downturn. To take advantage of such opportunities, however, private equity managers who are used to relying on financial engineering will have to roll up their sleeves and make substantial improvements in the companies in which they invest, staying with the job as long as necessary.[11]

In the climate of suspicion in which private equity now operates, it is also worth saying a word about the globalization of the industry, which Advent pioneered, and its relation to the issue of adding value. Much of the recent opposition to private equity (in Britain and Australia, for example, where proposed acquisitions by private equity firms of Sainsbury's and Qantas Airlines, respectively, galvanized the industry's critics) has expressed a sense that admired domestic companies were falling into the hands of foreigners. The rise of sovereign wealth funds as significant investors in private equity has given additional force to such fears. Yet private equity has become a global industry today not just because the free flow of capital across borders enables private equity firms to acquire companies almost anywhere in the world with capital raised from investors almost anywhere in the world but because a global presence has actually become imperative for adding value in much private equity investment today.

The Terapia story, for example, shows how important a global perspective and the ability to tap resources on a global basis have become for private equity firms in an era of intense global competition. In our work with

Terapia in Romania, it was crucial that Advent was able to bring in an expatriate CEO who had extensive global *and* local knowledge. The kind of global reach that made this possible is now a critical success factor in virtually every investment that Advent makes. In our successful restructuring of Moeller, a German manufacturer of electronics components that we acquired in 2003 and put on a path to growth in only two years, we were able not only to help transfer the company's less sophisticated production activities to lower-cost countries in Eastern Europe and Asia but also to help open up new markets for the company in these regions. Our acquisition of the global travel retailer Dufry, in 2004, has allowed us to bring global best practices to airport retailers in emerging markets, where travel is a rapidly growing industry.

As all these examples suggest, the globalization of private equity is creating opportunities for improving companies, and economies, that are almost limitless. The same is true for venture capital when it comes to helping young, entrepreneurial companies to establish themselves and grow. The times are ripe for both venture capital and private equity to recover the sense of mission that drove those of us who were present at the creation of these industries. This is a task that calls for leadership. The job of leading venture capital or private equity organizations in a mission-driven way has been complicated, however, by several developments that have occurred over the years since these industries were young. In the next chapter I consider some of the important changes in venture capital and private equity that I have seen and the challenges they pose for leaders with vision.

# CHAPTER 9

# LEADING WITH VISION IN VENTURE
# CAPITAL AND PRIVATE EQUITY FIRMS

· · ·

The globalization of venture capital and private equity for which a handful of other pioneers and I began laying the groundwork years ago is now proceeding at a rapid pace, creating many exciting opportunities for the industry. As countries in Western Europe and Asia, including the giants China and India, seek to develop the capacity for innovative, high-impact entrepreneurship in industries such as life sciences and "green tech," venture capitalists have a chance to help bring about the technological revolutions of the future and spread them around the world. As countries in regions such as Latin America, Africa, and the Middle East seek to develop their industrial infrastructures and, increasingly, find private investors willing to back these efforts, private equity also has a chance to be a real force for global economic development.

Since my fellow pioneers and I began our efforts in the 1970s and '80s, many of the most fundamental obstacles we faced in introducing venture capital and private equity into new environments have been overcome. The liberalization and deregulation of financial markets, for example, has made cross-border investment in vehicles such as venture capital and private equity much easier than it was when my colleague John Incledon and I formed our Trans-Atlantic Business Growth Fund in the late 1970s to try to channel capital from British institutions into venture capital investment in the United States (see chapter 3). The creation of the euro has also had an enormously beneficial effect for venture capital and private equity in Europe. The costs of global communications and travel have fallen dramatically. Most important, knowledge of venture capital and private equity and what they can do to improve economies has now spread across the globe. It is no longer necessary, as it was when I was traveling around Europe and Asia in the 1970s and '80s talking about venture capital and private equity, to explain to skeptical investors and government leaders what these forms of investment are.

At the same time that the globalization of venture capital and private equity is presenting a new set of opportunities, however, other developments in the industry have changed it in ways that have made it less mission driven than it originally was. During a career in which I have founded and built two venture capital/private equity firms, I have found that one of my fundamental challenges as a leader has been to keep the organizations innovative, adventuresome, and focused on realizing the goals that I set for them. At times I succeeded in meeting these challenges. At other times I did not. For some people, success breeds a desire to keep doing what they have already done successfully — not an unnatural desire, as I found when my partners at TA Associates declined to continue investing in the firm's international expansion, or when Advent International retreated from Asia in the early 2000s. Another factor is that as venture capital and private equity have become mature industries, they have become increasingly complex. Complexity has called for managers to rationalize their organizations and become more specialized. This has made it more difficult to sustain the sense of mission that drove those of us who were active in the early days of the business to see venture capital and private equity as part of a larger enterprise that could make the domestic and then the global economy more efficient and productive.

In their recent book *Good Capitalism, Bad Capitalism, and the Economics of Growth and Prosperity*, coauthors William J. Baumol, Robert E. Litan, and Carl J. Schramm make a compelling case that innovative entrepreneurship of the kind that venture capital exists to promote is the key to sustained economic growth. While demonstrating the critical importance of innovative new firms, the authors also discuss the key role in economic growth played by large firms that use the innovations developed by others to produce new products and services at prices that large numbers of customers can afford. Because large firms have their own part to play in disseminating innovation, they argue, it is important that they be kept on their toes.[1] I would add that because private equity performs precisely this function of keeping established firms from becoming complacent or stagnant, it makes its own very substantial contribution to economic growth and prosperity.

I wonder how many people in the venture capital and private equity industries today have such a broad understanding of the complementary roles of venture capital and private equity in promoting global economic well-being. To be fair, I suppose it was easy for me to create my vision of Advent International as the catalyst for a global, privately directed Marshall Plan at the time when I conceived it. Twenty-five years ago, when I started Advent, I had a blank canvas to work with. My colleagues and I, when we started, had little idea of what would work and what would not, because there was so little data and prior history to call upon. We invested in early-stage companies and mature companies, in many different sectors. As I looked beyond the United States to see where else venture capital and private equity could have an impact, every other region and country in the world was virgin territory. It was a simpler world, in many ways, than the one that venture capital and private equity managers today must learn to negotiate. That made it easier, perhaps, to see things whole and think about making a difference beyond maximizing returns for investors and ourselves.

How have venture capital and private equity changed so as to make it more difficult to pursue them with the sense of mission that drove so many of us who built these industries? What can leaders in venture capital and private equity do today to enable these forms of investment to realize their potential for advancing economic development and progress around the world? Let us begin with the first question and consider how much more complex venture capital and private equity have become since I got my start in the business fifty years ago.

## THE MATURING OF VENTURE CAPITAL
## AND PRIVATE EQUITY

In the 1960s, when I founded TA Associates and many of today's other leading venture capital and private equity firms were just getting started, the venture business was much different than it is today. It was smaller, for one thing. In Boston, the other venture capital firms were ARD and Greylock, and Bank Boston's and the Bank of New England's SBICs.[2] Charles River Ventures, the next of the major Boston venture capital firms to be founded, was established in 1970. The local venture capitalists all knew one another and shared deals. Venture capital was more like a club than an industry. Today the much larger number of firms and competition for deals has given the business a very different, more transactional feel.

Another major difference between the early days of the industry and today is in the size and complexity of the deals. Take TA Associates' early investment in New England Business Service (NEBS) as an example. In 1970, when we won out over Kidder, Peabody to organize a syndicate of investors to buy out the shares of the company's founder (see chapter 8), NEBS was an established firm with revenues of $4 million and profits after taxes of $400,000. Its business was the manufacture and distribution through the mail of business forms for small businesses such as car dealers, repair shops, and florists. We won the chance to make the investment because I made a case to management that we could provide part of the capital and organize a better syndicate than could Kidder, Peabody. NEBS was an easy business to analyze, and I did so with help from Tom Claflin. I negotiated the deal and organized a syndicate that included Greylock and Bessemer Securities. We completed all the work and closed the investment in two months.

To make the most dramatic comparison possible, consider that small, simple NEBS investment alongside a recent one made by Advent International. In 2005 Advent, along with Bain Capital and the senior management of the target company, acquired Boart Longyear (BLY), a global drilling service and equipment company serving the mining, construction, water, and environmental industries. BLY is a $1.6 billion company operating from sites in more than forty countries across Europe, the United States, Canada, Latin America, the former Soviet Union, the Middle East, the Asia-Pacific region, and Africa. It was being sold by its parent company, the global mining and natural resources conglomerate Anglo American, as part of that company's effort to rid itself of what it considered to be peripheral divisions.

Advent's objectives, along with making key operating improvements, were to consolidate BLY's existing operations, increase its market penetration in underrepresented territories, and help it diversify into new services related to its core areas of expertise. Before any of this, however, an Advent team based in North America had to coordinate a network of two dozen advisers drawn from the firm's global networks — lawyers, accountants, environmental consultants, and so forth — to perform due diligence on six continents. Environmental due diligence alone required site visits to twenty BLY plants and drilling sites worldwide, all within a few days. In London, where Anglo American is listed on the London Stock Exchange and the deal was put together, Advent's two lead people on the deal, managing partners Humphrey Battcock and Dave McKenna, worked together for a month and a half sorting out the financial, accounting, and legal complexities of investing in a company operating in nearly forty countries. Once the deal was done, Advent investment professionals from South America to Poland scouted the globe for potential acquisitions for BLY. In the meantime, Advent had moved BLY corporate headquarters from South Africa to the United States and begun a significant augmentation of the company's senior management team.

Boart Longyear, like most businesses in which private equity firms have traditionally invested, is an "old economy" company. Yet as this example shows, in a globalized world even investment in an old-fashioned industrial company can be dauntingly complex. For venture capitalists making investments in young technology-based companies, the challenge of understanding today's complex and rapidly evolving technologies is augmented by the frequent need for companies to globalize their operations and enter global markets at a comparatively early stage of their development. Sizing up "the market" for a new product may actually mean understanding several different national markets and how to penetrate them quickly.

Globalization and the advancement of technology — which have increased the importance of specialized knowledge of particular geographies and industries — are perhaps the principal causes of the greater complexity of the venture capital/private equity industry compared to when I entered it almost fifty years ago. There are other factors, however. In private equity, the financial side of the business has grown extremely complex, owing to the introduction of financial techniques and debt instruments such as toggle notes and PIK ("payment in kind") notes or the collateralized debt obligations that the banks that lend money for private equity deals sell (or *were* able to sell before the bottom fell out of the credit markets) to investors. Although knowledge of such financial tools is now widely shared among the major players in the private equity business, this knowledge is increasingly the province of financial specialists within a private equity firm. Moreover, as operational knowledge and skills have become more and more crucial to success in private equity investment, private equity firms have come to rely on assistance from a stable of "operating partners." These operating partners are experienced executives who, on a deal-by-deal basis, serve as close advisers and coaches to the management team of an acquired company, and as intermediaries between the management team and the private equity firm, usually in the role of chairman of the company's board of directors. (In its investment in Boart Longyear, for example, Advent employed the services of its operating partner Dave McLemore, a former General Electric executive who had previously worked with Advent on two investments, including Moeller in Germany.) In an age of complexity and specialization, in other words, private equity managers must sometimes outsource such a core function as providing management assistance to portfolio companies.[3]

Such changes have made the venture capital and private equity businesses not just more complex but also more specialized than they once were. In the early days of TA Associates, for example, we knocked on doors in and around Boston looking for any companies we could find that might be good investments, no matter in what industry or stage of development. Advent International's International Network Fund employed the same kind of strategy when we launched it in the mid-1980s. Today, not only has the industry largely segmented into firms specializing in early-stage ("venture capital") and later-stage ("private equity") investment; it has also become specialized along industry lines. For firms that do not actually specialize in particular sectors, as many now do, it has become important to develop a degree of sector expertise that was not necessary in an earlier time.

The formalization and rationalization of the venture capital and private equity industries since the 1980s represents what was probably a necessary adaptation to a changing environment. However, from the perspective of someone who has been in the business since its formative years and participated in some of its significant achievements, these adaptations threaten the industry, if not with stagnation, then with a certain loss of vigor. One colleague whom I brought into the industry thirty years ago and who has enjoyed great success now says (I don't know how many of his peers he speaks for) that the venture business is much more lucrative for him than it once was but also much less interesting. He misses the sense of adventure he had when he and the industry were young and we more or less had to make things up as we went along. I don't want to sound like an old-timer waxing nostalgic, but I have to say that I sympathize with this point of view.

I continue to have faith in the potential of venture capital and private equity to be forces for real good in economies and societies by fostering innovation and making companies more competitive. Yet in order to fulfill this potential, venture capital and private equity managers must also remember that, for all the complexity and sophistication that are now part of the industry, they practice an art, not a science. I believe that successful venture investment will never be reduced to a formula. This basic truth has three key implications for those who lead venture capital and private equity firms. First, finding and developing successful investors is mostly a matter of recognizing people who have the right traits and letting them learn through experience. Second, in order to get the best out of talented investors and maintain a sense of adventure in the organization, it is important to find ways to create structure and focus while still challenging people to push the envelope. Third, the key to striking the right balance between focus and adventurousness is to create an inspiring vision that the people in the organization believe is achievable.

### FINDING AND DEVELOPING
### SUCCESSFUL INVESTORS

Business schools today offer courses on entrepreneurship, venture capital, and private equity, but I am not sure what students learn in them. I never took such a course myself. Although I had a chance to study with the founder of the venture capital industry, Georges Doriot, when I was a student at Harvard Business School, I walked out of his legendary course on manufacturing, as I have related in chapter 1. It wasn't until I formally entered the emerging venture capital industry in 1961 that I met General Doriot again. I had my first lengthy conversation with him in the early 1970s, when I was involved in establishing Sofinnova in France, and we discussed pan-European versus country-by-country approaches to introducing venture capital to Europe (see chapter 3). Although he was gracious, I had the impression that he was merely tolerating me. The General had developed a cult following at HBS, and I did not qualify for membership in his cult.

My point is not to disparage General Doriot as a teacher. One does not disparage a god. Charlie Waite, one of the original partners of Greylock and a topflight venture capitalist, took the General's manufacturing course, spent a year as his teaching assistant, and followed him to ARD before leaving to join Greylock in 1966. Arthur Rock, Tom Perkins of Kleiner Perkins Caufield & Byers, and Sir Ronald Cohen, one of the founders of Apax Partners, were also students of the General at HBS, and future entrepreneurs such as George Hatsopoulos and Arthur Goldstein evidently benefited from what Doriot taught them as well. It has been my experience, however, that venture capital is an activity in which apprenticeship matters more than classroom learning. It is a business one learns by doing.

This approach to developing venture capital and private equity managers was unavoidable when I founded TA Associates in the late 1960s. Before venture investment came to require the in-depth sector knowledge and complex financial skills it now demands, new managers were recruited into the industry as generalists rather than specialists and trained in all aspects of the business. Since my goal from the beginning with TA Associates was to become a leading manager of capital for investment in high-value-added companies of all types and sizes, I had to have a team with multiple skills, one with the flexibility to do high-technology start-ups as well as later-stage restructuring financings. However, I was the only person at TA Associates with any venture capital experience at the beginning. I was also handling all the firm's fund-raising in addition to consulting and handling private placements of corporate debt and equity in order to pay salaries and cover other expenses. This meant that I had limited time for doing deals, which made it necessary that I push my young associates out of the nest as soon as possible.

I began by explaining the investment process to these new venture capitalists from start to finish. I taught them to prospect for deals as I had done in my days at the First National Bank of Boston, writing down the names of all the companies in any office park I visited and then finding a reason to go call on them. I took my recruits with me on visits to entrepreneurs. If one of them said something stupid in a meeting, I made my criticisms afterward as gently and indirectly as I could. They were all smart enough to get the message. I also taught them how to perform due diligence, negotiate a deal, monitor a portfolio company's progress, and manage the exit. I would sometimes take them along when I was fund-raising, to show them how it was done and to let prospective investors know that TA Associates was more than just a one-man show. Then I turned my team loose, giving them enough rope to make decisions on their own, albeit with a bit of guidance from me. These young associates even began sitting on boards of directors without having much business experience to speak of, as much to learn the venture business as to help our portfolio companies.

Today, by contrast, new managers in private equity firms are often recruited for their knowledge of a particular industry sector or because they have particular financial skills. They may work on only one phase of a deal and spend many years in the business before seeing the whole process from start to finish, which is what one needs to get a feel for how the industry works. As my former colleague Bill Egan puts it, the model for training people in private equity has changed from "apprenticeship" to "vertical education." To the extent that this change insulates recruits from the rough-and-tumble of the whole investment process, it represents a loss. It takes a long, long period of hands-on experience to develop a good deal doer. New investment managers have got to take their lumps and fail, while the more senior people in the firm just have to make sure that the failure isn't cataclysmic. If a deal looks as if it's going down the drain, as a leader you want to make sure that the person responsible has enough confidence in you to admit defeat rather than try to cover it up. After they've made their mistakes, you have to get the new managers back on their feet and hope that they've learned from those mistakes.

Just as there is no substitute for experience in venture capital and private equity, managing these kinds of investment requires certain innate qualities that a person either does or does not possess. Although I helped them learn the venture capital business, the people who succeeded at TA Associates — individuals such as Kevin Landry, Bill Egan, Craig Burr, Grant Wilson, David Croll, Andy McLane, Jacqui Morby, Roe Stamps, Steve Woodsum, and others — all had a number of traits that they brought with them when they joined the firm. They were competitive, diligent, tenacious, and skeptical, with a high energy level and a burning desire to succeed.

Kevin Landry certainly possessed all these characteristics, especially diligence and tenacity. When we were putting together our Advent II fund in the early 1970s, my secretary, whose name will live forever in the lore of TA Associates, inadvertently threw away approximately $2 million in checks, part of the $10 million capitalization of the fund. Kevin wasted no time setting out in pursuit of the lost checks. First he tracked down the trash collector in the building, who told him that all the rubbish for the day had already been loaded onto the truck, which had already left the building. Kevin then managed to locate the trucker who had picked up the trash; then the company that had hauled it to a processing plant in Revere, north of Boston, to be baled; and finally the recycling plant in Walpole, southeast of Boston, where the trash was going to be recycled. Once we got to the recycling plant, at 10:00 P.M., Kevin, with the help of a Tucker

Anthony partner, bribed the union trucker to dump the trash out on the floor of the recycler, where we could search for the missing checks.

Combing through bales of trash looking for a thin manila envelope is no easy task. While others were laughing and kicking the trash around, Kevin was deadly serious and in hot pursuit. After a search that lasted for what seemed like hours, we were able to isolate a bale from the financial district and found the missing checks. Although the investors involved had been informed of what had happened and issued stop orders on the checks, they admired our determination to find them. (I feared we would have looked stupid if we had not succeeded.) After the rescue, we negotiated our second successful bribe of the evening by convincing a tavern owner near the recycling plant to open his bar (it was by then after 1:00 A.M.), and I liberally rewarded all those who had participated in this adventure. But its successful outcome was attributable to no one more than Landry. I drove Kevin home at around 2:30 A.M., knowing that he was the person I wanted as a partner and, eventually, as my successor as head of TAA. Indeed, as the firm grew and became increasingly able to support itself from its investment activities, Kevin would be the person who eventually freed me of my own investment responsibilities and allowed me to devote my time and energy to building a global enterprise.

I was exceptionally lucky to have found Kevin Landry at a time when I was just going out on my own and there were very few people around with any experience or even interest in venture capital. I found myself in a similar situation when I founded Advent International in the mid-1980s, a time when the idea of a global venture capital organization was still a novelty, not to say an oddity, and I recruited my first set of employees through a combination of connections and luck.[4] Even if I had had my pick of all the brightest young business school graduates in the country when I founded TAA and Advent, however, I would not have been able to forecast which of them would make the best venture capitalists.

Even today there is no way to know who will adapt to the environment of a venture capital or private equity organization. Despite the fact that these industries are now well known and well regarded and attract plenty of people who are qualified by education and business experience, there is no way to get a handle on who will make it or who won't. You never know until you put them in the field. During my time at TA Associates and Advent International, more people didn't make it than did. Both organizations needed a lot of time at the beginning to find their way, and many of the people I hired who didn't make it were simply not able to abide an environment in which there was no clear path. This doesn't mean that those who didn't make it with us were not successful in a different environment.

I had the same experience in recruiting partners in Europe and Asia as I had in finding colleagues in the United States, for the successful managers in the network came from a variety of backgrounds. David Cooksey had been an industrialist; Lars-Olof Gustavsson was a banker; Rolf Dienst was an investment adviser. What they had in common was energy, ambition, creativity, and adaptability. When I started SEAVIC in Singapore, Koh Lee Boon was the only Singaporean member of the team to be trained in Boston, while Derrick Lee learned everything on the job. Yet Derrick proved to be the most entrepreneurial member of the SEAVIC team and the best investor. As I have seen repeatedly, you can give someone new to the business a manual to read, but if that person does not have the right instincts, following the manual will be of little use. People with the right instincts, like Derrick, will throw the manual away and do just fine.

This lesson, I should add, remained relevant when Advent expanded into central Europe and Latin America in the mid-1990s. The formerly communist countries of central Europe, for example, had no venture capitalists or private equity investors of their own when they made the transition from command to market economies. The only way to develop a cadre of professionals in the region has been to hire intelligent, ambitious young people — often with MBAs from schools like INSEAD or Wharton and some experience in industries such as investment banking and consulting — give them a lot of responsibility, and let them learn by doing. This is what global venture capital and private equity firms entering the Chinese and Indian markets must now do to recruit their own local teams and develop them into successful investors.

Giving people the freedom to learn, grow, and make mistakes has its risks, of course. Sometimes they do make mistakes. Craig Burr learned a painful lesson on his very first deal at TA Associates, which involved a mail-order seed business called Breck's of Boston. Kevin Landry visited the company after Craig did the deal and described it as a "shithouse." Breck's went bankrupt eighty-eight days after TA Associates inked the deal. Craig was chastened — perhaps too much — by this experience and became quite cautious afterward. He needed time to recover his confidence and reenter the fray, which he did successfully. It is rather ironic that the Breck deal was brought to TA Associates by Bill Egan, who at that time was a loan officer at the New England Merchants Bank. Shortly after recommending the deal, Bill joined TA Associates, and although he had egg on his face for the Breck introduction, he was not at all chastened. Bill was a warrior. He showed the same characteristics of diligence, tenacity, and a burning desire to succeed that propelled Kevin Landry to the top.

I have mentioned skepticism as one of the qualities of a successful venture capitalist, but as Bill Egan's career at TAA shows, it is equally important to have faith when your instincts tell you to make or stick with a particular investment. Bill's work on the Federal Express deal was a good example. FedEx's lead venture capital investor was Charlie Lea, who had been with Bessemer Securities and F. S. Smithers & Co. before joining New Court Securities. While at New Court, Charlie raised three rounds of financing for Fred Smith's new delivery company. TA Associates participated in the first round, where the company was valued at about $200 per share, then watched its investment plummet as the company floundered and was valued at $7 per share in the second round of financing, and $1 per share in the third. Bill Egan was managing TAA's investment in FedEx, and it would have been easy for him to lose faith. He never stopped believing in the company, however. Rather than balking at the final round, Bill doubled up TAA's investment. He got some grief for this from other people in the firm, but Bill's belief in Fred Smith and the concept of the company was strong, and he was right. FedEx was one of the most successful investments of TA Associates' early funds. Bill had great instincts, which is really what separates the winners from the also-rans in venture capital.

Another important aspect of Bill's performance in the FedEx deal was the close rapport he developed with Fred Smith, FedEx's founder and CEO. Bill managed this despite the fact that TAA was a relatively small investor in the company. The ability to empathize with entrepreneurs is another crucial quality in a successful venture capitalist, and something that it is impossible to teach. I have always felt energized working with bright people who are trying to do challenging things. In venture capital, if you don't identify with an entrepreneur and want to be his partner in making his dream come true, you shouldn't be in the business. And if the entrepreneur gets the feeling that you really want to be a partner and help him reach his goal, it creates an atmosphere conducive to success.

Obviously it is not enough, however, simply to collect a group of talented individuals in order to build a successful venture capital or private equity organization. This was true in the past, when venture capital and private equity were smaller, simpler, less formalized businesses than they are today. It is especially true in today's more complex and structured world, where one of the important issues for any venture capital or private equity firm of any size is how to balance the requirements of structure and focus against the need to stay on the lookout for new kinds of opportunities and challenges.

STAYING FOCUSED WHILE

REMAINING INNOVATIVE

The same changes in the industry that have transformed the process of recruiting and training new investment managers in venture capital and private equity firms have also affected how work is organized and managed there. When deals were small enough to be handled by a single member of a firm, the culture of the venture business was highly individualistic. Venture investment was a solo exercise, with an individual partner or associate finding a deal, analyzing it, negotiating the terms, monitoring the investment once it was made, and exiting with (hopefully) a substantial gain. This way of operating fostered individual initiative and independence. If an associate or partner succeeded as a deal maker, he or she became larger than life. One does not *manage* these types of people; one *handles* them. At TA Associates when it began to become successful, I often felt as I had when, as a student at Harvard Business School, I coached the Boston Lacrosse Club, which was loaded with former all-Americans. All the players were good, and knew it, and were difficult to control. The trick, aside from getting their respect, was to get them to put the team ahead of themselves.

In the venture capital and private equity businesses, getting the players to put the team first is even more important than it once was, given the more team-oriented nature of the work today. As Advent's investment in Boart Longyear illustrates, dedicated teams and teamwork are essential to success in today's environment, certainly in private equity. This is a good thing — inflated egos often poisoned the atmosphere in a firm in the days when individual achievement was the only measure for advancement. However, it is also important to allow for a certain amount of freedom for creative individuals.

My method of managing my investment managers was the same one I used for teaching them the business in the first place. I always let people have a fair amount of rope, even though this meant that they sometimes came close to hanging themselves. Tony Haight comes to mind as an example from the early days of Advent International. Tony was a charismatic guy with great gifts of persuasion and a firm idea of what he thought was a good investment. If he liked a guy and thought he was onto something, Tony would want to back him. He was also absolutely tireless in turning up these entrepreneurs. The nature of the business did not matter: golf club manufacture, sawmill operations, retail companies, whatever caught his fancy.

Tony's judgment as an investor could be flawed, but the pressure he exerted on Tan Keng Boon and Derrick Lee was often irresistible. If you have someone with the energy and drive of a Tony Haight, you ring-fence him with people like Keng Boon and Derrick who can do the more cool-headed analysis. But that tactic didn't always work, and Tony sometimes ran over Keng Boon and Derrick as well as the investment committee back in Boston. I remember questioning him on one occasion about his due diligence on a particular deal and what he had shared with the investment committee. "I gave them what I thought they needed to know," he replied. This was hardly the right answer. It went against all the principles of the venture investment process, by which the partner proposing a deal is supposed to find out everything he or she can about every aspect of the company and the market, and report absolutely everything to the investment committee so that it can make a good decision. Tom Armstrong headed the investment committee at Advent at the time, and his best defense against Tony's blandishments was to keep the firm's commitments in Tony's deals small.

For all the headaches he sometimes caused us, however, Tony was the tip of the spear in executing our Southeast Asian strategy. Without Tony pushing the envelope as hard as he sometimes did, SEAVIC would have been a less energetic and creative organization. As with my way of teaching new recruits the venture capital business through trial by fire, the idea of turning someone like Tony Haight loose in the field might seem outlandish in today's more structured, buttoned-down venture capital and private equity environments. Balancing control of the investment process with the need for creative thinking is always a challenge, but it is a challenge that really good leaders can handle.

This point is well illustrated by what happened at Advent International after Doug Brown took over as chief investment officer and subsequently succeeded me as CEO. It was only when Doug became chief investment officer that Advent's investment structure became efficiently utilized. He had the background and the credibility with the investment professionals to command their respect, and the strength to say no. After he became CEO, his decision to acquire SEAVIC, as I have explained in chapter 7, was designed partly to gain more control over an investment process that he did not believe was working to Advent's full advantage. These efforts to introduce more structure and discipline into the investment operation were all necessary and constructive. However, Doug's strengths in bringing discipline and focus to the organization were not matched by a complementary set of skills that a leader of a venture organization must have to keep it innovative as well as focused.

One of the most important of these skills is an ability to encourage genuine give-and-take within the organization, listen to many different viewpoints, and build consensus around decisions. When I recruited Advent International's first team of investment managers after the firm's founding in 1984, the new firm's global focus, combined with the fact that we cast the recruiting net as widely as possible, meant that we had a very interesting mix of people from a wide range of backgrounds and with many different kinds of experiences. This was partly a matter of necessity for a company that was breaking genuinely new ground and could not take its pick from a pool of seasoned venture capitalists, but it was also a conscious choice on my part. I believed that a varied group of people who were all adventurous enough to sign on with a firm like Advent would challenge and stimulate one another with their differing experiences and points of view. This proved to be the case. For example, Steve Tadler, one of our managing partners who now chairs Advent's executive committee, recalls that when he joined Advent as still a relatively young man in 1985, he learned a great deal from sharing a small office with George Reichenbach, who was fifty-seven years old and retired from a senior position with the Norton Company, and Miguel Zorita, a Spaniard who was with the Bank Bilbao Vizcaya.[5] Such interactions help build a culture in which differences are valued and contribute to the strength of the organization.

As I have said, entrepreneurial people of the kind that any venture capital or private equity organization wants to have are difficult to manage. When they come from different backgrounds and different countries, difficulties multiply, and conflict can often occur. To lead a group like this, one has to be able to live with a certain level of conflict. One also has to be able to adjudicate disputes when they arise. This takes a secure, patient, and judicious person, and a management style that respects other people's points of view. Doug found it difficult to tolerate this kind of environment, and his management style was top-down—not an effective approach in any organization whose major resource is the intelligence and creativity of its people. He listened to the observations of his partners and then decided what to do. There was seldom a dialogue where consensus was reached. People complained that he spent too much time holed up in his office and that when he made decisions, he did not communicate them clearly. My approach was more collegial. The door to my office was always open. Although I sometimes felt frustrated by the difficulty of incorporating different viewpoints and getting consensus, I realized that was what I had to do if I was going to keep people rowing together toward a common objective. There is no question that it is easier to tell people what to do, but in the environment I had created it simply did not work. I doubt that it works in any venture capital or private equity firm.

Doug Brown's tenure as CEO of Advent International also saw the emergence of an issue that had bedeviled me at TA Associates when my partners and I reached an impasse over the further international expansion of the firm. As I have related in chapter 2, once TAA had established itself and become very successful in the early 1980s, I wanted to keep trying new things—not just continuing to build the network in Western Europe but also expanding into Asia, where I believed that venture capital and private equity had great potential. My partners, however, were happy to stick with what they were doing. They had found a profitable formula for investing domestically. In short, TAA was doing extremely well by focusing on what it had already learned to do, and the partners saw no reason to take money out of their pockets to fund new activities in which there was a high degree of uncertainty.

At Advent International, the period between my founding of the firm in 1984 and Doug Brown's assumption of leadership there in the late 1990s was a time during which an initial experimentation with a variety of activities and structures eventually gave way to a more focused approach. In the beginning, out of necessity as well as a desire to create a new and innovative type of firm, Advent pursued a wide range of activities. As it became clear that it could become a direct investment organization rather than just a provider of services to others, the nature of the company began to change. Doug Brown transformed Advent's European operations from a network of affiliates coordinated from London into a group of Advent offices pursuing their own investments while also collaborating in ways that leveraged one another's knowledge and contacts. While creating a skilled and disciplined investment organization in Western Europe, Brown also played a key role in the firm's expansion into central Europe and Latin America. Later, as Advent's chief investment officer and then CEO, Brown consolidated a number of programs, de-emphasized a few, and focused the investment team on the larger private equity transactions that are now the firm's mainstay. Bringing order and focus to Advent's investment process, he put the firm on the path to the success it has enjoyed ever since.

The path that Advent followed during Brown's tenure, however, involved a certain amount of retrenchment. I have already written (in chapter 7) about the decision made in 2002 to spin off SEAVIC six years after Advent had acquired it, thus leaving Advent without a direct presence in Asia. Even before the decision to retreat from Asia, Brown had shown a reluctance to pursue new initiatives of a kind that fit with the mission of the company and would have helped advance our position as a global leader in private equity. In particular, Doug declined to have Advent participate in a US$1 billion Technopreneurship Investment Fund launched in 1999 by the government of Singapore as part of its "Technopreneurship 21" initiative for improving the environment in Singapore for technological entrepreneurship.

I thought this decision was a big mistake, and it was one that I tried to dissuade Brown from making. The Government Investment Corporation of Singapore, the sovereign wealth fund Temasek, and the Development Bank of Singapore (which had been one of the founding investors in SEAVIC back in 1983) all wanted Advent to participate in the Technopreneurship fund. We were uniquely equipped to manage such a program, and helping the Singaporeans could have helped us to attract more capital from Singapore. Over and above these practical considerations, as I reminded Doug, I have always believed that innovative programs are the lifeblood of a successful company. There was minimal risk in this case, and I thought that a decision not to participate would be demotivating to the development side of the organization. One of Advent's most admirable traits had always been its courage in pushing the envelope. But here was Brown treating what I saw as an opportunity as merely a set of potential problems.

Once Advent had spun off SEAVIC in 2002 and effectively retreated from Asia while I argued unsuccessfully for retaining some sort of presence there, I found myself wondering, as I had before in my career, why it was so hard to persuade my colleagues to take more risks and show more adventurousness. Success often makes people cautious because it gives them something to lose, but this has never been my way. Whenever in my career I have felt that I figured something out and knew how to make it work, I have always been eager to move on and try something new. The years when I had the most fun in business were the ones when things were toughest. In the 1970s, when TA Associates was a new firm in a young industry and I had to hustle just to feed the guys who were working for me, that was exciting. Starting new venture capital firms in Europe and Southeast Asia while having no idea if we would succeed or not was exciting as well. So was the founding of Advent.

To me, having something succeed and watching the money coming in is not as much fun as pushing something forward in the face of uncertainty. Besides, first-mover advantage can be a significant factor in new markets for venture capital and private equity: getting people on the ground to learn about the country and the market, even if you are not making big investments at first, can confer a sizable advantage over those who wait until a new market looks like a sure thing. My philosophy about new markets has always been to get there first and then figure out what to do. It seems to me that venture capital and private equity managers, by the nature of their business, must always be willing to take leaps into the unknown. I often ask myself why my colleagues have not been more inclined to see things this way.

Of course there are reasons for a successful private equity firm like Advent to stay on familiar terrain. The firm, and the industry, have enjoyed extraordinary success in recent years. At the same time, as we have seen, private equity has become an ever more complex business in which keeping up with the latest financial techniques, for example, demands time and attention. Developing new investment products and expanding into new markets are also expensive undertakings. Spending money on them not only means less money in the pockets of the partners but also leaves less for competing in today's highly competitive market for talent. Indeed the private equity business itself, like so many others, has become so competitive that one must run harder all the time just to stay in place.

Despite such reasons for prudence, however, it is important not to take prudence to extremes. I have always subscribed to C. Northcote Parkinson's idea that "perfection of planning is a symptom of decay." As Parkinson wrote, "During a period of exciting discovery or progress, there is no[t] time to plan the perfect headquarters. The time for that comes later, when all the important work has been done." We live in a period of exciting discovery and progress. Economic globalization, continued technological advancement, and the aspirations of people everywhere for better lives create opportunities to push the envelope and bring the benefits of venture capital and private equity to more and more places in the world. To me this is where the adventure in the business now lies, and it is hard for me to understand why others do not always share this sense of adventure.

Comparing myself and other veterans of the early days of venture capital and private equity with many of my younger colleagues now, I realize that my generation of venture capitalists was fortunate to have entered the industry at a time when just being in venture capital was an adventure. The industry was young, and the prospect of success was uncertain. We knew we were creating something new, and before we became prosperous we had nothing to lose. As long as we were paying our way, the thrill of doing something different was enough to sustain us, along with the belief that fostering innovation and entrepreneurship would help to build a stronger economy and a better society. We wanted to make money, but we believed that the financial rewards would come if we did a good job for our investors. We were also interested in building institutions. To me this meant not only helping to create sustainable companies but also reinvesting enough of our profits in the firm to enable it to develop and grow.

After I left TA Associates because my partners were no longer interested in investing in the international side of the business, I wanted things to be different at Advent International. As I have explained, I organized Advent as a corporation rather than a partnership, and the corporation received 25 percent of the override from its investments. For the first five years, I took none of the override for myself. I did this not to be noble but because I wanted to be able to build the firm. When Advent became a direct investment organization with the introduction of the European Special Situations Fund in 1990, however, pressure began to build to pass more and more of the corporation's share of the override to the managing directors. For many years afterward, virtually all the profits from operations and all the override were distributed to the professional staff. The thought of retaining capital for a rainy day or to reinvest in the business was not a subject for discussion.

In thinking over the changes I saw first at TA Associates and later at Advent, I have sometimes been tempted to think that they can be accounted for by generational differences. In the venture capital industry, I saw a shift in attitude occurring at about the same time that the success of venture capital was becoming obvious and money began flooding into the industry in the early 1980s. One important change that came about as a result of the new investment was that income from management fees increased dramatically, so that managers could compensate themselves handsomely exclusive of the carried interest they would receive from successful investments. In short, managers could do well for themselves without doing well for their investors. This is not the way the system was designed at the beginning. Back then, managers made real money only if the investors made a handsome return. Now they were making a lot of money regardless of their performance. And this change coincided with the entry into the industry of a new generation whose values were different from those of the pioneering generation of venture capitalists.

Generational differences do exist. I believe that many young Americans who came of age in the era of Vietnam and Watergate developed a deep cynicism about institutions, including government, universities, and business firms. Their attitudes contrasted strongly with those of their elders, whose formative experiences had included the Depression and World War II, and who in many cases went on to become the much-ridiculed "organization men" of the 1950s. The "If it feels good, do it" hedonism of the 1960s was eventually succeeded by the "Greed is good" materialism of the 1980s, but the common thread was a belief that satisfying one's own personal wants and needs was paramount. Institutions like companies and firms existed to serve the ambitions of individuals, not to achieve common aims.

In the business world of the 1980s, this new attitude was visible in the excesses that sometimes occurred amid the leveraged buyout movement, with viable companies being loaded down with debt, and sometimes destroyed, in order to enrich a handful of takeover artists. It was visible in the rise of celebrity CEOs who believed that they personally deserved most of the credit — and most of the rewards — for a company's success. In the venture capital business, the change came as increasing success brought in

large sums of new investment, attracted growing numbers of young people to the field, and changed the focus of the industry. It is true that, by
creating a successful new industry, venture capitalists had earned the right
to increased compensation. Yet among those who were now benefiting
from the work of others who had built the industry, high management
fees and quick exits increasingly became the order of the day rather than
the patient, exacting work of nurturing a young enterprise. The newcom-
ers to the industry saw it as a vehicle for creating wealth for themselves,
not an adventure, an engine for economic development, or a way of creating sustainable organizations.

Perhaps it is too easy for someone of my generation to criticize younger
people in the private equity business. After all, given the rewards that have
been dangled before them while reading about the precrash lifestyle of a
Stephen Schwarzman (stone crabs at $40 a claw and a $3 million sixtieth
birthday party), they have been subjected to more temptation than we
ever were. In a world in which organizations rarely exhibit the loyalty to
their people that they once did, perhaps it is understandable that individuals should care more about doing well for themselves than about building institutions. (Whether the hard times we are now living through will
prove to be a chastening experience, or whether they will only increase
the desire of individuals to grab what they can for themselves, only time
will tell.) In venture capital, where fostering innovation remains at the
center of the business and the new frontiers in China and India beckon
those who wish to explore new worlds, it is probably easier to preserve
something of the spirit that motivated the pioneers of the industry than it
is in private equity.

However, I believe there is still plenty of adventure for private equity
managers today apart from the excitement of the gigantic deals that recently motivated many in the buyout business. In a competitive global
business environment, even large, established companies must constantly
seek new forms of competitive advantage, and private equity managers, as
we saw in the last chapter, can play a vital role in helping them to reinvent
themselves. In the emerging markets of Eastern Europe, Asia, Latin America, and elsewhere, opportunities abound for helping countries undergoing fundamental transformations in order to exploit their own domestic
markets and compete in global ones. In private equity as in venture capital
or any other industry, however, fostering a spirit of risk taking and adventure means that leaders must give their people a vision.

CREATING AND REALIZING A VISION

*Vision* is not just a buzzword to me. I have spent my whole career in venture capital and private equity in pursuit of a vision of what these industries can do to advance economic development, in the United States and
overseas. In my exasperation with Doug Brown for his unwillingness to
have Advent participate in the Technopreneurship program in Singapore,
I sent him a memo at one point asking bluntly, "Do you agree that a company needs a vision to sustain itself and, if so, what is the vision for Advent
at this point in time?" Without an inspiring vision to pursue, venture capital and private equity, to me, would just be about making money, which
has never interested me as an end in itself.

Some now say that in the days when I was helping to establish organizations like Sofinnova in France or SEAVIC in Southeast Asia I was a
"missionary" for venture capital. If so, I was not the first. Georges Doriot's
greatest contribution to the industry he created was the sense of mission
with which he infused his followers. "The noble task is to build constructively in the hope that capital gains will be the reward for intelligent, hard
work," he told an audience of Harvard Business School alumni in 1966.
The General spoke with unabashed idealism in exhorting entrepreneurs
and venture capitalists to undertake such work: "Let us do more than our
share for the generations following us. Do we want to build or merely enjoy
what others ahead of us have made possible? Really, how can one enjoy
anything if one is not building for the future of others? Remember that
our happiness is in direct proportion to the contributions we make."[6]

It is possible that General Doriot spoke too loftily for some of his hear-
ers, and he perhaps did not have enough understanding of the more ordinary ways of motivating people. His employees at ARD received modest
salaries and were given no ownership stake in the organization, which
Charlie Waite cites as a factor in his decision to jump ship and join Greylock. At TA Associates, my partners were clearly motivated by their desire
to do well for their investors and to make money for themselves. My vision for making venture capital an international industry was of little interest to them. It did not motivate them in any way. I had to wait until I
founded Advent International to assemble a team that was interested in
pursuing my global vision for venture capital.

At Advent, I succeeded in hiring new colleagues who were excited by
the idea of a global venture capital organization. I have described Tony

Haight's background. Tom Armstrong, who became Advent's chief operating officer, had international experience but none whatsoever in venture capital or private equity. Clint Harris had been a management consultant with experience in Europe. Because Advent, as I originally conceived it, was not going to be a direct investment organization, and because the globalization of venture capital and private equity was not yet on most people's radar screens, it was impossible for me to lure the best talent from the domestic venture capital industry. What respectable venture capitalist would want to join a firm dedicated to the development of the international version? Later on, as the firm began to expand and eventually did become a direct investment organization, there were enough young people who wanted to get into the business to provide more job candidates than openings. Yet if someone had a choice between coming to Advent and going to an established firm like TA Associates or Greylock, recruiting that person for Advent could be a tough sell. We couldn't afford to pay the salaries that the other firms could, and a major question remained unanswered: would the returns on international venture capital approach those being realized in the United States by these other firms?[7]

Those who joined me at Advent International were taking a lot on faith. There was no certainty that my plan for the company would succeed, so they had to be inspired by the chance to make the idea work in practice. Of course, making money as a result of any success we gained was important to them. But the idea of an international adventure, something very new, aligned their interests with mine. While the early management team was a motley group composed of people with many different backgrounds, they were energized by the vision I had for the company and were dedicated to making that vision a reality. There was a great feeling of adventure and a wonderful camaraderie among the partners.

Notice, however, that I say that the visions of my Advent colleagues and I were "aligned" rather than that I persuaded them to follow mine. In thinking about why the idea of a global venture capital organization appealed to the Advent team but had not appealed to my partners at TA Associates, I realize that there was a major difference in circumstances that I have not explained. This had everything to do with timing.

After my TA Associates partners made it clear to me at the end of 1982 that they were not interested in pursuing my vision for international expansion, events in the world continued to move in the direction that was indicating to me that my idea was feasible. In Europe, the 1983 signing of the Solemn Declaration on European Union was followed, two years later, by the successful negotiation of the Single European Act, which created the framework for the European Union. The year 1985 also saw the beginnings of perestroika in the Soviet Union, which would lead, in turn, to the fall of the Berlin Wall and the dissolution of the Soviet bloc in central and Eastern Europe in 1989. Meanwhile, between 1984 and 1990 the Chinese government greatly expanded its opening of the country to international trade and investment, creating open economic areas not only in its coastal region but on its international borders and in inland locations as well. In short, my vision of venture capital becoming an increasingly global industry looked more plausible as the world continued to change in the ways that I had expected. This made it possible for my new partners at Advent to believe that a global firm like ours could play a role in a historic transformation of the world economy.[8]

Timing is always a factor in successfully creating a vision that can motivate others to reach beyond what seems possible in the immediate present. Another is demonstrating to your partners that they can personally benefit from advancing the goals of the organization. For me at Advent, this meant sharing the wealth as generously as possible and creating financial incentives for people to cooperate with one another and see the success of the firm as an important component of their own compensation. Doug Brown did not operate this way when he ran the company, which, along with his top-down management style, created a great deal of resentment among the partners.

Finally, in order to get people to buy into the vision it is essential to show them that you, and they, can execute. Demonstrating that you can execute means, first of all, having a plan. The business plan for Advent contained a description of the various business activities I envisioned. It was very flexible and called for people who could respond to events as they unfolded. These people, the Haights, Harrises, and Armstrongs of this world, had to be able to turn on a dime. They had to be confident and self-reliant. I, in turn, had to help them develop the investment skills that would make them successful, and then they had to learn from experience. They relied on me to show the direction in which I wanted to go. I had to rely upon their inventiveness, spirit, and judgment to get there. We executed the plan together, bolstering one another as we went along.

Even an inspiring, achievable vision with tangible rewards for reaching the goal is not enough by itself, however, to hold a venture capital or private equity organization together and enable it to reach its highest potential over the long term. My Advent colleagues' enthusiasm for my vision of international venture capital, coupled with my own successful efforts to bring in revenue until we had enough investment capital to produce management fees and carried interest, did sustain us through the firm's early years. Since the firm has become prosperous, however, it has been propelled forward not just by my vision for it or by the financial rewards the partners have been able to earn — rewards that they could have garnered at other firms, after all — but by a shared pride in how we create returns for our investors by adding value to our investments. A shared conception of "how we do things here" can be a powerful force for cohesion in any organization, and it has been one for Advent.

The emphasis on teamwork in Advent's style of investing globally has been an especially important factor in creating strong relationships and a sense of common purpose among members of the team: an indispensable ingredient in the success of the Boart Longyear deal, for example, was the close collaboration between Humphrey Battcock and Dave Mc-Kenna, fostered by a working relationship between the two of them and other key members of the investment team developed over many years. Advent, I should add, has had very low turnover over the years in its North American, Western European, and Latin American offices. I have asked myself on many occasions whether my failure to foster teamwork at TA Associates was what led to the departure of some very good people. I have come to the conclusion that the nature of the business in the early days of venture capital, when each individual found and did deals on his own, was very different from the nature of Advent's business today, when teamwork is required. I have also come to the conclusion that those who left TA Associates simply wanted to spread their wings. However, it is important for those who lead venture capital and private equity operations to realize that the low barriers to exiting one firm or beginning another make the issue of fostering group cohesion and retaining top performers an important one.

In any case, I believe that these developments in Advent International's culture over the years show that a compelling, achievable vision with something in it for everyone in the organization does not become fully effective until it is woven into attitudes and practices that enable the organization to reach its full potential. The leader of the organization has to work at infusing the vision into the day-to-day work of the firm. A successful leader has to provide the vision *and* the environment for creative people to develop. The leader must care for his people while at the same time prodding them to fulfill their own potential and that of the firm. But ultimately they have to make the vision their own.

It has been almost twenty-five years since I founded Advent International. I am eighty years old now and still pushing the envelope. I want Advent to focus on a vision of the future and not simply replicate the successes of the past. In my role as chairman, I have urged the managing directors to take risks, to try new things. In so doing, however, I have been reminded by past experience that a leader cannot convince people to follow a vision until they are ready to so. Most recently, following the firm's decision to retreat from a direct presence after the spin-off of SEAVIC in 2002, I pushed hard to persuade my partners not to retreat from Asia but to rethink how to take advantage of the opportunities there. When I encountered resistance, I felt as if I was fighting the same old battles all over again and wondered why my message about Advent's potential for becoming a truly global firm was not coming through.

As the managing directors discussed what the firm's strategy for Asia should be, I argued that many of the countries hit worst by the Asian currency crisis of the mid-1990s had made strong recoveries. Japan has become an increasingly attractive market for private equity, and, of course, China and India have emerged as new frontiers. I believe that many of today's investors in China and India will lose their shirts, and there may be good reasons, for now, for staying on the sidelines. However, I maintained, the only way to learn about a new market is to establish a presence on the ground. Again, there is never a perfect time to do anything, and if one spends all one's time planning and organizing, the opportunity might slip away. It is important to select a market, get there, and then figure out what to do — by learning about the region, making connections, and getting a feel for the rhythms of the economy and the markets. Then, when you commit to the region, you do it for the long term. The costs of such a commitment are considerable and are not primarily in fixed assets but in developing human assets to their fullest potential.

I would like to think that reminding my colleagues of my vision of Advent as a truly global private equity firm and hammering away at my points had some effect, but that's giving me too much credit. I believe that the managing directors always bought into the concept of a global private equity firm. What finally tipped the scale in favor of developing a truly global imprint, however — establishing a new office and fund for Japan,[9] begin-ning to invest in India, and considering the possibility of a new emerg-ing markets fund — was a combination of factors. Advent's investors have been impressed with its results in emerging markets such as central Eu-rope and Latin America and have encouraged us to spread our wings. In addition, there has been more money to spread around from increased capital under management and the success of our investments. But the most important factor has been confidence — confidence that the vision can be realized, and the confidence that members of the senior manage-ment group now have in one another. These last two factors, of course, are closely related.

Looking back over the last several years, I cannot emphasize enough the energy that was released when Advent International went from being a hierarchical firm under Doug Brown to the more collegially run organi-zation that it is today, led by an executive committee.[10] Suddenly everyone felt more a part of a firm that had a mission to become the leading global private equity organization. There are a number of people at Advent who should be recognized for managing through the turmoil that accompa-nied the transition to a new form of leadership, for they are the ones who are now keeping the vision I have had for the firm alive. In Europe, John Walker represented a stable force to whom people turned. Will Schmidt and John Singer, who had bought into the global concept from the begin-ning, showed unceasing dedication to achieving the company's mission. In the United States, Tom Lauer guided the transition process with great wisdom, and David Mussafer rebuilt a North American investment opera-tion that had languished under Brown. In the emerging markets in which Advent invests, Ernest Bachrach and Juan Carlos Torres in Latin Amer-ica, and Joanna James in central Europe, stayed focused amid the distrac-tions of the management transition and achieved market-leading results. Presiding over all this was Steve Tadler, who had been picked by his col-leagues to lead them because of his sense of the whole, his demeanor, and his fairness. No one person was the glue that held the firm together. They were all the glue. This is what pleases me most about the company, along with its successful fund-raising for Global Private Equity VI in a very chal-lenging environment.

As I consider what remains to be done to realize my vision of venture capital as a force for economic development the world over, both in the more economically advanced countries and in emerging markets, I also take pleasure in knowing that the vision has been taken up by others besides my colleagues at Advent International. In founding and building Advent while also helping to establish venture capital and private equity organizations in Europe, Asia, Australia, and Latin America, I have been fortunate to play a role in creating what has become a global infrastructure for venture capital and private equity and to spread awareness of these forms of investment. Today, thanks to that infrastructure and that awareness, others who share my vision of using venture capital and private equity in a global and social context have been discovering new frontiers to explore. In my last chapter, I describe some of the new frontiers for venture capital and private equity and some of the pioneering efforts in the industry today.

# THE PETER BROOKE VENTURE CAPITAL FAMILY TREE

## TA Associates

### NETWORK MEMBERS

- Advent Ltd.
  (England)
- S.A. Advent Management Belgium N.V.
  (Belgium)
- TVM Technoventure Management GmbH
  (Germany)
- Techno-Venture Co. Ltd.
  (Japan)
- The SEAVI Group
  - SEAVI Program
    (Singapore)
  - Maylaysian Ventures Management
    (Maylasia)
  - SEAVI Venture Services Pte. Ltd.
    (Thailand)
  - P.T. SEAVI Indonesia Ventures
    (Indonesia)
- Transtech Venture Management Pte Ltd.
  (Singapore)

### GRADUATES

- Claflin Capital Management
- Burr, Egan & Deleage
  - Polaris Ventures
  - Alta Partners
  - Alta Communications
- Summit Partners
  - Parthenon Capital
- Media/Communications Partners
  - Spectrum Equity Investors
  - Great Hill Partners

## Advent International

### NETWORK MEMBERS

- Alpha Associés S.A.
  (France)
- Innoventure Equity Partners AG
  (Switzerland)
- Horizonte Venture Management
  (Austria, Slovenia, Bosnia)
- Advent España S.A.
  (Spain)
- Itavent
  (Italy)
- Equinox Kft
  (Hungary)
- Copernicus Capital Management Sp.
  (Poland)
- Advent Management Group
  (Australia)
- Techno Ventures Hong Kong Ltd.
  (Hong Kong)
- Galicia Advent S.A.
  (Argentina)
- Partners with Banco Bozano, Simonsen S.A.
  (Brazil)
- Advent Morro
  (Puerto Rico)
- Gemini Capital Fund Management Ltd.
  (Israel)
- Turkven
  (Turkey)

### GRADUATES

- Nash, Sells & Partners Ltd.
- Grove Street Advisors
- Ticonderoga Ventures
- Argo Capital

## Brooke Private Equity Advisors

- Vectis Life Sciences

CHAPTER 10

# NEW FRONTIERS

. . .

Since the invention of organized venture capital just after the end of World War II, the frontiers of the industry have shifted a number of times. In the late 1950s and early 1960s, when I first began investing in small, growing companies, venture capital itself was still a frontier in the world of finance, practiced by small bands of investors in New York, Boston, and what would become known as Silicon Valley, and largely unknown elsewhere. In the late 1980s, when the industry had matured to the point where early-stage investing and what has since become known as private equity began to diverge into separate branches of finance, leveraged buyouts became a new frontier. Aided by friendly debt markets for much of the current decade, private equity firms in the mid-2000s began acquiring companies that would once have been thought too large for leveraged buyouts. Now that credit markets have tightened and the use of leverage will not provide the returns that it did during the recent buyout boom, the new challenge for private equity managers, as I have argued in chapter 8, will be to deliver the returns to which their investors have become accustomed by adding value to their portfolio companies.

As what we now call venture capital has grown and developed, its changing frontiers have most often been defined by technological trends and breakthroughs. From the end of World War II until the early 1980s, venture capital survived and eventually prospered mainly by financing innovations in electronics hardware, including computers. Later, as the success of the computer industry stimulated demand for software and the development of networking technology, venture capital helped launch companies that created a host of previously undreamt of applications and services for businesses and individual computer users, including the thousands of "dot-coms" that arose (and often fell hard to earth) amid the

Internet boom of the 1990s. On the technological front today, sectors such as biotechnology, nanotechnology, and, increasingly, green technology (or "clean tech") are areas of venture capital investment that could transform society as thoroughly as have the computer and communications revolutions. Buyout firms, in the meantime, have begun extending their reach from the sectors in which they have traditionally operated, such as manufacturing and distribution, into industries such as financial services, consumer goods, retail, and even technology.

Most significantly from my own perspective, the sixty-year history of venture capital and private equity has also seen a shifting of geographic frontiers. For the first twenty-five years or so after the founding of American Research & Development in 1946, venture capital investment was concentrated mainly in two regions of the United States: Silicon Valley and greater Boston. As I have related in Part I of this book, in the 1970s and 1980s I and a small number of other pioneers moved on to new frontiers in Western Europe, Southeast Asia, and greater China, introducing both venture capital and private equity into these markets. In the 1990s, Advent International played a key role in launching private equity in central Europe and Latin America. Today, although venture capital and private equity are pushing into new geographic frontiers in places such as Russia and other former CIS countries, the Middle East, and Africa, the areas that are seeing the most activity are China and India.

China has created the most intense excitement among venture investors. According to figures from the Emerging Markets Private Equity Association and *Asia Private Equity Review*, venture capital and private equity raised annually for investment in China grew from $152 million in 2001 to $14.461 billion in 2008. The cumulative total during those years was $25.654 billion. Both domestic and foreign investors are betting that the country will succeed in its strategy of moving beyond low-cost manufacturing for export and become a center of high-tech innovation. The country's growing middle class also presents apparently limitless opportunities in consumer sectors, while China's relatively advanced physical infrastructure is a boon for business development in a variety of industries. Private equity investment by outside investors has been somewhat hampered by the Chinese government's unwillingness to allow control investments by foreign entities (along with limits it has placed even on minority investments by foreigners in certain industries) and its efforts to build a yuan-denominated private equity sector. And Western investors in both venture capital and private equity still face substantial risks in China from a variety of other factors: a totalitarian government that can change the rules overnight, the lack of transparency in Chinese companies and of a body of commercial law for protecting investors, and very significant cultural differences between China and the West. While steps are being taken to mitigate some of these risks, they must be recognized and understood.

India has also seen a huge influx of venture capital and private equity in recent years, amounting to $19.247 billion in the period from 2001 to 2008, according to the Emerging Markets Private Equity Association and *Asia Private Equity Review*. In contrast to China's rise as a low-cost manufacturer, India has achieved its own rapid growth to date on the strength of its software, software services, and business process outsourcing sectors. It remains relatively underdeveloped in terms of infrastructure and basic industries like retailing, although its enormous domestic market provides plenty of incentive to foreign investors for entering these sectors. Here the risks for Western investors may not be as formidable as they are in China, although India's socialist past has left some sectors of its economy overregulated, and the country has a long way to go in areas such as education and infrastructure before it can hope to realize its full economic potential and lift the vast majority of its people out of poverty.[1]

Despite the challenges they face, however, both the Chinese and the Indians are highly entrepreneurial people, and both countries have benefited in recent years from an influx of returning expatriates who have acquired valuable business experience, even entrepreneurial experience, in the West.[2] Obviously only time will tell how successful China and India will be in achieving their goals for economic development on the extremely ambitious timetables they have set for themselves. Yet it is significant that both the Chinese and the Indian governments are taking steps to promote venture capital and private equity investment, and it seems clear that such investment will play a central role in both countries' development. Helping countries such as India and China, as well as other nations that are even less developed, to become prosperous through a combination of private capital and management assistance is a large project. But this remains my idea of what global venture capital and private equity are all about.

I also believe that venture capital and private equity managers today need to raise their sights and understand the potential of their industries for doing good. In the late 1980s, after I had left TA Associates and started

Advent International because my TAA partners were not interested in joining me on what were then the frontiers of international venture capital, I once remarked publicly that I had never seen an industry go from birth to senility as fast as the American venture capital business had. This raised a few eyebrows in the industry at the time. When I said this I certainly did not mean "senile" from the standpoint of innovation; indeed, in the years just after I made my remarks the industry moved the boundaries of technology in the Internet boom of the 1990s, giving birth to one of the major technological and business revolutions of the post–World War II era. What I did mean — probably because of my frustration at not convincing my partners at TA Associates to embrace international expansion — was that the industry did not seem to see the scope of what it could accomplish in a global and social context. It didn't seem to have occurred to many venture capitalists and private equity managers that they could be a force for economic and social progress in the world. To me, however, this is the whole point of what we do. The frontier in the industry is wherever the skills of venture capital and private equity managers can be applied to address economic problems such as poverty, underdevelopment, and lack of opportunity, along with the many social ills associated with them. To put it another way, the pioneers today are those who apply their entrepreneurial spirit and problem-solving skills not only to make a profit for their investors and themselves but also to improve the lives of others.

From this point of view, emerging markets are an especially important frontier for venture capital and private equity. Emerging markets ought to matter to the industry precisely because they offer a chance to use venture capital and private equity to stimulate basic economic development and improve the lives of people who have long been disadvantaged. Obviously emerging markets present their own challenges above and beyond those entailed in entering any new international market. Their often fragile political and economic institutions clearly pose particular risks for investors such as those that materialized for Advent International in the Asian currency crisis of the late 1990s. People in the less developed world are also especially sensitive to the possibility of being exploited by foreign investors, which makes it particularly important for venture capital and private equity managers there to earn the trust of entrepreneurs and local partners by adding value and rewarding themselves only when portfolio companies succeed and prosper.

Despite such challenges, however, emerging markets offer especially good opportunities for venture capital and private equity to carry out a mission of fostering economic development and contributing to global economic and social progress. For example, as we saw in the case of Terapia, one of Advent International's most successful investments in post-communist central Europe (chapter 7), companies in emerging markets offer scope for the value-adding capabilities that private equity managers provide. Local banks in many emerging markets are also now able to offer credit on better terms than their counterparts in the more developed economies currently reeling from the credit crisis that has emerged in the United States. (Deals in emerging markets, moreover, typically involve less leverage than those in developed markets.)

Even before the credit crunch hit in the summer of 2007, dampening the prospects for venture capital and private equity in the United States, increasing numbers of investors around the world — including sovereign wealth funds — were beginning to realize that emerging markets offer fertile ground for venture capital and private equity. The Emerging Markets Private Equity Association's 2007 *Fundraising Review* shows that venture capital and private equity funds for investment in emerging markets raised $59.2 billion in 2007 — a 78 percent increase over the $33.2 billion raised in 2006, which in turn represented a 29 percent increase over the $25.8 billion raised in 2005. (In 2004, the total was a mere $6.5 billion.) The fastest-growing region in terms of investor interest in 2007 was central and Eastern Europe including Russia, followed (in terms of growth rates) by the Middle East, Latin America, and the emerging countries of Asia. Investment in sub-Saharan Africa shrunk modestly in 2007 after nearly tripling between 2005 and 2006.[3]

The major reason for this increase in investor interest was, of course, that the returns in emerging markets were showing strong increases prior to the financial crisis of 2008. The Emerging Markets Private Equity Association has found that for the three-year period ending June 30, 2006, returns on emerging market venture capital/private equity funds were 22.6 percent, more than double the performance of the S&P 500 over the same period; the top-quartile emerging market funds during these years showed a return of 49.9 percent as compared with 42 percent for the top-quartile U.S. private equity funds and 28.4 percent for the top-quartile U.S. venture capital funds.[4]

Despite the promise of emerging markets, however, most American venture capital managers have so far been content to stay at home. They have been disinclined to invest abroad for a reason I have previously discussed: with the exception of Israel, the most vibrant technology centers in the world are in the United States. China and India, as we have noted, have been attracting significant interest and investment from venture capitalists, but they still account for a relatively small portion of all venture capital investment. A recent survey by Deloitte & Touche and the National Venture Capital Association found that less than half of the American respondents were investing abroad; as the national managing partner of Deloitte's Venture Capital Services described the results, "U.S.-based VCs are essentially dabbling in global markets."[5] Although, as we shall see, there are still frontiers for venture capitalists in the United States, what became evident to me twenty-five years ago at TA Associates appears still to be true today: American venture capitalists, for the most part, are either not especially curious about international markets, or not adventurous enough to invest the time and money it takes to learn about them and how to invest in them successfully.

Private equity is a different matter. The global private equity investing that Advent has pioneered over the last twenty years has become of interest to other American firms, especially to the managers of the largest ones, the Blackstones and Carlyles of the world. Sensing an underserved market, they are pouring private equity investment into Western Europe and China while also venturing into markets such as India, Japan, and the Middle East. Much of this is occurring without local presence or local commitment, which is different from how Advent has approached such markets. The absence of deep local roots could be a problem for these players in the future. Meanwhile, as the forays into new markets by mainstream private equity firms, including those outside the United States, are duly noted in the business press, a handful of other, less well-known private equity managers are exploring even more rugged terrain. For example, Acap Partners, a private equity firm established in 2004 with the support of Actis (a leading emerging markets private equity manager that split off from the British-born CDC Group that same year), has a mission to "to generate returns for its investors by providing innovative financing solutions to entrepreneurs in post-conflict and other frontier markets." Acap's Afghanistan Renewal Fund is providing risk capital for small and medium-size enterprises in that country—perhaps the closest thing to a real frontier in the private equity industry today.

Although Acap Partners is flying in the face of history in Afghanistan and has embarked upon what some might consider a quixotic adventure, these venture capitalists and those who back them[6] must be applauded for their courage and commitment to a difficult place. It is heartening that there are at least a few pioneers in venture capital and private equity today trying to push the boundaries of the industry far beyond what most practitioners are familiar or comfortable with. If the goal, however, is to help stimulate economic development wherever it is needed, it is not necessary for venture capital and private equity managers to travel to remote places to find challenges worthy of their best and most creative efforts. Here in the United States, for example, venture capitalists can find opportunities in cities and regions that have not yet begun to realize their potential for growing innovative technology companies and are hoping to use venture capital in order to do so. Moreover, for venture capital and private equity managers who can see their work in a social context, the not-for-profit sector in the United States offers many opportunities for them to use their skills to benefit society.

To illustrate this range of opportunities, I will first tell the stories of two individuals I know who are now trying to make venture capital and private equity a force for economic and social development in some of the countries in the world that need it most: Franz Krejs, founder of the Horizonte Bosnia & Herzegovina Enterprise Fund; and Linda Rottenberg, cofounder of the not-for-profit group Endeavor. Afterward I will describe two efforts in which I have been involved in the United States, one in the area of regional economic development and the other in the not-for-profit sector. Taken together, these stories suggest to me that there are still many new, as yet unrecognized frontiers to be explored in venture capital and private equity.

### TACKLING THE BIG CHALLENGES: FRANZ KREJS IN BOSNIA AND HERZEGOVINA

Of all the venture capitalists with whom I have been affiliated over the years, the one most dedicated to using venture capital as an economic development tool is Franz Krejs of Austria. Krejs, with Advent's help, formed the first venture capital company in Austria, Horizonte, in 1985. While not a notable financial success (the capital from its first and only fund might be returned to its investors with the eventual success of one of its technology investments), Horizonte at least introduced the idea of venture capital to a socialist country where government-guaranteed bank loans had been the only means of financing small, innovative companies. When the Iron Curtain came down and former Yugoslavia began to break apart, Krejs saw a new field of opportunity opening. In 1994 he formed the Horizonte Slovene Enterprise Fund in Slovenia, the most economically advanced of the former Yugoslav republics. About 40 percent of this €8.4 million fund has been invested in technology companies, and the fund itself should double its initial capitalization by the end of its run.

A managing director of one of the Slovene portfolio companies was quite impressed with the impact that venture capital was having on economic development in Slovenia almost from the start and, in 1995, introduced Krejs to the owner of the largest private Bosnian bank. This banker believed that venture capital and private equity would be useful in rebuilding Bosnia after the war with the Serbs had ended. This was the kind of challenge that really brought out the adventurer in Krejs. It was not unlike an adventure that had beckoned me at about the same time, when I collaborated with John Cullinane, one of the early and successful software pioneers in the United States, to establish a venture capital program connecting the technology centers in Northern Ireland and the Irish Republic. That project never came to fruition, but Franz Krejs was both more daring and more determined than the team of John Cullinane and Peter Brooke.[7]

Just days before the Dayton Accords were signed in December of 1995, Franz and his managing director friend traveled down the Dalmatian coast and up the Neretva Valley to Sarajevo, which was under siege. The trip was fraught with danger. Bandits frequently stopped and stole vehicles. Bridges had been blown up, and streams had to be forded before Krejs and his companion could reach the outskirts of Sarajevo. The one opening to the city was over Mount Igman on a narrow road with steep ravines on either side, with ruined and abandoned trucks lying at the bottom. Krejs and his party arrived in Sarajevo the day after the Dayton Accords were signed. They found that this proud city, which had hosted the Winter Olympics in 1984, had ceased to function. There wasn't an unbroken pane of glass in any of the buildings. Food and water had to be transported through an airport checkpoint during one short interval of each day. Krejs and his colleagues checked into the only hotel functioning at the time, the redoubtable Holiday Inn, the back half of which had been blown away. Here was a man who was really on a mission. Soon afterward, Krejs met with the Bosnian bank owner, who assured him that things could only get better and who agreed to invest DM 10 million in a venture capital fund once the war ended. This whole episode occurred during the height of the war.

Krejs eventually put together a €15.4 million Bosnian fund, the Horizonte Bosnia & Herzegovina Enterprise Fund, although not until after a tortuous road to closing. The owner of the Bosnian bank was thrown in jail for war profiteering and never fulfilled his commitment. The U.S. Agency for International Development, which had pledged $5 million to the fund, reneged on its commitment. The participation of those two investors had been pivotal to the EBRD's agreement to take part, although Krejs was able to retain EBRD's support when he found a number of additional investors: the IFC; government-sponsored funds such as the Swedfund (Sweden), Norfund (Norway), 10 (Denmark), and FMO (Netherlands); and commercial banks such as Uni Credito (Italy), Oesterreiche Kontrollbank (Austria), and the Hypo Alpe Adria Bank (Austria). Siemens also agreed to participate, and the fund finally closed in 1997.

The Bosnia & Herzegovina Enterprise Fund was not your typical venture capital fund. It did not invest in technology, for whatever intellectual capital existed in Bosnia before the war had long since departed. Instead the fund invested in companies that could rebuild the country's infrastructure, in sectors such as building materials and food processing and distribution. It would go on to achieve many significant milestones including the first privatization of a joint-stock company in Bosnia; the first lease financing for one of its portfolio companies (with Hypo Alpe Adria Bank, one of the investors in the fund); the first mining concession in the Canton of Una Sana; and the first capital increase in a joint-stock company effected by a foreign investor. In addition, at the fund's instigation, the Bosnian government removed a counterproductive article from the country's privatization law. All these achievements, however, were accomplished with nearly as much agony as Krejs had encountered on his voyage to Sarajevo.

The fund's first investment was in a brick company, Ternoziegl, one of the first privatizations in Bosnia. Management was introduced from Austria, but proved inefficient and dishonest. The labor union representing the workers then essentially took over the company, cordoning off the plant and physically preventing the directors from entering the premises. The directors appealed to the courts and the police, but to no avail. On one attempt to reenter the plant, the directors were threatened with death. The union's management has continued to run the enterprise ever since, selling the bricks on the black market, not paying taxes, and generally operating outside a law that is in place but not enforced. The fund's investment in the company is carried at zero.

Another such investment, in a brick and stone quarry company, has worked out in the end, but is another example of what can go wrong under the kinds of conditions prevailing in a place like Bosnia. Here, too, strife between a corrupt manager (German, in this case) and the union led to a revolt by the workers. When the company's directors finally understood the manager's plan to bankrupt the company and then acquire it for himself, they fired him. (The appropriate court was notified of the manager's removal, but it took four months for this notification to be registered under Bosnian law, during which time the manager was able to siphon off DM 700,000 to his own account.) The union allowed the directors to take control of the company once again, new management was brought in and dramatically improved operations, and the company is to be sold to a strategic buyer. The end result for the Bosnian fund will be a realization on the sale of the brick factory of 1.5 times cost, with ownership of the quarry being retained for a later sale.

Far and away the most heartrending case Krejs encountered was that of a fish-processing company owned by two brothers-in-law, one Serbian Orthodox and the other Muslim. When the war began and Messrs. Milosevic of Serbia and Tudjman of Croatia fanned the ethnic flames of their minorities within Bosnia-Herzegovina, families turned against families. In the fish-processing company, the brothers-in-law, who had previously coexisted peacefully, became involved in a blood feud. One brother attempted to run over the children of the other, and a spiral of vengeance threatened to unfold until the families were separated. The Bosnian fund purchased the share of the Serbian brother-in-law, and the company has survived. Such chilling tales have been repeated over and over again in this unfortunate land.

The fund has had many successes, however, and they are increasing as Krejs gets a handle on how to operate in the Bosnian environment. One notable example is a cement company that was privatized jointly by the Bosnian fund and an Austrian cement manufacturer. Krejs negotiated the privatization, cut a deal with the local unions, and brought in the IFC as the lead investor. The Austrian company provided the required management, and the results have been impressive. The Bosnian fund has a put arrangement with the Austrians and will exit with a 25 percent annual return. Franz Krejs believes that the Bosnia & Herzegovina Enterprise Fund as a whole has a good chance of returning all the capital to its investors, no mean feat for a first-time fund in this war-ravaged part of the world. His investors, all strategic in nature, will gain much more as the country recovers. Krejs's contribution, however, goes way beyond what he has accomplished for his investors. He will have given people in Bosnia hope that businesses can be started and survive and that jobs and a better way of life can materialize. He has also invested in Kosovo and will soon begin a Croatian fund whose prospects will be considerably better than those of the Bosnian fund at its beginning.

Franz Krejs, to me, is the quintessential venture capitalist. He is in it for the contribution he can make to giving others a better life. Krejs's effort to help rebuild Bosnia after a devastating war is also as pure an example as one could find of a venture capitalist working in the spirit of the Marshall Plan. In many other countries in the world, however, it is simply poverty and a lack of opportunity that hold people back from realizing their economic and human potential. Most venture capitalists assume that the developing and emerging markets are not ready for venture capital, and that it therefore has no role to play in stimulating economic development in the poorer countries of the world. One entrepreneur I know, however, is challenging that assumption and convincingly demonstrating that venture capital can take root and grow in unlikely places.

### JUMP-STARTING VENTURE CAPITAL IN EMERGING MARKETS: LINDA ROTTENBERG AND ENDEAVOR

Linda Rottenberg, the cofounder and CEO of the nonprofit Endeavor, is a forty-year-old Harvard College and Yale Law School graduate whose passion for making a difference in the world and energy for doing it seem boundless. I met Linda in the mid-1990s when I was at Harvard Business School to speak about venture capital at an event sponsored by the Latino Student Organization. Linda was in the process of starting an organization to stimulate venture capital in emerging and developing markets and had been told that she should speak with me.

Knowing that the Harvard Business School students would swarm all over the podium at the end of my talk and make it difficult for her to get my attention, Linda followed me when I stepped out to go to the men's room just before my talk began. When I emerged from the men's room, Linda was waiting for me, introduced herself, and briefly explained what her new nonprofit was about. After I gave her my card and suggested that she call me at the office the following week, Linda went to see Bill Sahlman, a professor of entrepreneurial finance at HBS, and asked him if he would serve as cochair of her new organization's global advisory board. Bill replied, "Go and see Peter. If he agrees to be the other cochair, I will join him." Linda then came to see me and made a persuasive case. She was very passionate about the mission of Endeavor, and my defenses were breached. Sahlman was surprised that I collapsed so quickly and did join me as cochair of Endeavor's global advisory board.

Linda had conceived the idea for Endeavor while working at Ashoka, the organization of "Innovators for the Public" founded in 1980 by the social entrepreneur Bill Drayton. Along with its work of promoting social entrepreneurship, Ashoka was engaged in microlending in the developing world, and while Linda saw that microfinance was a good tool for alleviating poverty, she also saw its limitations. She became concerned that between the microlenders, on the one hand, and the multilateral and government sponsors of large-scale public works projects, on the other, no one was focused on the people in developing countries with ideas for enterprises that could create jobs on a large scale and help build a middle class.

Linda's ideas about using venture capital as a tool for large-scale economic development in the poorer countries of the world naturally resonated with me. I also agreed with her analysis of the limits of multilateral- and government-sponsored economic development projects for bringing about real, sustainable economic progress in these countries. Latin America, however, is a region that presents even more hindrances to venture capital and entrepreneurship than Western Europe and Southeast Asia did when I was trying to introduce venture capital to those areas beginning in the early 1970s and early 1980s, respectively. It lacks institutional support for the research that produces technological innovation and institutional and cultural support for entrepreneurship. Linda Rottenberg knew from experience in Latin America that the region had many potential high-impact entrepreneurs but also that these individuals did not believe that they could actually go out and start a business. While in Latin America working for Ashoka in the early 1990s, she once told a group of Argentinean students the story of Steve Jobs and Steve Wozniak developing the first Apple computer in their garage, only to have a young man respond: "That's a nice story, but nobody in Latin America is going to give me money to start a business, and I don't even have a garage."[8]

The situation in Latin America that Linda described is not so different, in many ways, from conditions I had encountered in countries such as Germany and Japan in the 1980s when I was trying to introduce venture capital there. There was never any question of introducing early-stage investing in Latin America when Advent International expanded there in the mid-1990s, however. While the region was ripe for private equity investing, for which Advent had a proven model, the lack of social and institutional support for entrepreneurship in Latin American countries, and the resulting lack of entrepreneurial experience and models (similar to what Advent International's affiliate SEAVIC had discovered in Southeast Asia in the 1980s), created obstacles for early-stage venture capital. The establishment of a venture capital industry in the region needed to be preceded by the creation of an entrepreneurial class. Linda wanted to prove that she could jump-start that process.

Linda founded Endeavor in 1997 with Peter Kellner, an entrepreneur and investment manager whose experience in postcommunist central Europe and Russia had taught him that would-be entrepreneurs in emerging markets needed both management skills and mentoring. Endeavor's mission is to help emerging-market economies make the transition from international aid to international investment by creating the conditions in which venture capital can thrive in these markets. It does this by identifying and supporting "high-impact entrepreneurs," which Endeavor defines as those with the potential for creating successful companies employing hundreds or even thousands of people and generating millions of dollars in wages and revenues. Such entrepreneurs have impact not just with the companies they start but also through their ability to inspire others to follow in their footsteps in countries where the unfamiliarity of entrepreneurship constitutes a significant cultural barrier to the creation of new businesses. Linda and her colleagues believe that by helping to produce successful entrepreneurs who can serve as models in Latin America, the Middle East, Africa, and the emerging countries of Asia, they can also help bring about other changes — in laws and regulations, education, and capital markets — that are needed to stimulate new business development and bring the private sectors of developing and emerging countries into the global economy.

The lack of an organized venture capital market in regions like Latin America poses many challenges for promoting entrepreneurship. For example, the lack of formal mechanisms for entrepreneurs and investors to find and connect with one another creates search costs that would be prohibitive for most venture capitalists. With few American and European venture capitalists, as we have seen, investing internationally in any serious way, outside investors are hard to come by in emerging markets. In addition, the handful of local venture capitalists in these markets insist on terms that no Western entrepreneur would agree to. (At a recent Endeavor Entrepreneurship Summit, entrepreneurs from emerging markets were amazed to hear that a Western venture capitalist would leave them with 30 to 40 percent of their own companies.) Linda and Peter Kellner found that they needed to provide entrepreneurs in emerging markets not only with management advice and mentoring but also with introductions to potential investors who would accept reasonable terms.

Endeavor began its efforts in Argentina and Chile and has since expanded into Brazil, Colombia, Egypt, India, Jordan, Mexico, South Africa, Turkey, and Uruguay. It is currently laying the groundwork for expansion into the Middle East and Peru. Endeavor's "venture catalyst" model involves, first of all, a rigorous search and selection process of scouring emerging markets for potential high-impact entrepreneurs. Screening panels consisting of local and international businesspeople, including venture capitalists, meet four times a year to select entrepreneurs who deserve support. Endeavor then provides these entrepreneurs with mentoring, management advice, and access to networks, managerial talent, and potential investors through its own global network.

To date, Endeavor has screened over 17,000 entrepreneurs and worked with over 400 of them in 266 companies. As of the end of 2007, the companies founded by Endeavor entrepreneurs had created over 86,000 jobs paying considerably more than the minimum wage in their countries and generated over $2.5 billion in revenues. Year by year, Endeavor is seeing exponential growth in the figures for jobs and revenues, showing how large an impact a relatively small number of highly talented, well-supported entrepreneurs can have. Ten years after Endeavor's founding, moreover, 95 percent of the companies founded and managed by its entrepreneurs survive, despite the fact that entrepreneurial ventures in the countries where Endeavor operates typically close within forty-two months.

These impressive results naturally raise the question of what resources Endeavor uses to achieve them and how it obtains these resources. They also reflect success, so far, in dealing with intricate problems of how to organize and manage a global entrepreneurial venture. My experience in dealing with such questions and problems is the reason Linda Rottenberg asked me to advise her on how to grow and develop Endeavor, where in addition to cochairing the global advisory board I serve as a special adviser to the global board of directors. To give an example of how Advent International's experience in entering new markets has been relevant to Endeavor's efforts, consider the question of how to support local affiliates. When I reviewed Endeavor's plan for expansion, the organization was raising money at the core and distributing it to its local offices. It seemed to me, however, that the local offices should be financially supported by local champions of substance who embraced the concept and who could adapt the model to conditions in their countries. This had been my model for expanding into new markets back in the days when I was building the original TA Associates, later Advent, networks in Western Europe and Southeast Asia. I also thought that money that Endeavor raised at the core level should be used to provide value-added services to the local offices, as Advent had provided such services to its affiliates.

Endeavor has followed this advice. Because it wants the impetus for its efforts in a country to come from the local business community, Endeavor has assisted its local champions in each new market it has entered in raising between $1.5 and $3 million from top local business leaders. These business leaders, in turn, have been extremely forthcoming with support— they are anxious to find local entrepreneurs to assist but lack the time to find them on their own. Many of them also become investors in Endeavor entrepreneurs' companies as well as mentors for the entrepreneurs and supporters of the local Endeavor operation.

Meanwhile, Endeavor makes this proposition to local supporters and staff: if you think the Endeavor model will work in your country, Endeavor will share best practices and connect you with our global network, but it will be up to you to figure out how to adapt our model to your local context. Linda believes that this approach has been the key to Endeavor's success. As I have learned from my own experience, however, it is important to balance local adaptation and responsiveness with direction from the core. So I have also advised Linda to make sure that managers of Endeavor's local operations understand the mission and maintain the Endeavor "brand" while at the same time adapting to local circumstances.

With a view to making the local offices self-sufficient in the future, Endeavor entrepreneurs are required to give a percentage of their profits or revenues back to the local offices. Moreover, Endeavor entrepreneurs are already becoming investors in future entrepreneurs in their own countries. In Argentina, for example, Jonatan Altszul, the founder of the IT security provider CORE, is now setting up the first pure high-tech venture capital firm in the country. If Endeavor can succeed, through such means, in making venture capital a self-replicating organism in emerging markets, it will have gone a long way toward fulfilling my own dream of venture capital as a private-sector Marshall Plan bringing economic and social development to countries everywhere.[9] Moreover, with its approach to promoting economic development by helping entrepreneurs to succeed and then using them as role models for others to follow, Endeavor is instilling confidence in people in the developing world in their ability to solve their own problems. This emphasis on building confidence was an aspect of George Marshall's approach that has always appealed to me.

I am excited to be helping Endeavor succeed not only because the organization is pursuing a dream in which I believe or because, as a venture capitalist, I enjoy helping entrepreneurs like Linda Rottenberg to realize *their* dreams.[10] I am also excited and pleased to see American venture capitalists giving of their time and their talents to help promote entrepreneurship in other countries. Many of the American venture capitalists who serve as mentors and advisers in Endeavor's Venture Corps program are younger people. I see in them the idealism and desire to play a constructive role in society that motivated many of my own generation of venture capitalists.

I hope that the example of Endeavor will be broadcast throughout the venture capital and private equity communities. It is true that few countries in the world possess the cultural and institutional supports for entrepreneurship that we have in the United States, but we do not have a monopoly on inventiveness. I do not believe that there is anything in the American character that makes us inherently superior to others as innovators. We have been fortunate, because of geography and history, to have had the opportunity to develop our talents. Give Europeans, Asians, or Latin Americans the same advantages, and you will find energetic people equally capable of innovation. From this standpoint, there are many more frontiers for venture capitalists to conquer. Moreover, some of these frontiers exist right here in the United States. While venture capital is still more of a success story in America than in almost any other country, its success in America has been confined mostly to pockets on the East and West coasts. This need not remain the case indefinitely, however, as illustrated by another story from the venture capital frontier.

GROWING THE VENTURE CAPITAL
SECTOR IN THE UNITED STATES TODAY:
THE VECTIS LIFE SCIENCES FUND

It is rare among American venture capitalists today to go off to war-ravaged places like Bosnia or even to invest in emerging markets such as those in which Endeavor is working in Latin America, Africa, and Asia. However, it is not just in the emerging markets of the world, or even in the developed countries of Europe and Asia, that more and more people are looking to create a vibrant venture capital sector to spark economic development. Here in the United States, in regions still trying to recover from deindustrialization and the loss of the high-paying manufacturing jobs that once sustained their economies, venture capital is rightly seen as a key ingredient in creating renewed prosperity. In the last few years, I have participated in a determined and creative effort by one American city to foster innovation, entrepreneurship, and sustainable economic development through the use of venture capital.

The Boston area's success in using venture capital as a tool for developing a local biotech industry has made it a model, along with Silicon Valley, for other cities and regions in the United States that hope to develop their own assets in the life-sciences sector. In 2002, the St. Louis Regional Chamber and Growth Association visited Boston with a group of 125 local business and civic leaders to study how venture capital had been used to develop the life-sciences sector in the Boston area. I was invited to address this group. After my speech I was asked if I could suggest a way of jump-starting investment in the new health-sciences ventures that were emerging around Washington University. At the request of two members of the delegation, William Danforth (chancellor emeritus of Washington University in St. Louis) and John McDonnell (former head of McDonnell Douglas), I agreed to investigate whether the research and the existing infrastructure in St. Louis, and Missouri as a whole, could support a venture capital presence.

I worked on this project with my son John Brooke. In the early 1990s, John and I had established the Brooke Family Partnership. Its purpose was to participate in funds managed by both established and emerging venture capital and private equity managers and to coinvest with them in deals that we thought particularly attractive. The successful performance of this family partnership encouraged John to recommend that it be expanded to include other families and to address other opportunities in the venture and private equity fields, so we established Brooke Private Equity Advisors. One obvious opportunity for the firm was the use of venture capital and private equity for economic development in regions like St. Louis. I had begun my own career as a venture capitalist by looking for ways to help the economy of Massachusetts to recover from its own decades-long economic slump, so this activity was a return to my professional roots as well as an extension of my whole life's work.

With the help of Belden Daniels of Economic Innovation International Inc. — a firm that Daniels founded to build innovative, privately capitalized institutions for public purposes such as regional economic development — Brooke Private Equity Advisors undertook a yearlong study of St. Louis's potential as a center for biotechnology and life-sciences ventures. We examined the life-sciences research and technology at Washington University and other research centers in the area, consulting with experts to determine if this research and technology was important and deep enough to support significant venture activity. We looked at the technology-transfer mechanisms at the local research institutions and the enabling organizations such as business incubators. Finally we looked at the local venture capital community and assessed its capabilities.

We found that St. Louis was indeed a major biotechnology and life-sciences center. We also found that it was being underserved by its venture capitalists, who did not have enough capital or connections to fund companies that could exploit the available research. Research institutions including the Washington University School of Medicine, the Washington University Medical Center, and the schools of medicine and public health at St. Louis University have generated innovations that their own technology-transfer programs have made available to those who have the capital and entrepreneurial energy to exploit them. The problem was that there was not enough capital or expertise available. The St. Louis venture capital community today actually reminds me of Boston's in the 1960s and '70s, which consisted of a very small group of individuals and firms doing a few deals here and there, scrambling for every dollar we could get from individual investors, friends, or families.[11]

The question put to John Brooke and me was how the St. Louis region should respond to the lack of venture capital and the lack of experienced venture managers. It was obvious that some type of civic intervention was required — a conclusion that was also reached by a Batelle Memorial Institute study that found that, in the absence of such intervention, growing a world-class plant and life-sciences industry fueled by venture capital would take anywhere from twelve to twenty years. John and I responded by suggesting that a program be developed to address the shortage of venture capital, the lack of connections between the local venture capitalists and those in other parts of the country, and the lack of venture management expertise.

The program we created to address these shortcomings was the Vectis Life Sciences Fund. Vectis is a fund of funds whose sponsoring investors are the Danforth Foundation, the James S. McDonnell Foundation, and Washington University (which had invested in Advent International's International Network fund back in the 1980s). It has raised $81 million and invested in funds managed by venture capital firms in St. Louis as well as in others managed by East and West Coast firms with deep experience in the life-sciences sector. While I was involved in the design of the Vectis program, John was the one who has carried out its execution. He organized the research effort, interviewed the various constituencies, drew the conclusions, raised the capital with help from me, and has managed the activity from the beginning.

The creation of a network, via the Vectis fund, linking East and West Coast venture capitalists with experience in the life-sciences sector with local venture capitalists in St. Louis is a unique and crucial element of the Vectis program. The national and local venture capital managers are working together to coordinate deal flow, due diligence, and deal syndication, with significant benefits for all. The national managers (Advent International,[12] MPM Capital, and Accuitive Medical Ventures in the East, and Prospect Venture Partners and CMEA Ventures on the West Coast) are gaining access to a deal flow in an area of the Midwest with great potential in the life-sciences sector. The local St. Louis managers (Prolog Ventures, Oakwood Medical Investors, and RiverVest Venture Partners) are benefiting not only from new sources of capital to manage but also from the ability to work alongside the experienced national firms.

The result will be a strengthening of the local venture capital industry that will, in turn, play a crucial role in the effort to turn St. Louis into a major center for innovation and entrepreneurship in the life sciences.[13]

Although the structure of the Vectis program is unique, St. Louis is just one of many American cities and states currently attempting to use such programs as a path to greater prosperity.[14] As more and more people concerned with local and regional economic development in the United States now realize, using venture capital and other forms of entrepreneurial finance to create innovative new businesses offers a more promising route to sustainable prosperity than tax incentives and subsidies designed to lure established companies to particular locales. Such policies are too often used to attract businesses that offer low-wage jobs with meager benefits, costing states and cities more in lost corporate tax revenues and increased spending for infrastructure and social services than they gain in employment and payroll tax revenues. (Even when companies with better jobs to offer are lured to open facilities in a new locale, it is often without meaningful guarantees that they will stay put any longer than it takes to realize the more immediate benefits of the initial move.) These tactics set off a race to the bottom that, in today's world of global competition, pits localities in the United States not only against one another but also against low-wage countries all over the world. This is not a race that Americans can win, in the long run, without doing grave damage to our economy, our social fabric, and our whole way of life.

Venture capitalists need to be concerned about such problems, and there are things they can do to help solve them. I have long believed that venture capitalists can do good in ways that have hardly been explored. Following conscientious investment strategies and practices is one way they can contribute to economic development and social progress. Designing and participating in innovative programs like Vectis is another. Venture capitalists can also invest their time and skills in efforts in the social or nongovernmental sector to improve opportunities for the economically disadvantaged, whether individuals, regions, or nations, and to contribute in other ways to the betterment of society. The involvement of American venture capitalists in an organization like Endeavor offers an example of venture capitalists using their unique sets of skills to help others improve economic conditions in the places where they live. The problem-solving skills of venture capitalists can also be put to use in the social or not-for-profit sector to help meet society's important nonmaterial needs.

## VENTURE CAPITAL SKILLS IN THE
## NOT-FOR-PROFIT SECTOR

As many people have observed since Alexis de Tocqueville first noticed Americans' propensity to form "voluntary associations," the United States has an unusually large number of what are now called nonprofit or, as I prefer to say, not-for-profit organizations. The not-for-profit sector in America brings private resources to bear in countless spheres of activity that go into making a dynamic civil society. I have been involved in the not-for-profit sector since I started TA Associates back in 1968, mostly in education as a trustee of the schools my children attended, as a trustee of Colgate University, and as a member of the Board of Overseers of Harvard University. However, the institution that has given me the most pleasure serving has been the Boston Symphony Orchestra. I was an overseer of the BSO for eight years, a trustee for fifteen years, and its chairman from 1999 to 2005. I played the piano as a boy and was introduced to classical music at an early age, so the BSO was a natural fit. I also deeply believe in the arts as a vital part of a child's education.

When I became chairman-elect of the BSO in 1998, my predecessor, Nick Zervas, had just led a successful quest by a search committee for the best person available to fill the role of music director. The orchestra's skills and performances had slipped over the later years of Seiji Ozawa's tenure, and the players who served on the committee felt that there was one man who could raise the BSO to a higher level. His name was James Levine, artistic director of the Metropolitan Opera. The understanding we reached with Jim was an expensive one, but it was necessary to spend some money if the BSO was to reach the goal that the trustees had set of becoming the world's great orchestra. This involved financial support for additional rehearsal time (Jim believed, and the trustees and players agreed, that the orchestra should always be prepared to play at the highest level), for expansion of the repertoire, and for the inclusion of the very best guest artists.

Realizing these ambitions was a challenge to a budget that was already stretched. There was only one answer to these considerable increases in expenses: a targeted capital campaign that we named the "Artistic Initiative." My first job as chairman was, with the help of the BSO's very competent managing director, Mark Volpe, to frame the campaign message and get the support of the board of trustees. The fact that we had already agreed upon the Levine program did not necessarily mean that the trust-

ees were eager to dig deep into their own pockets. They had to be convinced that the BSO had the opportunity, under Levine's leadership, to
become the best, and that to fail to respond to that challenge would be a
dereliction of their duty as trustees.

I had a great deal of support from my eventual successor, Ed Linde, as
well as my old friend Tom Stemberg. When Tom, the founder and then-
CEO of Staples, heard my challenge to the board, he came to me and said,
"Peter, I am going to go to all the venture capitalists and private equity
guys in this town who you put in business over the years and tell them it's
payback time." Tom did that, and the response from my former colleagues
was heartening, becoming the cornerstone to what will be a successful
conclusion of the Artistic Initiative campaign. As Jim Levine has said on
countless occasions, this was the first time in his career that he did not
have to go through a laborious committee process to receive approval of a
program, and where the leadership of the organization grasped the nettle
and got the job done.

Our approach to the venture capital community was just one outgrowth
of my fund-raising strategy for the BSO, a strategy that involved segment-
ing the Boston business community and approaching each segment with a
pitch that would secure its support. The pitch was a simple one: "We Bos-
tonians have the enviable opportunity of making our orchestra into one
of the world's greatest, an opportunity that not many other cities have. If
we want Boston to retain its claim to be a great intellectual center that at-
tracts the best talent, we have to come forward with our financial support."
As an article in the *Wall Street Journal* reported,[15] we targeted the technology, money management, legal, medical, and private equity sectors
and then had board members use their personal connections in whatever
sector they were affiliated with to solicit potential donors, whether these
people had supported musical organizations in the past or not. I thought
that lawyers would be most effective at communicating with lawyers, doctors with doctors, and so forth. I also contended that old money had to
be supplemented with new, fresh money — and a lot of it — if we were to
achieve our mission. The trust fund money was just not as available as it
had been in the past (almost precisely the situation that the Massachusetts
economy had faced in the 1950s, when the old money in Boston was not
being invested in innovation and risk).

My career in venture capital and private equity prepared me for the
challenge that the BSO faced when I became chairman. I knew Jim Levine

to be the kind of extraordinarily talented and innovative individual who needed to be given the ability to pursue his vision, much like an entrepreneur in whose enterprise I wanted to invest. I, in turn, helped to create the vision for the BSO board of how Jim could take us where we wanted to go, made the case for that vision, organized the effort, and helped execute the plan, all with the help of dedicated trustees and an administration that believed in our mission. This was old hat to me, because I have been doing this kind of thing all my life. Venture capitalists and private equity managers are problem solvers. They know how to define and set objectives, they know how to organize, and they know how to execute. If they dedicate part of their lives to solving the problems of others, whether it be in the arts, education, the inner city, or elsewhere, they will make improvements that those in the public sector will find hard to duplicate. When my wife Anne and I were honored by the Boston venture capital and private equity communities with the naming for us of the main corridor in Symphony Hall, I urged them to use their considerable wealth and the problem-solving talent to improve the lot of others. Many have already done this, and my hope is that more will do so as well.

One promising use of the talents of venture capital and private equity managers in the not-for-profit world can be seen in the field of what is called "venture philanthropy," where foundations and individuals adopt a high-engagement, outcome-focused approach to the support of fledgling not-for-profit organizations that mirrors, in many ways, the support that venture capitalists provide to their portfolio companies. Venture philanthropists (or at least those who are not just borrowing the language of venture capital to make themselves look glamorous) understand that in order to help new not-for-profits succeed in their missions, they must help build organizations that are capable of carrying out and sustaining innovative programs. This means not only making grants for operating support but also providing hands-on management assistance, setting organizational benchmarks that make continued funding contingent on demonstrable progress toward desired outcomes, and helping not-for-profits find enduring sources of financial support.

Not by coincidence, many of the original, most respected venture philanthropy organizations are led by successful venture capital or private equity managers. The list of such venture capital and private equity managers includes George Roberts, cofounder of KKR (also founder and chairman of the Roberts Enterprise Development Fund, now known as

REDF); Josh Bekenstein, managing partner of Bain Capital (chairman of New Profit Inc.); Rick Burnes, cofounder of Charles River Ventures (partner with the Boston affiliate of the Social Venture Partners network); and Peter Barris, managing general partner of New Enterprise Associates (founding investor and honorary board member of Venture Philanthropy Partners).[16] In Britain, meanwhile, Apax Partners cofounder Sir Ronald Cohen has founded Bridges Community Ventures, a venture capital firm with a mission of investing in enterprises that can have a positive social or environmental impact and that employ local people in areas ranked among the poorest 25 percent in the country. Permira, which ranks with Apax as one of the leading private equity firms in Britain, has invested £1 million in creating a philanthropic endeavor, Breakthrough, that is investing both money and the time of its partners and staff in social enterprises.[17]

Thinking about the many problems in our society, domestic and global, that require innovative solutions from the private sector and the ability to put them into effect, one realizes that there are, indeed, many frontiers for pioneering venture capital and private equity managers to explore. The excitement and the fun of constantly pushing into new territory has been the greatest reward I have received from my career in venture capital and private equity. Since I also believe, along with General Doriot, that "our happiness is in direct proportion to the contributions we make," I recommend the path of adventure to anyone in the industry who wants to realize the full range of rewards it has to offer. Venture capital and private equity may have spread all over the globe, but they still have many worlds left to conquer.

ACKNOWLEDGMENTS

It is difficult to acknowledge everyone who has been part of this book. I undoubtedly have left some names out, and I apologize for that. This exercise began three years ago when Richard Sobel and my wife, Anne, convinced me that I should describe my odyssey through the world of venture capital and private equity. I was reluctant to do this until I met Davis Dyer and Dan Penrice, who convinced me that there was a story to be told and a message that would be useful to others. I owe a lot to Dave and Dan. They shepherded this novice with great patience through a process that bewildered him at times. They are true professionals without whose guidance this book would not have been published.

I did not realize how long and arduous the journey would be. However, when I talked to my first partner at TA Associates, Kevin Landry, and others such as Bill Egan, Roe Stamps, and Steve Woodsum, I realized that reliving the old days was great fun. These colleagues also shared their recollections of the early days of TAA with Dan Penrice, as did Tom Claflin and Mike Ruane. The conversations I had with portfolio company principals like Bill Frusztajer, Don Troxel, and Amram Rasiel were essential to set the scene in the early days.

In describing the time when the international network concept took shape in my mind, the economic conditions that impeded our progress in France were recalled by Antoine Dupont-Fauville, Christian Marbach, Jean Deléage, and Jean-Bernard Schmidt, and in the United Kingdom by John Incledon. Probably the most fun was talking to my partner in building the international network, Sir David Cooksey. David and I relived the founding of Advent Ltd. in the United Kingdom and the establishment of the European network with such pivotal managers and directors as Jochen Mackenrodt and Rolf Dienst in Germany, Lars-Olof Gustavsson and Gösta Oscarsson in Sweden, and Franz Krejs in Austria and Slovenia. Neal Pearce, now retired from Advent Venture Partners (the successor to Advent Ltd.), helped fill in important background about the early days of venture capital in Britain, as did Friedrich Bornikoel of TVM Capital in the case of Germany.

The early, colorful days of the network in Asia were recalled by Tan Keng Boon, Derrick Lee, Koh Lee Boon, and Hoe Boon Kwee in Singapore and Malaysia, and by Victor Fung and Chris Leong in Hong Kong and China.

David Gill, formerly of the International Finance Corporation, also contributed his recollections of the founding of SEAVIC. Others who spoke with Dan Penrice or me on aspects of venture capital and private equity in Asia include Brooks Zug, Phil Bilden, Mintoo Bhandari, Chuan Thor, and Vincent Chan.

Conversations with Tom Armstrong, Tony Haight, and Clint Harris reminded me all too well of the tenuous, fragile days when Advent International was formed. Doug Brown helped me recall the growth of our offices in Europe. The emergence of Advent as an industry leader were described by many of those who made it so: John Walker, Steve Tadler, Will Schmidt, Chris Neizert, Ralf Huep, and Humphrey Battcock in Western Europe; Nick Callinan, Joanna James, Chris Mruck, and Emma Popa-Radu in central Europe; and the two transplants from Europe to Latin America, Ernest Bachrach and Juan Carlos Torres. Numerous conversations with David Mussafer, David McKenna, and Tom Lauer in Boston provided useful perspective on the growth of the company's investment and administrative functions.

In describing my hopes for venture capital as an economic development tool in emerging markets both abroad and in the United States, I received valuable comments from Linda Rottenberg of Endeavor and John Brooke of Brooke Private Equity Advisors. Linda's colleague Greg Durst in Johannesburg and Donn Rubin of the Coalition for Plant and Life Sciences in St. Louis supplied Dan Penrice with valuable background on the Endeavor and Vectis stories, respectively. In describing my hopes for venture capital in the not-for-profit sector, Mark Volpe, the managing director of the Boston Symphony Orchestra, was very helpful as was Jack Davies of Venture Philanthropy Partners. Throughout the entire project, my assistant Nancy C. Smith provided excellent administrative support.

Although all the people I have named here have contributed recollections and/or important insights, it is important to note that the views expressed in the book, except for those expressly attributed to other individuals at certain points, are my own and not those of Advent International or TA Associates.

Finally, I have to thank the people who have been a great encouragement to me in this effort: Bill Sahlman, who read and provided helpful comments on an early version of the manuscript and who, in his foreword, has put this story into the context of our times; and Anne Brooke, who encouraged me to write this to keep me out of her hair but who, in the final analysis, decided it was "not bad."

# APPENDIX
## DRAMATIS PERSONAE

It took the efforts of a great many people to build TA Associates, Advent International, and the international network of venture capital firms that TAA and Advent created. Many of the key people are listed below, along with brief descriptions of the parts they played in the story I tell in Part I of the book.

### TA ASSOCIATES

Craig Burr. Joined TA Associates in early 1970s. With Bill Egan and Jean Deléage, formed Burr, Egan, Deleage in 1979.

Tom Claflin. First employee at TA Associates. Left TAA in 1978 to form Claflin Capital Management.

David Croll. Joined TA Associates in 1976 and developed media and communications unit into a leader in cable television financings. Became managing partner of TAA in 1982. Became managing partner of M/C Partners, the independent media and communications investing firm eventually formed from the unit he led at TAA.

Bill Egan. Joined TA Associates in 1973. With Craig Burr and Jean Deléage, formed Burr, Egan, Deleage in 1979.

Kevin Landry. Second employee at TA Associates. Became partner in 1972, managing partner in 1982. Currently a managing director at TAA. His assumption of increasing responsibility for the investment side of TAA's activities in the course of the 1970s allowed me to spend my time developing the international network.

P. Andrews (Andy) McLane. Joined TA Associates in 1979. Became a managing director of the firm in 1982 and senior managing director in 1997. Currently a senior adviser at TAA.

Jacqui Morby. Joined TAA in 1978. Became a managing director in 1982, served on the firm's executive committee from 1986 until 2001. Currently a senior adviser at TAA.

E. Roe Stamps. Joined TA Associates in 1979. With Steve Woodsum, formed Summit Partners in 1984.

Grant Wilson. Joined TA Associates in mid-1970s and inaugurated the firm's cable television investment activity. Left TAA in late 1970s to launch his own investment operation.

Steve Woodsum. Joined TA Associates in 1981. With Roe Stamps, formed Summit Partners in 1984.

Tom Armstrong. Joined Advent International as COO in 1984, serving until 1998.

Ernest Bachrach. Joined Advent's London office in 1990. Since 1995 has led the firm's Latin American operations.

Doug Brown. Joined Advent in 1985. Took charge of Advent's European operations in 1990. Became chief investment officer in 1994, CEO in 1995, serving in that capacity until his resignation in 2003.

Nick Callinan. Led the development Advent International's central European operations between 1994 and 1998. Founded Western Pacific (forerunner of today's Advent Private Capital), which became Advent's network member in Australia, in 1984.

Clint Harris. Joined Advent in 1984 and developed the firm's highly successful corporate venturing programs. Led Advent effort that established Gemini Israel Venture Funds Ltd. Formed Grove Street Advisors in 1998.

Henry Huntley (Tony) Haight IV. Joined Advent in 1984. Comanaging director of the Southeast Asia Venture Investment Company (SEAVIC) 1984–1996; comanaging director of Techno Ventures Hong Kong, the management company for the Hong Kong Venture Investment Trust (HKVIT), 1985–1989. Spearheaded the development of the firm's Southeast Asian operations. Left Advent in 1997 and founded Argo Global Capital.

Joanna James. Joined Advent in 1995, assumed leadership of central European operations in 1998.

John Littlechild. Joined Advent International in 1984 from Advent Ltd., the TA Associates and then Advent International network member in London. Left Advent in 1992 to join HealthCare Ventures.

Julio Nuñez. Founding director of Advent International. As CEO of Entreprises Quilmes, the Bemberg-controlled industrial and financial company, invested in the early programs of TA Associates and in funds of TAA's and Advent International's Asian affiliates. Pivotal in Entreprises Quilmes's decision to provide the bulk of the capital for the formation of Advent International.

Juan Carlos Torres. Joined Advent International's Mexico City office in 1996 from former network member Advent España.

David J. S. Cooksey. Cofounded Advent Ltd. in the United Kingdom in 1981. Played a key role in the development of the TA Associates/Advent International network in Western Europe. Chief executive of Advent Ltd. (now Advent Venture Partners) 1981–1987; chairman 1987–2006. Director of Advent International, 1985–1990.

Jean Deléage. Joined Sofinnova in 1971. Established Sofinnova's American subsidiary, Sofinnova, Inc., in 1976. With Craig Burr and Bill Egan, formed Burr, Egan, Deleage in 1979.

Leo Deschuyteneer. Chief investment officer of Sofina (Belgium) and cofounder of Advent Belgium.

Rolf Dienst. Cofounder of the investment firm the Matuschka Group in Germany; cofounder of TVM Technoventures. Founded Wellington Partners, a pan-European venture capital firm based in London and Munich, in 1991.

Antoine Dupont-Fauville. Chairman of Crédit National, cofounder and chairman of Sofinnova.

Lars-Olof Gustavsson and Gösta Oscarsson. Cofounders of network member Four Seasons in Sweden.

Franz Krejs. Founded Austrian network member Horizonte in 1985 after apprenticing at TVM Technoventures. Established the Horizonte Slovene Enterprise Fund in 1994 and the Horizonte Bosnia & Herzegovina Enterprise Fund in 1997.

Jochen Mackenrodt. Siemens executive, cofounder and founding chairman of TVM Technoventures.

Christian Marbach. Deputy minister in the French Ministry of Industry, cofounder and director of Sofinnova.

Count Albrecht Matuschka. Cofounder of the investment firm the Matuschka Group in Germany; cofounder of network member TVM Technoventures.

Gösta Oscarsson. See Lars-Olof Gustavsson above.

Jean-Bernard Schmidt. Joined Sofinnova in 1973, chairman since 1986.

Piet van de Ven. Managing director of Orange Nassau. Key player in the development of the TA Associates/Advent International network in Western Europe and Southeast Asia.

ASIA

Yaichi Ayukawa. Founder of the Japanese venture capital firm Techno-Venture; cochairman of the venture capital fund Advent Techno-Venture.

Koh Lee Boon. Joined SEAVIC in 1984. Retired in 1996 as senior vice president, currently serves on board of SEAVI Advent.

Tan Keng Boon. Joined SEAVIC as comanaging director in 1985. Currently managing partner of SEAVI Advent.

John Brooke. Joined Advent in 1985. Cofounded Brooke Private Equity Advisors in 2002.

Victor K. Fung. Cofounder of the Hong Kong Venture Investment Trust (HKVIT) and chairman of HKVIT 1985–1989. Group chairman of the Li & Fung group of companies.

David Gill. As head of the capital markets group at the International Finance Corporation (IFC), encouraged me to expand the TA Associates network into Southeast Asia and provided IFC sponsorship for SEAVIC. In the mid-1990s, as an adviser to the Inter-American Development Bank, recommended that Advent International develop a private equity program in Latin America.

Ang Kong Hua. President of National Iron and Steel of Singapore and former officer of the Development Bank of Singapore (DBS). Persuaded DBS to spearhead local fund-raising for SEAVIC, of which National Iron and Steel also became a sponsor.

Derrick Lee. Joined SEAVIC in 1984 as senior vice president. Currently managing partner of SEAVI Advent.

Chris Leong. Comanaging director of Techno Ventures Hong Kong, the management company for the Hong Kong Venture Investment Trust (HKVIT) 1985–1989.

Augustin (Toti) Que. As an officer in David Gill's capital markets group at the IFC, persuaded Gill to encourage the development of venture capital in Southeast Asia. First comanaging director, with Tony Haight, of SEAVIC.

Bob Theleen. Founder of the venture capital/private equity group ChinaVest.

Alan Yeo. Chairman of Yeo Hiap Seng and of the Trade Development Board of Singapore. Chairman of SEAVIC (now SEAVI Advent) 1983–present.

LATIN AMERICA

Francisco (Pancho) Ravecca. Chairman of the Uruguayan trade bank Surinvest. Helped to assemble a group of Advent International affiliates and to launch Advent's own operations in Latin America.

# NOTES

### INTRODUCTION (xiii–xviii)

1. Marshall's vision continues to inspire people concerned with alleviating poverty and providing opportunity for people around the world, as Bill Gates testified when he delivered his own Harvard commencement address sixty years after General Marshall gave his. See Robert A. Guth, "The Speechmaker: How Bill Gates Got Ready for Harvard," *Wall Street Journal*, June 8, 2007, p. A1.

2. Tony Judt, *Postwar: A History of Europe since 1945* (New York: Penguin Press, 2005), p. 94.

3. Relaxation of trade barriers has been critical to the growth of both developed and emerging markets. Unfortunately, the deregulation of financial markets, which has nothing to do with the efficient movement of goods and services, has caused a crisis that will harm the progress that has been made. Recovering from this crisis will take a long time.

### CHAPTER 1: BECOMING A VENTURE CAPITALIST (3–21)

1. Semenenko was said to have loaned $2 billion to the major Hollywood studios between the mid-1930s and 1956, when he put together a syndicate that purchased 33 percent of the common stock of Warner Bros. from Jack, Albert, and Harry Warner. See "Boston to Hollywood," *Time*, May 21, 1956, accessed at http://www.time .com/time/magazine/article/0,9171,808529,00.html (4/1/08).

2. Although MIT spin-offs played a key role in making the Boston area America's leading center of innovation in electronics during the 1960s, it must be noted that MIT was not as energetic in promoting relationships between the institution and new, technology-based enterprises as were Stanford University (where the legendary Frederick Terman, mentor to William Hewlett and David Packard in the 1930s, became dean of engineering in 1946) and the University of California at Berkeley, which developed many of the technologies that spurred the creation of Silicon Valley. Although MIT in the postwar period encouraged its faculty to do research with commercial applications, its institutional ties were mainly with Washington and the larger, more established companies that dominated the defense and aerospace industries. Meanwhile, the idea of an academic institution exploiting its technology to stimulate the creation of whole new industries and enterprises in the Boston area remained internally controversial at MIT. For a brief but authoritative account of the rise of Silicon Valley and Route 128, and of the role played by the local

universities in each instance, see AnnaLee Saxenian, *Regional Advantage: Culture and Competition in Silicon Valley and Route 128* (Cambridge, Mass., and London: Harvard University Press, 1996), pp. 11–27 and 66–67. Saxenian states (p. 15) that a "calculated distancing from the region's new technology enterprises would typify MIT's relationship to Route 128. In spite of the university's commitment to commercially relevant research, it kept firms at arm's length."

3. The High Technology Lending Group also sponsored the First Small Business Investment Corporation, which was the first small business investment corporation (SBIC) chartered by a commercial bank in the United States after Congress created this new kind of entity in 1958. The small business investment companies were allowed to borrow three times their capital, with the loans guaranteed by the federal government. Congress passed the Small Business Investment Act, which established the SBIC program, in response to Sputnik. Although most SBICs did not perform well, they helped to stimulate the rise of the venture capital communities in Boston and Silicon Valley. See Paul A. Gompers and Josh Lerner, *The Money of Invention: How Venture Capital Creates New Wealth* (Boston: Harvard Business School Press, 2001), pp. 170–171.

4. In 1965, after I had left the First National Bank of Boston to run the venture capital operation at Bessemer Securities, I joined Wang Laboratories' board. I remained on the board through the company's rise as one of the great computer companies of the 1960s and '70s, its decline in the late 1980s, Dr. Wang's death in 1990, and the company's journey through bankruptcy in 1992–1993. During the thirty-two years I knew him, I played an active role in advising Dr. Wang and furnishing him with connections.

5. My successor as head of the High Technology Lending Group at FNBB was Charlie Cunningham, a private investor (as well as a great collector of seventeenth-century Dutch art and a trustee of Boston's Museum of Fine Arts for many years) who was a good interim leader. Charlie, in turn, was succeeded by Tom Lee, who took the group to a whole new level and then left in 1974 to start Thomas H. Lee Company, which became a major force in the buyout industry in the 1980s.

6. Laurance Rockefeller went on to found Venrock Associates as the venture capital arm of the Rockefeller family in 1969. For a short account of the Rockefellers' early venture activity, the creation of Venrock, and the firm's investment philosophy, see Udayan Gupta, ed., *Done Deals: Venture Capitalists Tell Their Stories* (Boston: Harvard Business School Press, 2000), pp. 107–112.

7. Knowing Dr. Wang for over thirty years, I saw him change a great deal. In the early days of our relationship he was a humble man, living in a modest house and driving his own car. After Wang Laboratories went public in 1966, his behavior be-

came quite different. By the time the company introduced its first word processor in 1976, Dr. Wang had a fleet of cars, chauffeurs, and an airplane. The company's headquarters had moved from Tewksbury, where the Doctor was available to everybody, to the towers in Lowell, where he isolated himself. He became interested in having buildings named after him: the Wang Performing Arts Center, the Wang Ambulatory Care Wing at Massachusetts General Hospital, and the Wang Institute for Computer Science. He became a Harvard overseer and a director of the Bank of Boston. He had become a big man, a deity. He did not take advice from a very good board of directors, especially when it suggested that his son Fred needed seasoning before he became president. The board recommended that an experienced, professional manager become president and that Fred Wang be tutored and evaluated as future CEO material. Dr. Wang rejected this advice out of hand. Two highly respected members of the board resigned as a result. Eventually I had to tell the Doctor, who by then was a sick man, that unless he removed Fred, the banks would. Fred subsequently resigned. For another account of the Wang story and my own role in it, see Charles C. Kenney, *Riding the Runaway Horse: The Rise and Decline of Wang Laboratories* (Boston: Little, Brown and Co., 1992). For Dr. Wang's account of the relationship with Warner & Swasey, see Dr. An Wang, with Eugene Linden, *Lessons: An Autobiography* (Reading, Mass.: Addison-Wesley, 1986), pp. 115–118.

8. Hayden Stone, which Arthur Rock joined after graduating from Harvard Business School in 1951, had engaged in some significant venture capital activity in the 1950s, most famously its 1957 investment in Fairchild Semiconductor, which would give birth to Intel when Robert Noyce and Gordon Moore left Fairchild in 1968 to start their own company. Arthur Rock relates this episode in his early career as a venture capitalist in Gupta, *Done Deals*, pp. 139–142. Tom Wolfe's 1983 *Esquire* article "The Tinkerings of Robert Noyce," which describes the foundings of Fairchild Semiconductor and Intel and the beginnings of Silicon Valley, is reprinted (as "Two Young Men Who Went West") in *Hooking Up* (New York: Farrar Straus Giroux, 2000), pp. 17–65.

9. In recent years, historians of New England have found that entrepreneurship in Boston from colonial times well into the nineteenth century was not confined to the traders, merchants, and textile manufacturers who built the city's reputation as a commercial center but was also widely practiced by groups including artisans, women, and African-Americans. Some of this history is recounted in Conrad Edick Wright and Katheryn P. Viens, eds., *Entrepreneurs: The Boston Business Community, 1700–1850* (Boston: Massachusetts Historical Society, 1997).

10. Quoted in Rudolph L. Weissman, *Small Business and Venture Capital: An Economic Program* (New York and London: Harper & Brothers, 1945), p. 49. For my

own brief summary of the origins of venture capital in New England I have also drawn from David H. Hsu and Martin Kenney, "Organizing Venture Capital: The Rise and Demise of American Research & Development Corporation, 1946–1973," in *Industrial and Corporate Change*, vol. 14, no. 4, pp. 579–616, available at www .management.wharton.upenn.edu/hsu/files/ARD_ICC.pdf; and Susan Rosegrant and David Lampe, *Route 128: Lessons from Boston's High-Tech Community* (New York: Basic Books, 1992).

11. Hsu and Kenney, "Organizing Venture Capital," p. 589. It is also worth noting that it was not unheard of for ARD to make investments in technologies from which it expected no financial return, simply because the technology would be socially beneficial. According to one of the entrepreneurs who founded High Voltage Engineering Corporation, whose original mission was to develop X-ray machines for cancer treatment and which was the second company in which ARD invested, MIT president Karl T. Compton (one of the cofounders of ARD) told Doriot, "They probably won't ever make any money, but the ethics of the thing and the human qualities of treating cancer with X rays are so outstanding that I'm sure it should be in our portfolio." See Rosegrant and Lampe, *Route 128*, p. 112.

12. "Despite its early pioneering role [in helping to finance ARD], . . . MIT curtailed its financial support for ARD in 1955. Articulating the conservatism of New England universities and financial institutions of this era, MIT concluded that investing in startup companies was too risky and not consistent with how 'men of prudence, discretion, and intelligence manage their own affairs'" (Saxenian, *Regional Advantage*, p. 15, citing Rosegrant and Lampe, *Route 128*, p. 134). As I note in chapter 2, Boston University, in the late 1970s, became the first university in the Boston area to invest with TA Associates, followed soon thereafter by Harvard.

13. Bill Elfers wrote his own brief accounts of the Damon-IEC merger and the Wang IPO in his book *Greylock: An Adventure Capital Story* (Boston: Greylock Management Corp., 1995), pp. 22–23 and 25–26, respectively.

CHAPTER 2: BUILDING TA ASSOCIATES (22–39)

1. In Advent Company, $2 million out of the $6 million raised was from foreign investors. For Advent II, $2 million out of $10 million was from foreign investors, and for Advent III, $5 million out of $15 million.

2. I also acquired a 25 percent interest in Advent II, the second venture fund managed by TA Associates, which closed in 1972. I subsequently bought out Tucker Anthony's 75 percent interest in these earlier partnerships upon the establishment of Advent III in 1978, and distributed the carried interest among the general partners of TA Associates.

Tucker Anthony was not particularly helpful in raising money for TA Associates' managed funds. In 1972 I was approached by Nick Brady, who was then the head of Dillon Read and is an old friend of mine, about launching a venture capital effort in New York. I informed Bill Claflin, the managing partner of Tucker Anthony, about this, and told him that I preferred to stay in Boston but needed a commitment from the firm to help raise the second of TA Associates' venture funds. Bill committed to doing this but did not follow through. When he tried to talk me out of raising TAA's third venture fund, I decided that it was time to cut Tucker Anthony out of the carry of the proposed fund and to buy out its capital interest in the first two funds. The negotiation with Tucker Anthony about this was quite interesting. To try to get Tucker Anthony behind my efforts to raise capital for TAA's funds, I had long tried to convince Claflin of the underlying value of the portfolios of Advent Company and Advent II, and that these funds would yield a handsome override. He did not buy my argument and agreed to accept my offer to buy out Tucker Anthony's position based on the conservative valuations we were providing our investors, a steep discount from what I believed the portfolios would be worth in the future. So I was able to buy out Tucker Anthony's interest in these first two funds for a song, and TA Associates became an independent company owned by its partners.

3. The story of ARD's relationship with Digital is told in some detail in Spencer E. Ante's biography of Georges Doriot, *Creative Capital* (Boston: Harvard Business Press, 2008).

4. For fuller accounts of the story, see Dick Lehr and Gerard O'Neill, *Black Mass: The True Story of an Unholy Alliance between the FBI and the Irish Mob* (New York: Perennial Books, 2001) and Howie Carr, *The Brothers Bulger: How They Terrorized and Corrupted Boston for a Quarter Century* (New York: Warner Books, 2006).

5. Troxel continues to appreciate our work today. Since being sold by Addressograph Multigraph in 1983, ECRM Imaging Systems, as it is now known, has been built into a world leader in imaging systems for the graphic communications industry by the men who bought it from AM, chairman William Givens and president and CEO Richard Black. Don Troxel remains on the company's board.

6. Gompers and Lerner, *The Money of Invention*, pp. 146–148.

7. Tom Perkins has written about Kleiner Perkins's investment in Genentech in his book *Valley Boy: The Education of Tom Perkins* (New York: Gotham Books, 2007), pp. 117–125.

8. It is not unusual to see an American corporation lurching, as INCO did following Schaeffer's retirement, from a diversification effort back to a focus on its traditional business, and then sometimes back to diversification. It has been my experience that an intelligent diversification effort such as the one Schaeffer under-

took rarely survives the departure of the individual in charge of executing it. Long-range strategic planning and corporate-wide commitment to executing a plan patiently over many years are not strengths of American management. Only rarely do U.S. corporations have the patience and courage to see a strategic diversification effort through to a useful conclusion. (Gompers and Lerner find that "[t]he typical corporate venture capital program has been terminated within four years of being launched" [*The Money of Invention*, p. 145].) I should add that it is only rarely, in my experience, that corporate venture capital has been used for diversification rather than for financial purposes.

9. In 1996, Bill Egan and other members of the communications group at the firm formed Alta Communications, of which Bill remains a general partner. Craig Burr retired from the industry at this point.

10. http://www.masscapital.com (accessed 5/1/08).

11. http://www.mtdc.com/role.html (accessed 5/1/08). In the late 1990s, the Massachusetts Industrial Finance Agency and the Massachusetts Government Land Bank were folded into a new organization, MassDevelopment, which provides financing and real estate development services to for-profit companies (in manufacturing, technology, and other sectors), nonprofits, and municipalities for purposes of job creation and community development.

12. One Boston venture capitalist who was interested in collaborating with TA Associates on a purely private-sector initiative to address the capital gap was Tom Lee. I was actually thinking, about the same time that Tom started his own company in 1974, that it would be a great idea for TAA to hire him — not that I am sure that he would have agreed to come on board. But when I mentioned this to my partners, there was a certain resistance. They knew that if we hired Tom we would be putting a pretty powerful character into the mix. At any rate, while I was involved in the capital gap study, Tom identified mezzanine financing (i.e., the last stage of venture capital investment prior to an IPO) as a particular need in Massachusetts. He came to my office to see if there was anything we could do together in this area, and we hit upon the idea of a joint venture between Thomas H. Lee Company and TA Associates to introduce a mezzanine fund to be managed jointly by both organizations.

Tom and I went down to Hartford a few times to try this idea out on the insurance companies there. We went to Aetna, Travelers, and a few others. On one of these trips, as we were driving down together, Tom said, "I'm going to lay a big number on these guys." (I forget which company it was that we were visiting that day.) I said, "Good, don't be bashful." When we got there, the figure Tom laid on them was $50 million to invest in this new fund we were going to put together. I nearly had a heart attack — I had been thinking that a big commitment would be something like

$10 million. At any rate, Tom's strategy didn't work. It turned out that all the insurance companies were as transfixed with their own problems at the time as were the commercial banks up in Boston, so nothing happened. Still, I suppose you have to admire Tom's brashness in "laying a big number on those guys."

## CHAPTER 3: GOING INTERNATIONAL:
### FRANCE AND BRITAIN (40–57)

1. Quoted from the ARD press release announcing the formation of the European Enterprise Development Company in Udayan Gupta, ed., *The First Venture Capitalist: Georges Doriot on Leadership, Capital, & Business Organization* (Calgary: Gondolier, 2004), p. 59.

2. Doriot's biographer Spencer E. Ante attributes the failure of EED to the inexperience of its managers and directors, the difficulty of doing business across national boundaries in Europe at the time, and the burden of excessive debt. See *Creative Capital*, pp. 242–243.

3. Jean Deléage, who went to San Francisco in 1976 to open an office for Sofinnova there, invested capital from Innova, during his first week in California, in Printronix, Tandem Computers, and Genentech. Needless to say, that fund was a winner. Deléage left Sofinnova in 1979 to join two former partners of TA Associates, Bill Egan and Craig Burr. The firm became Burr, Egan, Deleage, a very successful venture capital operation.

4. In the spring of 1976, when the Sofinnova experiment was proving successful and Christian Marbach decided to spread his wings in the United States, EED — which by then was in serious trouble — approached me to see if TA Associates would be interested in making an investment. TAA and INCO had recently embarked on their relationship (see chapter 2), and INCO was interested in establishing an imprint in Europe and thought that a TAA/INCO bid for EED was something we might wish to pursue. I met with Jean Gueroult, EED's executive vice president, and, after hearing his story, thought that the only way to evaluate the company's portfolio was to evaluate each investment. I was willing to spend the time and money to conduct such an investigation, because otherwise I thought we would be buying a pig in a poke. EED rejected our proposition, however. Through this whole affair, I had the feeling that General Doriot did not have high a regard for what I was doing in France and in Europe. I believe he regarded me as something of an interloper, encroaching on his territory.

5. In 1974, I actually sold 15 percent of TA Associates to Hambros Bank in London. The significance of this was not in the capital that the sale itself raised but rather in Hambros's commitment to raise considerable capital from its clients in

Europe and America for our use in investments or anything else we thought useful. The agreement with Hambros was carefully worded so that I could remove it at
any time after three years if it had not honored its commitment in exchange for the
return on capital it had invested. Hambros (which had fallen upon hard times after
lending heavily to Hilmar Reksten, the supertanker builder and owner in Norway
whose fleet had been beached due to the Arab oil embargo of 1973–1974) was not
able to fulfill its obligation and was removed from ownership in 1977.

6. I was and am a great admirer of Margaret Thatcher. While an overseer of Harvard University in the 1990s I twice put her name forward for an honorary degree.
My recommendation was twice rejected. The Committee on Honorary Degrees
gave as its reason for these rejections that Mrs. Thatcher had not been so honored
by Oxford and Cambridge, and that she had reduced the government's financial
support of the British university system. It apparently did not occur to these aca-
demics that she had turned the British economy around—saved it, for that matter—and in so doing was able to increase financial support for the universities in
later years. I thought it would be a wonderful thing for the New World to do what
the Old World could not. Harvard did not see it that way. It amazes me what academic faculties are unable to see.

7. Another person in Britain who has tried to play a role in fostering innovation
and entrepreneurship is Prince Charles. In 1993, at a celebration of the tenth anniversary of the founding of the British Venture Capital Association, I was asked to sit at
the head table with him and the former presidents of the association. He gave a brilliant speech on what he hoped the private equity business in Britain would do and
not do. "Don't buy things from yourself," he told them. (I'm paraphrasing.) "Don't do
leveraged buyouts of existing companies unless you really feel you can manage them
more appropriately. Better to invest in new, technology-based companies." It was a
real challenge to the British venture capital industry to do something productive.

8. MacDonald lived out on the Firth of Forth. While driving to his home, you
would take a hard left toward the firth and then a sharp right. On many occasions
Douglas would miss the sharp right and end up in the sand. The turn was affection-
ately called "MacDonald's Triangle," after the Bermuda Triangle.

9. In 1983, the ICFC was merged with the Finance Corporation for Industry to
form the venture capital and private equity firm 3i.

CHAPTER 4: THE BEGINNINGS OF A GLOBAL NETWORK:
WESTERN EUROPE AND SOUTHEAST ASIA (58–77)

1. Orange Nassau eventually started its own venture capital concern in the Netherlands, a company called Halder Holdings. Neither TAA nor Advent International

ever had an ownership interest in Halder Holdings. We called the company a "network member," but in every other country in Europe our network members were management companies of which TAA, and later Advent International, owned a piece. The first venture capital firm in the Netherlands was the Gilde Venture Fund, established in 1982 by Bert Twaalfhoven, president of the Dutch manufacturing firm Indivers N.V., in which American Research & Development had invested. (See Ante, *Creative Capital*, pp. 243–244.)

2. Even so, Mackenrodt still had to face down opposition at Siemens from those who thought that the company should have 100 percent control of any venture capital operation in which it participated. Mackenrodt, who knew from his own research that venture investing required patient capital, and that many of the most disastrous forays into venture capital up to that point in the United States had been in corporate venturing, insisted that Siemens not have control—and also that he not have to report any results for seven years—so that what became TVM could not be shut down when profits for Siemens did not materialize right away. Only two Siemens representatives sat on the original five-person board of TVM: Mackenrodt himself and Siemens's president of worldwide research at the time, Karl-Heinz Beckurts, whom Mackenrodt had finally brought round to support the whole idea. In 1986, Beckurts became one of several prominent German businessmen murdered by the Red Army Faction during its reign of terror lasting from the early 1970s to the early 1990s.

3. Van Agtmael, who founded EMM, is generally credited with coining the term *emerging markets* and was responsible, while at the IFC, for other breakthroughs including the creation of the world's first emerging markets equity index.

4. The Spanish fund, SEFINNOVA I, was launched in January 1978 following a study done by Sofinnova in France on the feasibility of venture capital in Spain. Sofinnova became an active sponsor of the fund, which was managed by the Sociedad Espanola de Financiacion de la Innovacion (SEFINNOVA), the venture capital management company within the Banco de Bilbao that is credited with being the first not only in Spain but in the entire developing world (of which Spain was then considered a part). On SEFINNOVA I, see Charles Weiss, "Science and Technology at the World Bank, 1968–83," accessed at http://www9.georgetown.edu/faculty/khb3/Osiris/papers/Weiss.pdf (12/15/06).

5. Singapore split off from Malaysia to become an independent nation in 1965. Economically underdeveloped and possessing few natural resources, the new city-state, under the government of Prime Minister Lee Kuan Yew, set out in the 1970s to create an export-oriented manufacturing sector that increasingly turned out products such as computer parts and peripherals, software, and silicon wafers. In

1981, the government established its National Computer Board for the purpose of turning Singapore into a center for computer software and services. The Singapore Economic Development Board (EDB), founded in 1961, would partner with the governments of Japan, Germany, and France in the 1980s to set up technology institutes to train workers for high-skill jobs in electronics and engineering, and went on to establish its own $100 million fund in 1986. The Singapore government also financed the construction of the Singapore Science Park, which opened in 1984 (in a location near key research institutions including the National University of Singapore, the National University Hospital, the Institute of Systems Science, and the Institute of Molecular and Cellular Biology), to house both government and private R&D organizations. See http://www.edb.gov.sg/edb/sg/en_uk/index/about_us .html, accessed 11/13/06; and Robert Chia Kay Guan and Wong Kwei Chong, *Venture Capital in the Asia Pacific Region with Special Reference to Singapore* (Singapore: Toppan Co., 1989), pp. 21–46.

6. Kong Hua would succeed in doing this in the course of the 1980s by taking NIS into the electronics and computer-components manufacturing businesses.

7. Quoted in Poonam Sharma, *Chasing Success: Lessons We Can Learn From the Lives of Harvard's Entrepreneurs* (Salt Lake City: American Book Business Press, 2004), p. 95.

8. Two key events contributed to the revival of the venture capital industry in the 1980s: Congress's 1978 decision to return the capital gains rate to 28 percent (it had been raised from 28 to 49 percent in 1969), and the Labor Department's 1979 clarification of the "prudent man" rule in the Employee Retirement and Security Act of 1974. The latter development opened the way for pension funds to invest in venture capital for the first time.

CHAPTER 5: PUSHING AHEAD:

ADVENT INTERNATIONAL AND EXPANSION IN ASIA (78–99)

1. I discuss the establishment of our Japanese affiliate, and what proved to be a short relationship between this affiliate and Advent International, later in this chapter.

2. On the positive side, my separation from TA Associates cleared up for the outside world who was actually managing the investment process there — Kevin Landry — and gave him the authority and recognition he so richly deserved. Kevin was and is a superb manager and, with the separation, had a clean sheet of paper on which to draw his own design. Through the transition period after I left TAA to start Advent International, Kevin played a very steadying role. He had no fear of competition from Advent or anyone else because he was completely secure in

his ability to meet the challenges of managing and building the firm. His cool hand had a great deal to do with maintaining the civility that soon allowed the two firms to seek their own identities. This outcome probably had everything to do with the battles Kevin and I had fought together in the early days and the genuine affection we had for each other.

3. The incident with the Dato' Azman is but one example of Anne's contributions to the success of TA Associates' and Advent International's foreign ventures. The relationships she established with individuals and families of prominence in France, Germany, Belgium, Singapore, Hong Kong, and Japan were helpful and sometimes crucial. Her relationship with Masako Ayukawa, the wife of my Japanese partner Yaichi Ayukawa (described later in this chapter), became an enduring friendship. Her relationship with the Yeos in Singapore and the Victor Fungs in Hong Kong led to an ease and comfort that was conducive to success. Her friendship with Julio Nuñez (see chapter 6) and the Bemberg family in Paris gave them the sense that, if this gracious woman had confidence in me, they should as well. I could give other examples. Never underestimate an observant mind, wisdom, graciousness, beauty, and where a sense of adventure can take you.

4. In May 2006, AspenTech opened a sales office and R&D facility in Shanghai, which is now the company's regional headquarters for Asia Pacific. Its Chinese customers today include CNOOC, PetroChina, and Sinopec.

Advent International has made three investments in AspenTech since its founding. In 1986, it invested $2 million for its corporate clients and affiliates to help fund the company's expansion. In 1991, Advent invested $4.2 million from its European Special Situations Fund to finance Aspen's acquisition of a U.K. software company. Advent exited these two investments in 1996. In the late 1990s, AspenTech embarked on an acquisition binge financed mainly by debt. A combination of heavy leverage, lack of control of its acquisitions and of expenses, and poor management generally almost killed the company. Recognizing the soundness of the core business, Advent invested $100 million in a recapitalization of AspenTech in August 2003 and proceeded to clean up the mess. Advent reorganized the board of directors and senior management, disposed of the noncore acquisitions, and refocused the company on its original business.

The CEO at the time of the recapitalization, David McQuillin, was forced to resign in 2004 when the company's audit committee found that previously reported financial results would need to be restated. The revenue recognition problem led to a July 2007 "cease and desist" order from the SEC alleging that the company had fraudulently inflated revenue over a period of three years. Advent was not represented on the Aspen board during this period and, unfortunately, none of the transgressions were uncovered by Advent's auditors during the preinvestment investigation in 2003.

5. Merck (Shanghai) Trading Co., Ltd. was established in 1997 in the Pudong Wai Gao Qiao Free Trade Zone of Shanghai and now operates under the name Merck Chemicals (Shanghai) Co., Ltd.

6. For an explanation of the SBIC program, see chapter 1, note 3.

7. On Advent International's expansion into central Europe in the 1990s, see chapter 7.

8. The primary source of capital for promising Japanese companies in the early 1980s was JAFCO, an affiliate of the Nomura Securities Group. It did not supply early-stage capital but rather expansion capital to companies that Nomura was priming for public offerings.

CHAPTER 6: TRIAL AND ERROR IN EUROPE AND ASIA (100–127)

1. I discuss Advent International's transition to an investment organization and the International Network Fund later in this chapter.

2. From 1988 to 1997, Seillière served as vice president and a member of the executive council of the CNPF (Conseil national du patronat français [National Council of French Employers], now known as MEDEF), and from 1997 to 2005 as president of that organization. Since 2005 he has been president of BusinessEurope (formerly UNICE), where he is a strong advocate for the integration of the European market.

3. Alain Blanc-Brude is today chairman of the Supervisory Board of Alpha Associés, and Nicolas ver Hulst is a managing director. Dominique Peninon is now chairman and managing partner of Access Capital Partners, a European private equity firm that he cofounded in 1999.

4. The first venture capital management company in Spain was the Sociedad Espanola de Financiacion de la Innovacion (Seffinova), founded in the mid-1970s within the Banco de Bilbao. The Banco de Bilbao had previously invested in Sofinnova in France, partly to learn whether a similar entity could be established in Spain.

5. Advent eventually ended its corporate programs after Clint Harris departed in 1998 to found Grove Street Advisors. Harris's unbounded resourcefulness in designing and executing the programs he ran at Advent made a major contribution to the early growth and success of the firm.

6. Anthony Ramirez, "Foreign Affairs of a Venture Capitalist," *Fortune*, February 2, 1987, p. 84.

7. Julio Nuñez was a significant figure in the history of TA Associates and Ad-

vent International. As the CEO of Entreprises Quilmes, he invested in the early programs of TA Associates and in the various funds of the affiliates of TAA and Advent
in Asia. He was also pivotal in Entreprises Quilmes's decision to provide the bulk of
the capital for the formation of Advent International and was a founding director of
Advent. His wisdom and probing questions, along with his friendship, were important to both TAA and Advent and to me personally.

8. Before I went out to raise funds on my own for the INF, however, a Boston
group called Beacon Hill Financial, run by Bob Johnston and Jim O'Brien, approached us about their interest in exploring these uncharted waters, and ended up
doing a magnificent job. Johnston and O'Brien, who also raised funds in those days
for the private equity firm Forstmann-Little, subsequently helped Advent with the
fund-raising for its European Special Situations Fund, Asia-Pacific Special Situations Fund, and Global Private Equity Fund II.

9. After leaving Advent International and returning to Advent Ltd., David rebuilt
the firm brilliantly, was knighted, and became a director of the Bank of England and
of the Wellcome Trust. Our close relationship could never be what it had been, but
we remain friends. The fact also remains that David, besides cofounding Advent
Ltd. with me, participated in the establishment of virtually all the Western European affiliates including Advent Belgium, Alpha Associés in France, TVM in Germany, and Innovent in Switzerland. He was also directly responsible for changing
Advent's course in Australia when he identified Nicholas Callinan as the person to
head our affiliate there. In addition to this he was a superb strategist and visionary
whose belief in the Advent concept was critical to the development of the firm.

10. Advent opened offices in Frankfurt and Milan in 1991 and a Paris office in 1997.
More recently in Western Europe, Advent has opened offices in Madrid (2002) and
Amsterdam (2006).

11. After Advent made the transition to a direct investment organization in Western Europe with its own offices in the region, some of the network members there
chose not to continue the relationship: Innovent in Switzerland, Itavent in Italy, and
Advent España, for example. None of these firms survived on their own, but their
decision to sever their relationship with Advent was not the decisive factor. Some
of the differences between those network members that succeeded and those that
failed could be ascribed to circumstances such as industry structure and attitudes
toward entrepreneurship that obtained in the various countries. However, among
those network members that survived and, in some cases, even prospered, the main
reason for success in every case was the quality of the management. It took courage
and enterprise to introduce a venture management company in a country that had
previously been less than hospitable to the concept. It took flexibility to adapt the

model in whatever ways were necessary to make it succeed in a given country. Those
network members that were led by individuals who did not possess these qualities all fell by the wayside, while those that had the requisite leadership all made
an impact, if only by the example of their pluck, in their own countries and around
Europe.

After we had opened our own offices in Britain, Germany, the Benelux countries,
and France, Advent retained relationships with its network members in those countries. I remained on the investment committee of Advent Ltd. in Britain for several years and remain honorary chairman of TVM in Germany; we also remained
in contact, and shared deals, with Advent Belgium and Alpha Associés in France.
Today Advent International's only formal affiliate in Western Europe is Verdane
Capital AS in Norway, a descendant of Four Seasons.

12. The relatively poor results for early-stage investment in Europe as compared
with the United States make for an interesting contrast with another place where
Advent formed a connection and played a role in launching a local venture capital industry at the same time we were investing the ESSF in Europe. As I mention
in chapter 4, there was an Israeli investment manager, Meyer Barel, on the staff of
TVM in Germany who had invested in some Israeli companies that had done well,
which alerted me to the potential of Israel as an arena for venture capital. In 1991,
Clint Harris of Advent International began leading an effort that resulted in the establishment of Gemini Israel Venture Funds Ltd., one of the first private venture
capital funds to be set up under the Israeli government's Yozma ("initiative") program for stimulating venture investment in the country and creating a domestic
venture capital industry. Clint helped Gemini to raise its first two funds, attracting
capital from several important corporate and institutional investors to Israel for the
first time and negotiating key tax and regulatory issues involved in building a viable
venture capital industry there.

13. I would have preferred that Advent International have both an early-stage
venture capital program and a later-stage private equity program under one roof.
For a while I thought it could have been done if we had the right management, but
Doug Brown, when he became CEO of Advent in 1996, did not believe it was possible to do both. And as Advent began raising larger and larger funds, it became necessary to employ larger amounts of capital in each deal. This essentially removed us
from the early-stage venture capital business. Before that happened, Advent raised
three Digital Media & Communications funds between 1996 and 2000 totaling
$475 million; two $30 million health-care and life-sciences funds in the mid-1990s
for a major pharmaceutical firm; and two additional life-sciences funds in 1999
($100 million) and 2004 ($125 million). Advent's participation in early-stage ven-

turing was not insignificant, and although I understood the reasons for abandoning the activity, the decision to do so was not without sadness for me.

14. In a book published in 1996, the IFC explained its strategy for introducing venture capital into emerging markets as having both a regional and a local aspect. According to the IFC authors, it was in order to cope with the difficulty of finding experienced venture managers interested in managing small funds in often difficult environments that the organization set up regional management companies and funds. The purpose of this structure was "to provide international management input to several country funds in a region — which each have their own manager as well. This structure achieves critical mass for the individual manager, but also develops local expertise" (*Investment Funds in Emerging Markets*, IFC Lessons of Experience Series [Washington, D.C.: The World Bank, 1996], p. 41). I do not recall this strategy being articulated when we set up SEAVIC or the country funds that followed, leading me to believe that the IFC was using its experience with SEAVIC in order to develop what subsequently became its approach to introducing venture capital into emerging markets.

15. In 1991, the IFC also invested in SEAVIC's second Malaysian fund, Malaysian Ventures II Sdn. Bhd. Country funds remained at the center of the IFC's efforts in Southeast Asia, and the organization did not invest in SEAVIC's second regional fund ("SEAVI II Ltd") when that fund was organized in 1999.

16. One can understand a lack of prudence in an emerging market like Indonesia. However, one would not have expected the lack of prudence exhibited in the developed markets during the years 2000–2007. While debt/worth ratios in the United States and Europe did not reach those that obtained in Indonesia in the late 1990s, the availability of massive low-interest debt led private equity managers in those developed markets to overpay for their acquisitions. Debt-to-worth ratios of four to five times equity were not uncommon. The carrying cost for servicing this debt often caused the acquired companies to reduce R&D and product development expenses and to delay geographic expansion, thereby decreasing their ability to compete in the global marketplace. It would seem that madness is not confined to Southeast Asia.

17. I must admit that my hope that Victor would run Advent's Asia operations was quite unrealistic. Advent was still a fledgling organization at the end of the 1980s, and Victor was a man of considerable stature — a fact that was borne out when the Prudential Life Insurance Company of America put $100 million at his disposal to invest in Asia and gave him one-third of the capital gains for his effort. PruAsia became a force in the region, concentrating on expansion capital and restructurings, and dwarfed the venture capital activity of HKVIT. Although Victor

was loyal to HKVIT, it was obvious that he was attracted by the bigger prize. In any event, Techno Ventures Hong Kong merged in 1989 with Transtech — a firm that Tony Haight had helped found three years earlier, and that was also affiliated with the Development Bank of Singapore, National Iron and Steel, and the Economic Development Board of Singapore — to form Transpac Capital.

18. For my views on Soros as I expressed them at the time the Asian currency crisis was still unfolding, see David Warsh, "The Greatest Villain," *Boston Globe*, January 13, 1998, p. D1. From the time the currency crisis struck until the end of 2006, Soros and Mahathir bin Mohamad, the former prime minister of Malaysia, waged a feud over Mahathir's criticism of Soros's role in instigating the Asian currency crisis, criticism characterized by blatant anti-Semitism. While it is difficult to sympathize with Mahathir given his racist remarks and human rights abuses, I did and still do agree with him on the need to curb currency speculation in emerging markets. If this means closing markets to the free flow of capital in and out of a country, so be it. The risks created by the free flow of capital into emerging markets have been demonstrated more recently in former Soviet satellites, including Latvia and Hungary.

CHAPTER 7: MORE NEW VENTURES:
CENTRAL EUROPE, LATIN AMERICA, AND BEYOND (128–146)

1. After the collapse of the Soviet bloc, the introduction of venture capital into formerly communist central Europe took place through the formation of country enterprise funds created with the encouragement of the U.S. government. One of these funds, the Polish-American Enterprise Fund, was chaired by John Berkland, formerly head of Dillon Reed, and managed by Enterprise Investors, whose strategy for the region was to focus initially on Poland.

2. The Abu Dhabi Investment Authority has been in the news recently as such sovereign wealth funds have grown larger in size and have become significant investors in alternative investments including private equity. A recent report from the McKinsey Global Institute estimates Adia's current holdings at between $200 billion and $875 billion, with as much as 10 percent of the total invested in private equity. In November 2007, Adia acquired stakes of $7.5 billion in both the Carlyle Group and Citicorp.

3. What happened to the IFC when it became politicized shows how multilateral organizations can change over time depending on who runs them and whom they select to lead the critical units. Later in the 1990s, as I explain below, the IFC became an effective promoter of private equity in Latin America. I believe this change can be attributed to James Wolfensohn's leadership of the World Bank. Wolfensohn, a bright and admirable man who served as president of the World Bank from 1995

until 2005, understood the investment world, especially venture capital and private equity, and the need for quick response to the needs of investors rather than prolonged discussion. Perhaps I am giving Jim too much credit, but whatever the reason, the climate at the IFC changed.

4. As this book was going to press, Gordon Bajnai was Hungary's economics minister and was expected to become prime minister in the wake of the resignation of Ferenc Gyurcsány on March 23, 2009.

5. Nick Callinan had considered setting up a Romanian affiliate with the local sponsor of Advent's Hungarian affiliate, the Austrian bank Creditanstalt (now part of Bank Austria), where Nick knew the head of the investment banking unit that was managing the bank's private equity activities. This person's hidden agenda was to duplicate the Advent network in the region for Creditanstalt. He made overtures to take over our affiliate in Poland and help solve our problem in the Czech Republic and Slovakia by setting up an affiliate for us there. He was clearly trying to use us to set up his own network. So Nick dropped the idea of establishing an affiliate in Romania, hired two top people from Creditanstalt, and set up Advent's Bucharest office. In 2007, Advent entered a new market in Eastern Europe with the opening of an office in Kiev, Ukraine. I should add that Advent has been investing in Turkey since 2003 through an affiliation with the firm Turkven Private Equity, the first and leading independent private equity firm in Turkey.

6. Another uncertainty that private equity investors faced in central Europe at the beginning of the transition to market economies there was whether the countries in the region would adopt Continental- or Anglo-American-style systems of law. It has been fortunate that Anglo-American law, with its greater protections for investors, has become the dominant model in the formerly communist countries of central Europe.

7. In 1998, Nick left London, from where he had directed the central European program, to take on other responsibilities for Advent in the United States. He passed the leadership in central Europe on to Joanna James, who has proven to be an able successor. The success of Advent's central European program, as of so many of its others over the years, has everything to do with the pioneer, Callinan, and the successor who built on his work, James.

In spring 2005, Advent closed its third central European regional fund, ACEE III, at €330 million. The fund is investing in high-growth companies across the region in the media, communications, health care, construction materials, financial services, and retail sectors. AIC closed ACEE IV, at €1 billion, early in 2008. ACEE IV is investing in companies requiring €30 million to €100 million of equity to build market leadership and to expand across borders.

8. In May 2007, Advent and the investment firm Novator, which had been a coinvestor with Viva Ventures and had purchased an option to buy all of Viva's shares in BTC at a future date, decided to exercise its option, purchase Viva's shares in BTC, and sell on Viva's 65 percent stake in the company to the AIG Global Investment Group in a deal that valued these shares at €1.08 billion. Advent had paid €230 million for its stake in 2004 and invested nearly €500 million in BTC during the three years that it owned the company, as per agreement with the Bulgarian privatization authority. During this period, Advent succeeded in transforming BTC from a state monopoly operating an analog landline system into a modern, digitized telecommunications company offering a full range of services. In 2006, BTC made a profit before tax of €76 million on revenues of €516 million. The sale to AIG closed in August 2007.

9. The Southern Common Market, or Mercosur, was established in 1991 with Brazil, Argentina, Uruguay, and Paraguay as its original members. It has since expanded to include Venezuela as a full member, and Bolivia, Chile, Colombia, Ecuador, and Peru as associate members.

10. Advent was not much affected by the depreciation of the Argentine peso since it was not using leverage in its Latin American deals at that point.

11. It is important to note that the IFC, which had created headaches for Advent in central Europe in the mid-1990s, played a very constructive role for us and the for the private equity industry generally in Latin America in the late 1990s and early 2000s. After the negative returns from most of the early private equity funds in the region (although not for Advent's LAPEF I) created a perception that Latin America was a poor risk for private equity, the IFC helped Advent raise its second Latin American fund and invested $15 million of its own money in it. It also played a broader role in addressing some of the key factors affecting performance in the region: poor corporate governance, lack of awareness and understanding of private equity, and the need for appropriate legal, fiscal, and accounting practices to attract and support private equity investment.

As part of my vision for Advent International as the catalyst for a global, privately managed Marshall Plan, I once imagined Advent becoming the preferred partner of multilaterals such as the IFC and the Inter-American Development Bank in helping to establish venture capital/private equity sectors in emerging markets. Since Advent last worked with such institutions in central Europe and Latin America, however, these two regions have developed to the point where there is plenty of private capital available for investment (at least for private equity). For private equity investors operating in today's frontier markets where private capital is not so readily available, the multilaterals should continue to play an important supporting role.

12. A noteworthy development in Latin America since Advent International began investing there in the mid-1990s has been the concurrent rise of a Brazilian firm, GP Investments, that has become a major presence in Latin American private equity. GP Investments raised a $500 million fund from foreign institutional investors in 1994; its fourth and most recent fund, GPCPIV, closed in 2007 at US$1.025 billion. In 2000, the firm raised a fund of R$130 million from local investors. The firm has recently expanded into Mexico, opening a Mexico City office in June 2007.

13. In a recent article in *Foreign Policy* on Latin American countries' continuing failure to better the lot of their poorer citizens, the magazine's editor in chief, Moisés Naím, notes that "[w]ith its high wages and low technology, Latin America is having a hard time fitting into the hypercompetitive global economy." Naím's economic prescription for the region is an eschewal of silver bullets and an increased willingness to take patient, long-term measures: "Unless the patience of all influential actors is raised," he writes, "efforts will continue to fail before they are fully tested or executed. Investors will continue to ignore good projects that cannot offer quick returns, governments will only pick policies that can generate rapid, visible results even if they are unsustainable or mostly cosmetic, and voters will continue to shed leaders that don't deliver soon enough" ("The Lost Continent," *Foreign Policy*, November/December 2006, p. 46). Naím's analysis makes it clear that in Latin America in the present, as in Southeast Asia in the 1990s, patient capital of the kind that private equity investors provide is key to increased and sustainable prosperity.

14. Tony Haight, who opposed the acquisition of SEAVIC, left Advent in 1997 to start his own firm, Argo Global Capital, where Simon Wong, formerly of HKVIT and Transpac, is now one of his partners.

### CHAPTER 8: VENTURE CAPITAL, PRIVATE EQUITY, AND THE ART OF ADDING VALUE (149–168)

1. While private equity managers were becoming celebrities, at least one celebrity—the rock star Bono—became a private equity manager, having joined the Silicon Valley private equity firm Elevation Partners as a managing partner in 2004.

2. Boruch B. Frusztajer, *Surviving Siberia and Thriving Under Capitalism* (Scranton, Pa.: University of Scranton Press, 2007), p. 385.

3. On Bessemer's investment in what was originally Damon Engineering, see chapter 1.

4. Two partners in the deal, the European Bank for Reconstruction and Development and the Dutch development bank FMO, put in small amounts of money and played only a minor role thereafter.

5. As the International Finance Corporation has recently noted, private equity

firms such as Advent are also demonstrating that environmental and social responsibility can be integral parts of profitable private equity investment in emerging
markets. See the IFC's November 2006 report *The Promise of Private Equity: Environment, Society, and Corporate Governance — New Criteria for Success in Private
Equity Investments* (http://www.ifc.org/ifcext/enviro.nsf/AttachmentsByTitle/p
_SI_PromiseofPrivateEquity/$FILE/PromiseofPrivateEquity_full.pdf, accessed
7/25/07). Advent's investment in Terapia is the subject of one of five case studies
from emerging markets included in the report.

    6. The Warner Music buyout is described in a well-documented summary
in "Behind the Buyouts: Inside the World of Private Equity," a report published
in April 2007 by the Service Employees International Union that is available at
http://www.behindthebuyouts.org (accessed 7/5/07). See also Bernard Condon,
"Swan Song," *Forbes*, June 6, 2005, accessed at http://www.forbes.com/business/
forbes/2005/0606/050a.html (3/12/08). The Debenhams buyout is briefly summarized in Jenny Davey, "Debenhams Scours Europe for Merger deal," *Sunday
Times* (London), July 1, 2007, accessed at http://business.timesonline.co.uk/tol/
business/industry_sectors/retailing/article2009325.ece (7/5/07). For a description of one of the more egregious uses of dividend recapitalizations, among other
means, to reward private equity investors handsomely long before the results of the
attempted turnaround were in, see the account of the Burger King buyout in Greg
Ip and Henny Sender, "In Today's Buyouts, Payday for Firms Is Never Far Away,"
*Wall Street Journal*, July 25, 2006. On the effects of the recent financial meltdown on
highly leveraged, private equity–financed companies, see Andrew Ross Sorkin and
Michael J. de la Merced, "Debt Linked to Buyouts Tightens the Economic Vise,"
*New York Times*, November 3, 2008.

    7. Even before the onset of the present economic downturn, the skills of such
private equity managers were more needed than has been generally recognized.
Sclerosis is a disease of many of our once formidable American companies. The environments there encourage game playing and ladder climbing, not innovation and
risk taking. The future success of U.S. industry may depend to a considerable extent
on private equity managers who can breath life into nonproductive assets.

    8. The Wharton study has been published as a paper by Andrew Metrick and
Ayako Yasuda, "The Economics of Private Equity Funds" (September 9, 2007),
available at http://www.frbsf.org/csip/research/200710_Ayako_Yasuda.pdf (accessed 3/13/08). See table VI, "Summary Statistics: Revenue Estimates."

    9. On the excessive fees charged to the investors in many private equity funds,
along with other abuses, venture capitalist Tom Perkins writes, "Today I stand in
awe at the way the managing partners of some of the huge buyout funds reward

themselves: fees for raising the fund, fees for managing the fund, fees for doing the deals within the fund, and profit participation from individual investments whether or not overall profits are achieved" (*Valley Boy*, p. 105). Such practices, however, are certain to be curtailed as those private equity firms that survive the present downturn deal with investors who have seen their returns plummet.

10. The McKinsey research is summarized by Diana Farrell of the McKinsey Global Institute in "Private Equity Isn't Fading Away," *Business Week*, November 20, 2007, accessed at http://www.mckinsey.com/mgi/mginews/private_equity.asp (3/13/08).

11. I am happy to say that Advent International has leveraged its portfolio companies judiciously in the first decade of the 2000s. This has allowed it to liquidate its portfolios at substantial profits compared with other private equity firms that did not have the same standards. It has also positioned the firm to invest its recently raised capital at a time when prices are moving lower and where its value-added approach can create substantial future profits.

CHAPTER 9: LEADING WITH VISION IN VENTURE CAPITAL
AND PRIVATE EQUITY FIRMS (169–196)

1. William J. Baumol, Robert E. Litan, and Carl J. Schramm, *Good Capitalism, Bad Capitalism, and the Economics of Growth and Prosperity* (New Haven and London: Yale University Press, 2007). See especially chapter 7, "The Big-Firm Wealthy Economies: Preventing Retreat or Stagnation."

2. For an explanation of the SBIC program, see chapter 1, note 3.

3. Although operating partners are engaged on a deal-by-deal basis, they generally enjoy close relationships with the private equity firms for which they work, since they need to understand a particular firm's approach to investing. Advent International, with its emphasis on operating change and EBITDA improvement for its portfolio companies, has a network of over thirty operating partners, generally former CEOs and COOs, and all with expertise in particular sectors.

4. I met Tom Armstrong, who became Advent's chief operating officer, through Yaichi Ayukawa, who worked as a consultant for Tom in Japan while Tom was vice president of international operations for the Allen Group. I knew Tony Haight because one of his sons and one of my mine were schoolmates and friends. John Littlechild was with Advent's London affiliate, Advent Ltd. I found Clint Harris, who was then a consultant at Bain & Co., through a headhunter, my friend Chris Smallhorn.

5. Zorita is now vice chairman of a company formed by the 2002 merger of the Spanish operations of Arthur Andersen and Deloitte.

6. Quoted in Gupta, *The First Venture Capitalist*, pp. xix, xxv.

7. Of course at these established firms, just like at Advent, no one was going to get a share of the override right from the start. But for someone who was interested in making a lot of money, Advent did not look like the best bet.

8. I faced a similar challenge in seeking new investors for Advent. Here I dealt with people who could see economic globalization on the horizon and wanted to test the waters. They knew they had to do *something* to respond to changes such as European integration, the rise of the East Asian tigers, the opening of China, and the weakening of the Soviet Union. So I sold them on the idea of venture capital as a way of tapping into the economic energy about to be released by these events. I did this by listening carefully to learn what their particular interests were and then adjusting my presentation to appeal to these interests. If they were interested in Western Europe, I talked about Sofinnova and the success it had enjoyed in introducing venture capital to France. If they were interested in the tigers of Southeast Asia, I would talk about our success in Singapore and Malaysia and our expansion into Thailand and Indonesia. If they were interested in technology, I talked about our technology transfer activities in Hong Kong and Singapore. In other words, I gave them what they were looking for. I was confident that we could deliver on the expectations of our investors, both from a returns perspective and a strategic one. I was selling them my vision of what was possible, just as an entrepreneur would sell me on the prospects for his company.

9. Advent has recently raised ¥60 billion ($550 million) for its Japan Private Equity Fund.

10. When I realized that the dissatisfaction in the firm with Doug's leadership, if allowed to continue, could have a very negative effect on the company, I suggested to Doug that he select an executive committee to help him manage the firm. I counseled the committee, ensuring that its voice counted, and that it gained confidence and power. This led to its suggestion, with which Brown concurred, that it would be wise to study the governance of the firm and to suggest how the executive committee should be used. This led to a partnership structure managed by an executive committee selected by the managing directors. The managing directors selected both the committee and its chairman, Steve Tadler, in 2003. Doug Brown was not elected to the executive committee and resigned his post as CEO shortly thereafter. In thinking back on all this, I have come to the conclusion that Doug was tired of managing Advent. When engaged in the early days he was very focused. In the later days he lost focus and interest. His parting from the firm was amicable, and since he left Doug has had great success in industry. Despite some decisions, including serious ones, that annoyed his colleagues, he made a very valuable con-

tribution to the firm. We would not be where we are in Europe or Latin America without his contribution. It is good to remember his success in building the European team and bringing order to the investment process. I also recognize now that I bear responsibility for the discontent that Doug Brown's leadership created. When I handed the CEO position to Brown, I in effect took a sabbatical. I did not stay actively involved, and I did not monitor either his performance or his compensation. This was a mistake, and it was my fault. After all, I was the founder and the chairman.

### CHAPTER 10: NEW FRONTIERS (198–221)

1. In 2007, Advent International made its first investment in India when it acquired a minority stake in Computer Age Management Services LTD (CAMS), India's leading provider of business process outsourcing services to the asset management industry. CAMS's core business is to provide transaction processing and investor record-keeping services for independent financial advisers and mutual funds in India. HDFC, one of India's leading financial institutions, is also an investor in CAMS.

2. Western Europe has for several years been benefiting from a similar reverse migration, as future entrepreneurs and venture capitalists have returned to their home countries after gaining business experience in the United States. On the other hand, as Western Europe continues to lag behind the United States in providing financing and other necessary support for innovation and the creation of new enterprises, many fear a "brain drain" that will hold Europe back in coming years.

3. "Emerging Markets Private Equity Funds Raise US$59 Billion in 2007," press release from Emerging Markets Private Equity Association, February 29, 2008 (http://www.empea.net/research/fundraising2007/EMPEAFundraising_2007_PressRelease.pdf, accessed 3/28/08); and Emerging Markets Private Equity Association (EMPEA), *Emerging Markets Private Equity 2006 Fundraising Review* (http://www.empea.net/docs/EMPEA_Fundraising_Review2006.pdf, accessed 7/25/07), pp. 5–11. It should be noted that EMPEA defines "emerging markets" to include some countries that others would describe as "developing" rather than "emerging." EMPEA's list of emerging markets consists of Asia except for Japan, Australia, and New Zealand; Latin America and the Caribbean except for Puerto Rico; the EU accession countries in central and Eastern Europe and the now-independent states (including Russia) of the former Soviet Union; the Middle East (including Afghanistan and Pakistan and excluding Israel) and North Africa; and sub-Saharan Africa. Of the emerging markets funds closed in 2007, the EMPEA review finds that 21 percent were buyout funds, 25 percent venture funds, and 51 percent growth funds. See

*Emerging Markets Private Equity 2007 Fundraising Review* (http://www.empea.net/pdf/2007FundraisingReview_FINAL.pdf, accessed 11/22/08), p. 8.

4. *Emerging Markets Private Equity Association, Quarterly Review* (vol. II, issue 4, Q4 2006), pp. 2–3. My source for the comparison with the S&P 500 over the years 2003–2006 is "Private Equity: New Gates to Storm," *The Economist*, January 18, 2007 (http://www.economist.com/finance/displaystory.cfm?story_id=8559787, accessed 7/25/07).

5. Mark Jensen, national managing partner of Deloitte's Venture Capital Services, quoted in Deloitte & Touche USA LLP/National Venture Capital Association, *Global Trends in Venture Capital: 2007 Survey* (http://www.nvca.org/pdf/US_Rpt_Global_VC_Survey_7-25-07.pdf), p. 5. The survey found that European venture capitalists, for their part, are focused mostly on Europe. When asked where they would like to expand their investments, 67 percent of European venture capitalists cited locations in Europe.

6. Investors in Acap's Afghanistan Renewal fund include the Asian Development Bank, CDC, the Overseas Private Investment Corporation, and the Rebuilding Agricultural Markets Program (RAMP) funded by the U.S. Agency for International Development as well as high-net-worth private investors. This volatile and troubled country is no place for a pension fund investor. For an introduction to Acap Partners, see http://www.acap.com.af/default.htm (accessed 5/16/08). CDC is a fund of funds owned by the British government that invests in emerging markets, particularly in South Asia and sub-Saharan Africa.

7. This project appealed to me because I saw it as part of the peace process being spearheaded by President Clinton. It also appealed to me because one Sir Henry Brooke from England (no direct relationship to my family can be substantiated, although, as with Sir James Brooke, the White Rajah of Sarawak, the family crest indicates that there might have been a connection) had been awarded a landholding in County Fermanagh in the seventeenth century. Sir Henry, who had fought for Parliament during the Civil War, was the son of Sir Basil Brooke, an English soldier who served in Ireland under Elizabeth I and who had obtained large territorial grants in County Donegal. Brookes had played an important role in the history of Ulster, and I had developed a close relationship with the Brookes of Ireland and always hoped that I could play a role in building bridges between the North and the South. The opportunity was provided to me by John Cullinane, who had advised President Clinton on what could be done in the economies of the North and the South to encourage the two communities to work together peacefully. John's work created the platform for the introduction of a venture capital fund that could capi-

talize on the excellent technologies being developed at Queens College, Belfast, and Trinity College, Dublin.

After a due diligence trip to Belfast and Dublin in the fall of 1995 that indicated that the technology in both places could produce a deal flow justifying a substantial fund, John and I designed one that would include two of the best venture capital managers in the region, Hambro Northern Ireland and Delta Partners of Dublin. Half of the capital from the new fund would be downloaded to these managers, and the remainder would be coinvested with them in deals that Cullinane and I thought the most attractive. There would also be a technology- and business-transfer aspect of the fund linking the United States and Ireland. A private placement document was drafted, and John hit the road in search of commitments. He was successful, and it appeared that the fund would become a reality. Then John began to have second thoughts. He was not comfortable taking money from others, many of them his friends. John was and is an entrepreneur and wanted to do deals on his own, free of the responsibility to others. Although I understood where he was coming from, it is unfortunate that we abandoned the project. We had the chance to create an institution that could have played a role in the peace process, offering a tangible example of the North and South working together and sending a clear message that the Irish could give up their obsession with the past and focus on the future together.

8. Latin America presents other obstacles to entrepreneurship, one of which is exemplified by a story Linda Rottenberg tells about speaking to a group of top Mexican business leaders who asked her, "Why don't we have more entrepreneurship in Mexico?" Linda's answer was direct: "Because you big fish eat the little fish. Why don't you let us create some aquariums where you can feed the little fish instead?" Her observation reminds me of the environment in Japan in the 1980s, where big companies tended to crush the small ones before they had a chance to grow.

9. After many decades and the expenditure of billions of dollars in government- and multilateral-sponsored aid programs that, in many cases, have done little to promote sustainable economic development in the poorer countries of the world, a welcome consensus has emerged that the promotion of vigorous private sectors in the developing world is the path to follow. This new consensus is exemplified by the United Nations' formation of a Commission on the Private Sector and Development in 2003, cochaired by former Canadian prime minister Paul Martin and former Mexican president Ernesto Zedillo. The commission's 2004 report to the UN secretary-general, *Unleashing Entrepreneurship: Making Business Work for the Poor*, mentions venture capital only in passing but notes that "the savings, investment and innovation that lead to development are undertaken largely by private

individuals, corporations and communities" and calls for small and medium enterprises to be brought from the informal economy in which they now too often operate into the formal economy where, for example, they can gain access to capital. See
http://www.undp.org/cpsd/documents/report/english/fullreport.pdf (accessed
4/23/08), p. 1.

10. *U.S. News & World Report* named Linda one of "America's Best Leaders" in
2008.

11. The venture capital community in St. Louis includes one old friend from my
days at TA Associates, Costas Anagnostopoulos, who while running Monsanto
Europe in the early 1980s had invested in Advent Ltd.'s Advent Eurofund and later
in the first SEAVIC fund. After his retirement from Monsanto, Costas served as
managing director of the St. Louis venture capital firm Gateway Associates, which I
helped to establish. He now serves on the boards of several biotechnology companies including Kereos, in which the Vectis Life Sciences Fund is a direct investor.

12. Advent has invested in the health-care and life-sciences sectors since 1986;
as I mention in chapter 6 (note 13), Advent also raised three health-care and life-
sciences funds between 1993 and 2004.

13. The Vectis program is part of a larger economic development effort in the
St. Louis region being spearheaded by the Coalition for Plant and Life Sciences,
a group put together by the organization Civic Progress (consisting of the CEOs
of the thirty largest companies in the region) and the St. Louis Regional Chamber
and Growth Association to act on the recommendations of the Batelle Memorial
Institute's study (commissioned in 2000 by the Regional Chamber and Growth Association). As a result of the coalition's efforts to promote programs such as Vectis,
locally managed venture capital funds focused on the life-sciences sector grew from
zero to $500 million over the five-year period 2001–2006. The Batelle Memorial In-
stitute has projected that if its strategy for growing the life-sciences sector in Missouri (based mostly in St. Louis and environs) is implemented, the state will add
more than 21,000 "permanent, mostly high-paying jobs in the life science industries," and gross regional product and real disposable personal income will increase
between 2003 and 2012 by $7.2 billion and $3.9 billion, respectively.

14. A recent report from PricewaterhouseCoopers and the National Venture
Capital Association points to five "pockets in non-traditional venture capital regions" in the United States where the number of start-ups increased by anywhere
from 70 percent to 600 percent between 1997 and 2007. These regions are New
Mexico and the metropolitan areas of Pittsburgh, Seattle, Los Angeles, and Washington, D.C. See the NVCA/PricewaterhouseCoopers press release "Fastest Growing Regions for Venture Capital Investment Lie outside Silicon Valley," March 11,

2008, available at http://www.nvca.org/pdf/Fast_Growing_07Q4.pdf (accessed 4/3/08).

15. Jacob Hale Russell, "Hunger vs. the Arts," *Wall Street Journal*, October 14, 2006.

16. For an introduction to the subject of venture philanthropy, two good sources are Christine W. Letts, William Ryan, and Allen Grossman, "Virtuous Capital: What Foundations Can Learn from Venture Capitalists," *Harvard Business Review*, March–April 1997; and a series of reports issued since 2000 by Venture Philanthropy Partners and available on the organization's Web site at http://www.vppartners.org/learning/reports/index.html.

17. Siobhan Kennedy, "Bridges Builds Venture Capital with a Heart," *Times Online*, June 11, 2007 (http://business.timesonline.co.uk/tol/business/industry_sectors/banking_and_finance/article1917684.ece, accessed 4/3/08); and James Quinn and Caroline Muspratt, "Permira Pledges £1m Cash for Social Enterprise," *Telegraph*, July 24, 2006 (http://www.telegraph.co.uk/money/main.jhtml?xml=/money/2006/07/24/cnperm24.xml, accessed 4/3/08).

venture capitalists *(continued)*
   developing, 175–81; hostility of
   American, 38; international investment by America and European, 211;
   motivations of, 150; New York area,
   35; in nonprofit sector, 217, 218–21;
   numbers of (1970s), 36; obligations
   of, 38–39; qualities of, 180; roles of,
   19, 220; West Coast, 26–27
venture catalyst model, 211
Venture Corporation Ltd., 89
Venture Corps program, 213
Venture Economics, 76
venture groups, U.S., in Europe, 58
Venture Investment Singapore (VIS),
   118
Venture Investment Singapore (VIS I),
   86
Venture Manufacturing Singapore
   (VMS), 88–89, 91–92
venture philanthropy, 220
Venture Philanthropy Partners, 221
ver Hulst, Nicolas, 104, 240
vision/goals: Advent International
   Corporation's, 107, 145, 155–56, 190,
   242–43, 246–47; American venture
   capitalists, 75; creating/realizing
   a, 190–97; TA Associates', 191–92;
   venture capital for economic
   development, 115–16, 149–50
Viva, 246
volatile countries, 120
Volpe, Mark, 218
von Amerongen, Otto Wolff, 160
Vranitzky, Franz, 105

Wagnisfinanzierung Gesellschaft
   (WFG), 48

Waite, Charlie, 19, 175, 190
Walker, John, 112
*Wall Street Journal,* 219
Walsh, John, 4
Wang, An, 10, 11, 230–31
Wang, Fred, 14
Wang Laboratories, 10–11, 20
Warburg, Eric, xvii
Warburg Pincus, xvii, 155
Warner Bros., 229
Warner Music, 165, 248
Warner & Swasey, 10–11
Warsaw Pact nations, 72, 129
Watson family investments, 19
Weissman, Charles, 31
Weld, Philip, 53
Wendel Group, 103
Wendel Investissement, 103
Western Europe, 203; 1970s views of
   venture capital in, 49; acquisitions
   of East German firms, 161; building
   networks in, 75; cold calling in,
   88; early-stage investment in, 127;
   establishing TAA affiliates in, 86;
   Maastricht Treaty's effect on, 156;
   private equity in, 117; reverse migra-
   tion in, 251; TA Associates (TAA)'s
   network in, 60
Western Pacific, 93–94
Wharton School study on private
   equity funds, 166, 248
Wheeler, Roger, 29
Whitney family investments, 13
Wiesner, Jerome, 95
Wilson, Grant, 23, 32–33, 177, 225
Witt, Peter, 160
Wolfensohn, James, 244–45
Wong, Simon, 91, 247